Reich's theory of orgone energy—that total mental and physical health is impossible in the absence of complete sexual gratification—is perhaps the most radical, most widely acclaimed theory of contemporary psychology.

In THE SEXUAL REVOLUTION, Freud's most controversial disciple shows that orgone energy cannot be suppressed without permanent damage to the social structure. And that only when the genital rights of adults *and* adolescents are protected by law will there be no need for external regulation of the individual, for, indeed, one who is biologically satisfied has no impulses which call for moral inhibition.

"Wilhelm Reich blazed the trail which led, after his tragic death, to what is now known as the Permissive Society. That is why, in the Underground Press and among the younger generation in revolt against the Establishment, the name of Reich is honored today, whereas most of the other early disciples of Freud are either ignored or forgotten."

—Eustace Chesser, in *Salvation Through Sex*

THE SEXUAL REVOLUTION
was published in hardcover by
Farrar, Straus & Giroux, Inc.

Books by Wilhelm Reich

The Function of the Orgasm
The Sexual Revolution

Published by POCKET BOOKS

 *Are there paperbound books you want
but cannot find in your retail stores?*

You can get any title in print in **POCKET BOOK** editions. Simply
send retail price, local sales tax, if any, plus 25¢ (50¢ if you
order two or more books) to cover mailing and handling costs to:

MAIL SERVICE DEPARTMENT
  POCKET BOOKS • A Division of Simon & Schuster, Inc.
  1 West 39th Street • New York, New York 10018

Please send check or money order. We cannot be responsible
for cash. *Catalogue sent free on request.*

WILHELM REICH

THE SEXUAL REVOLUTION

TOWARD
A SELF-REGULATING
CHARACTER STRUCTURE

Translated by Therese Pol

PUBLISHED BY POCKET BOOKS NEW YORK

THE SEXUAL REVOLUTION

Farrar, Straus edition published 1962

POCKET BOOK edition published September, 1975

Standard Book Number: 671-78765-9.
This POCKET BOOK edition is published by arrangement with Farrar, Straus & Giroux, Inc. Copyright, 1945, ©, 1962, 1969, 1974, by Mary Boyd Higgins as trustee of the Wilhelm Reich Infant Trust Fund. This is a new translation of *Die Sexualität im Kulturkampf*, which was originally published in English in 1945 by the Orgone Institute Press. All rights reserved. This book, or portions thereof, may not be reproduced by any means without permission of the publisher: Farrar, Straus & Giroux, Inc., 19 Union Square West, New York, N.Y. 10003.
Front cover art by Al Pisano.

Printed in the U.S.A.

Love, work, and knowledge are the wellsprings of our life. They should also govern it.

WILHELM REICH

Contents

PART ONE

THE FIASCO OF COMPULSORY SEXUAL MORALITY

PART TWO

THE STRUGGLE FOR A "NEW LIFE" IN THE SOVIET UNION

Preface to the Fourth Edition (1949)

Twenty years have passed since the material for the first part of this book was gathered in Austria and, under the title of *Geschlechtsreife, Enthaltsamkeit, Ehemoral*,[1] was turned over to the Münster Verlag in Vienna for publication. Twenty years are of little account in the realm of biology, but in that stormy portion of the twentieth century more misery was inflicted on humanity than in preceding centuries. We may say that all concepts formulated by men to explain and shed light on their lives have been brought into question and have remained unresolved for two decades. Among those concepts none has collapsed so completely as that of compulsory sexual morality, which unshakably ruled human existence a mere thirty years ago. We are living through a true revolution of all values regarding sexual life. And among those values most seriously undermined are those relating to infant and adolescent sexuality.

In 1928, when I founded the Socialist Society for Sexual Consultation and Sexual Research in Vienna, the genital rights of children and adolescents were denied. It was unthinkable for parents to tolerate sexual play, let alone to regard such manifestations as part of a natural, healthy development. The mere thought that adolescents would satisfy their need for love in the natural embrace was horrifying. Anyone who even mentioned these rights was slandered. Resistance to the first attempts to guarantee the love life of children and adolescents united groups of peo-

[1] *Sexual Maturity, Abstinence, Marriage Ethic.*

ple who otherwise were violently opposed to each
other: members of all religious denominations, socialists, Communists, psychologists, physicians, psychoanalysts, etc. In my counseling office for sexual
hygiene and in our meetings to promote mental
hygiene, which many Austrians may still recall, there
were moralists and sophists who predicted the down-
fall of the human race as a result of immorality.
Politicians who irresponsibly promised the masses
"heaven on earth" expelled us from their organizations because we fought for the rights of children
and adolescents to have a natural love life. Our purely
clinical defense of biological needs pointed to necessary changes in the whole social and economic
structure of society. It would be necessary to have
apartments for adolescents; a secure livelihood for
parents, educators, and adolescents; characterological
restructuring of educators; criticism of all political
trends that base their activities and existence on the
on the characterological helplessness of man; the
inner self-sufficiency of human beings and, with it, of
the masses of humanity; the development of self-
regulation in children which would lead eventually
to independent adults. These would be the beginnings
of a great revolution in the biological constitution of
man.

The pressure exerted from all sides on this social-
hygiene work was so strong that I decided to move
to Germany. In September 1930 I gave up my
flourishing medical practice and my psychoanalytic
teaching in Vienna and went to Berlin. Since then
I have been back to Austria only once, in April 1933.
During that brief sojourn, in an address to a large
gathering of Viennese university students, I was able
to outline some of my conclusions about Fascism.
To me, as a psychiatrist and biologist, the German
catastrophe resulted from the biological helplessness
of masses of human beings who had come under
the spell of a handful of power-hungry bandits. I
was grateful for the understanding that Vienna's

academic youth afforded me at that time; but not a single politician deigned to listen to me.

Since then, the problem of the biology of the human animal has grown infinitely. Today, March 1949, in the United States, we are in the midst of severe struggles for the recognition of a biological revolution which has gripped humanity for several decades. It would lead us too far afield to go into detail at this point. But one fact must be strongly emphasized.

What appeared so alien and dangerous in the Austria of 1920–1930 is today, in 1949, the subject of lively public debate in America. This change came about circa 1946, shortly after the end of World War II. It became evident in an increasing number of articles in the daily papers which endorsed the naturalness of genital self-gratification for the child. The all-encompassing mental-hygiene movement has penetrated public consciousness in the United States. It is now recognized that *the future of the human race depends on resolving the problem of human character structure.*[2] Particularly during the last two decades the concept of self-regulation has become popular in child education and is now beginning to appeal to large masses of people. Of course, here as elsewhere, we find the highly placed sexual hypocrite, the government bureaucrat, the political climber of the worse sort, who becomes indignant when he hears of self-regulation. But there can be no doubt that the mental-hygiene movement and the affirmation of the natural biological sexuality of children and adolescents are steadily progressing. They can no longer be stopped. The negation of life is being confronted by the affirmation of life.

I am not saying that victory has already been gained. We still face decades of arduous dispute. But I do say that the basic affirmation of natural love life is advancing inexorably, in spite of numerous and

---

[2] Character Structure (Human Structure). An individual's typical structure, his stereotyped manner of acting and reacting. The orgonomic concept of character is functional and biological, not a static, psychological, or moralistic concept.

dangerous foes. To my knowledge, America is the only country where life, liberty, and the pursuit of happiness are anchored in the Constitution. Let me assure the reader that I, too, am fully aware of reactionary trends in the United States. But here, as nowhere else, there is the possibility of striving for happiness and for human rights. Thousands of copies of Alexander Neill's book *The Problem Family,* which fully endorses the principle of sex-economy[3] in education, were sold soon after publication. The present volume, *The Sexual Revolution,* has also been favorably received. In America, there are powerful and well-established parent-teacher organizations which defend the principle of self-regulation and, with it, of sex-economy for the child. Universities teach the life principle, including its sexual elements. Here and there one encounters hesitation, silence, even hostility, but sexual hygiene for the masses is making strong progress.

It would have pleased me to enlarge this book and bring it up to date with contemporary knowledge, but I had to forgo this. The book forms a comprehensive whole in reflecting the sexual-political conditions of the 1920's; essentially, it is still valid today. The scientific and medical findings made since 1930 in the field of sex-economy have all been published *in extenso.* Hence, I present *The Sexual Revolution* in virtually unchanged form. In so doing, I must emphasize once again that for more than seventeen years my work has been independent of all political movements and parties. It has become a piece of work about human life, a work which has often been in sharp conflict with the political threat to human life.

Forest Hills, New York
March 1949

---

3 Sex-economy. The body of knowledge within orgonomy which deals with the economy of the biological (orgone) energy in the organism, with the energy household.

Preface to the Third Edition (1945)

The current, third edition of my book *Die Sexualität im Kulturkampf*[1] is presented here for the first time in the English language. It contains no changes in subject matter, but it was necessary to make many changes in terminology.

The European freedom movement forms the framework for the material in this book, gathered originally between 1918 and 1935. It labored under the illusion that authoritarian ideology was equivalent to the life process of the "bourgeoisie," while freedom reflected the life process of the "proletariat." The European freedom movement foundered on this basic error. The social events of the last twelve years have provided a bloody refutation of this error: authoritarian and progressive ideologies have nothing to do with economic class distinctions. The ideology of a social stratum is not an immediate reflection of its economic condition. The emotional and mystical excitations of the human masses must play at least as large a role in the social process as do purely economic interests. Authoritarian coercion crisscrosses *all* social strata in all nations, just as do

[1] First ed., 1930; 2nd, enlarged ed., 1936.

progressive thought and action. There are no class boundaries in character structure, as there are economic and social boundaries. It is not a matter of "class struggles" between proletarians and the bourgeoisie, as theoretical sociology has mechanistically postulated. On the contrary, workers who are structurally capable of freedom war against workers with authoritarian structures and against the parasites of society, members of the upper social classes with the capacity for freedom have risked their existence to fight for the right of *all* workers against dictators who have arisen from the ranks of the proletariat. The Soviet Union of 1944, with its origin in a proletarian revolution is—and I deeply regret to say so—reactionary in terms of sex politics, while the United States, originating in a bourgeois revolution, must be described as at least progressive in its sexual policies. Social concepts of the nineteenth century which were defined purely in economic terms no longer fit the ideological stratifications in the cultural struggles of the twentieth century. In its simplest formulation: today's social struggles are being waged between those forces interested in the safeguarding and affirming of life and those whose interests lie in its destruction and negation. Today the principal social question no longer is: "Are you rich or are you poor?" but: "Do you endorse and do you fight to secure the greatest possible freedom for human life? Are you doing everything in your power to enable the millions of workingmen to become so independent in their thinking, acting, and living that the complete self-regulation of social life will be taken for granted in the predictable future?"

It is clear that the basic social question, as concretely formulated above, must take into account the living functioning of even the poorest member of the human community. And, in this context, the significance I had ascribed to sexual suppression fifteen years ago takes on gigantic proportions. Social and individual sex-economy have established the fact that suppression of the love of children and adolescents is the central mechanism for producing enslaved subordinates and economic serfs. So it is no longer a question of whether one carries a white, yellow, black, or red party membership card as proof of this or that mental persuasion. It is quite unmistakably a question of whether one fully affirms, supports, and safeguards the free life expressions of newborn infants, of small children, adolescents, and adult men and women, or whether one suppresses and destroys these expressions, regardless of which ideology or subterfuge is used, regardless of whether it is done for this or that country, regardless of whether "proletarian" or "capitalistic," regardless of religion, be it Jewish, Christian, or Buddhist. This is universally true and will remain so as long as there is life; it must be recognized if we want to eradicate for all time the organized swindle perpetrated on the working masses of humanity, if we want to prove in action that we take our democratic ideals seriously.

Today, realization of the necessity for a radical change in the conditions of sexual life has penetrated social thinking and is rapidly taking hold. An appreciation and concern for the child's sexuality is becoming more and more widespread. It is true that there is still little social support for adolescent love life, that official science still avoids picking up the "hot coals" represented by the sexual problem during puberty. But the idea that sexual intercourse during puberty is a natural and self-evident need seems no longer as horrendous as it did in 1929 when I first discussed it. The success that sex-economy enjoys in so many countries is due to the many good educators and understanding parents to whom the sexual needs of infants and adolescents are completely natural and justified. Although we still have disgraceful medieval legislation and dreadful correctional institutions, which have caused tremendous harm, the rational thinking about infantile and adolescent love life has indelibly left its mark.

A new period of enlightment will have to assert itself against the powerful residual forces of medieval irrationalism. Although there are still some exponents of "hereditary degeneracy" and "criminal deviation," knowledge of the *social* causes of crime and emotional illness has made a breakthrough everywhere. Although there are far too many physicians who recommend that the hands of infants be tied to prevent masturbation, many mass-circulation dailies have gone on record against such practices. Although heathy adolescents are still sent to correctional institutions because they have gratified their natural love functions, there are many judges who know that such jurisprudence and such institutions are social crimes. Although there is still an abundance of ecclesiastical snooping and moralizing which condemn natural sexuality as the work of the devil, there is a growing number of candidates for the priesthood who are practicing social work and casting off conventional morality. There are even bishops who favor birth control, although they restrict it to legal marriages. Although too many young people come to grief in the exhausting battle for happiness in love, a father has been publicly censured on the radio for condemning his daughter because she had a child but no marriage license. Although there are still compulsory marriage laws which turn divorce into blackmail, the abhorrence of such laws and such divorce procedures is growing and affecting the general community.

We are experiencing an authentic revolutionary upheaval of our cultural existence. In this struggle there are no parades, no uniforms, no medals, no beating of drums, and no cannon salutes. But the fight is costing no fewer victims than a civil-war battle of 1848 or 1917. The responses of the human animal to his natural life functions are awakening from the sleep of millennia. The revolution in our lives strikes at the root of our emotional, social, and economic existence.

It is mainly the tremendous upheavals in family

life, the Achilles' heel of society, that are emerging in a state of chaos. They are chaotic because our authoritarian family structure, derived from ancient patriarchy, has been deeply shaken and is about to make way for a better, more natural family organization. This book does not attack the natural family relationships but opposes the authoritarian form of the family, which is maintained by rigid laws, human structure, and irrational public opinion. It is precisely the events in the Soviet Union following the social revolution of 1917 (which will be dealt with in the second part of this book)that demonstrate the emotionally and socially dangerous nature of this upheaval. What Soviet Russia tried to resolve by force within a brief time span during the 1920's, is being accomplished today throughout the whole world in a slower but far more thorough manner. When I speak of revolutionary upheavals in the conditions of our cultural life, I have in mind primarily the removal of the patriarchal authoritarian family form in the favor of natural relationships. But it is precisely these natural relationships between husband and wife, and between parents and children, which are confronted with extremely dangerous obstacles.

The word "revolutionary" in this as well as in other sex-economic writings does not mean the use of high explosives but the use of truth; it does not mean secret meetings and the distribution of illegal handbills, but an open and public warning directed to human conscience, without pretext or circumlocutions; it does not mean political gangsterism, assassinations, the signing and breaking of treaties, but it does mean "rational revolution, grasping the root of the matter." Sex-economy is revolutionary in the same sense that the following events were revolutionary: the discovery of microbes and the unconscious emotional life in medicine, the discovery of mechanical laws and electricity in physics, and the discovery of the nature of productive power, labor force, in economics. Sex-economy is revolutionary because it reveals the laws of the formation of human character structure and because it no longer bases human aspirations for freedom on slogans but on the functional laws of biological energy. We are revolutionary in the sense that we view the life processes from the standpoint of *natural science* instead of from that of mysticism, mechanistics, or politics. The discovery of cosmic orgone energy, which functions in living organisms as biological energy, provides our social efforts with a solid foundation rooted in natural science.

The social development of our time strives everywhere for a planetary community and for internationalism without ifs and buts. Government by politicians must be replaced by the natural scientific regulation of social processes. What is at stake is human society, and not the state. We are concerned with truth, not with tactics. Natural science confronts its greatest task: to assume the responsibility for the future destiny of a tortured humanity. Politics has finally been reduced to mere politicizing at cross-purposes. Natural scientists, whether they like it or not, will have to guide social processes, and the politicians will have to learn, willy-nilly, to accomplish some useful work. One of the tasks of this book is to help the new, rational scientific order of life, which is embattled everywhere, to break through and to make its birth and growth less painful and entailing fewer victims. Anyone who is decent and has a sense of responsibility toward life cannot, and will not, misconstrue or abuse this book.

November 1944   WILHELM REICH

Preface to the Second Edition (1936)

In October 1935, three hundred of the best-known psychiatrists called upon the world's conscience. Italy had just carried out her first assault on Ethiopia. Thousands of defenseless people, among them women, old men, and children, were slain in that first attack. People began to realize how vast would be the scope of mass murder if there should be another world war.

That a nation like Italy, with millions starving, would follow the cry of war with such enthusiasm and without rebellion, save for a few exceptions, was to be expected, but it is incomprehensible. It strengthened the general impression that the whole world allowed itself to be governed by men whom psychiatrists would have described as mentally disturbed, and more than that: people in all parts of the world are indeed emotionally sick; their emotional reactions are abnormal, in contradiction to their own wishes and real potentialities. These are the symptoms of emotionally abnormal reactions: to strive amid abundance; to be exposed to cold and rain in spite of available coal reserves, construction machinery, millions of square miles of empty land on which to build, etc.; to believe that a divine power with a long white beard guides everything and that people are completely at the mercy of this power; to be jubilant over murdering people who have done no harm to anyone and to believe it is necessary to conquer a country one has never heard of; to go about in rags and think one is representing the "greatness of the nation" to which one belongs; to desire the classless society and to regard the "people's community" with its profiteers as that kind of society; to forget what a national leader promised before he came to power; generally to entrust individual persons, even if they are statesmen, with power over one's life and destiny; to disregard the fact that even so-called leaders of state and economy must eat, sleep, have sexual disturbances, follow their bladder and bowel urges, and be governed by uncontrollable emotions just as the average mortal is; to look upon corporal punishment of children in the service of "culture" as a matter of course; to forbid adolescents in the bloom of life the happiness of sexual embrace. . . . One might continue indefinitely.

The psychiatrists' appeal was an official politicization, on the part of an otherwise unworldly and allegedly nonpolitical science. But this act was incomplete. It did not touch the roots of the phenomenon which it correctly described. The psychiatrists did not proceed from the *nature* of the general emotional sickness of contemporary man. They did not question the basic cause of the masses' boundless willingness to sacrifice themselves in the interests of a handful of politicians. They did not note the difference between real gratification of needs and the illusionary gratification in nationalistic frenzy, which is related to the ecstatic state of religious fanatics. They did not attempt to understand why the masses accepted hunger and misery despite increased economic productivity which should have led to a rational planned economy. This problem was not the psychology of the statesmen but that of the masses.

Modern statesmen are the friends, brothers, cousins, or fathers-in-law of financial tycoons or dictators. The fact that the mass of thinking people, whether or not they are educated and cultured, do not see this and react accordingly is a problem in itself. It cannot be solved by the "psychodiagnostic examination of individuals." Emotional illnesses, revealing confused thinking, resignation, emotional enslavement, self-injury, unquestioned faith in a leader, etc., all express a disturbance in the harmony of vegetative, particularly of sexual, life which is inherent in the social mechanization of life.

The grotesque symptoms of the mentally ill are merely distortions and magnifications of the mystical, credulous attitudes of the masses who try to ward off war by prayers. The mental institutions of the world, which house about four in every thousand people, pay no more attention to the ordering of sexual life than does politics. The chapter on sexuality still remains to be written by official science. Yet the origin of abnormal emotional reactions in the pathological channeling of ungratified sexual energy can no longer be doubted. Therefore, when we raise the question about the social ordering of man's sexual life, we strike at the roots of emotional illness.

Sexual energy is the biological energy which, in the psyche, determines the character of human feeling and thinking. "Sexuality" (physiologically, the parasympathetic function) is the productive life energy per se. Its suppression results not only in psychic and somatic disorders but in a general disturbance of social functioning manifested in most purposeless actions, mysticism, readiness for war, etc. Sex politics must therefore proceed from the question: *Why is human love life suppressed?*

Let us briefly summarize how sex-economy relates emotional life to the socioeconomic order. Human needs are formed, altered, and, in particular, suppressed by society; this process establishes the psychic structure of man. It is not inborn but develops in each individual member of society in the course of the never ending battle between his needs and society. There is no innate structure of the impulses; this

structure is acquired during the first years of life.
What *is* innate is the larger or smaller amount of
biological energy in the organism. Sexual suppression
produces a subordinate individual who simultaneously exhibits slavish obedience and rebellion. We
want man to be "free." Therefore, not only must we
know how modern man has been structured; we
must also understand how free men have been structured and what forces have been used to create them.

Since the core of emotional functioning is the sexual
function, the core of political (pragmatic) psychology
is sex politics. This is apparent in literature and motion
pictures which cater almost exclusively to sexual
needs.

The biological needs—food and sexual pleasure—
create the necessity for the social community of men.
The conditions of production thus created by community change the basic needs, without, however,
destroying them, and also create new needs. The
transformed and newly created needs in turn determine the further development of production and its
means (tools and machines), and, along with them,
the social and economic relations among men. Based
on these conditions of production, certain ideas about
life, morals, philosophy, etc., develop. They generally
correspond to the level of technology at a particular
time, i.e., to the ability to comprehend and master
life. The social "ideology" thus created forms the
human structure and is turned into a material force
to be preserved in that structure as "tradition." Now,
everything depends on whether the whole society
or only a small minority participates in the formation
of the social ideology. If a minority holds political
power, then it also determines the type and content
of the general ideology and the formation of human
structure. Therefore, in an authoritarian society, the
thinking of the majority corresponds to the economic
and political interests of the rulers. Conversely, in
a work-democratic society, where there are no minority power interests, the social ideology would corre-

spond to the vital interests of *all* members of society.

Until now, social ideology was envisioned only as a sum of ideas forming "in the heads of men" about the economic process. But after the victory of political reaction in Germany's gravest crisis and the experience of the irrational behavior of the masses, ideology can no longer be regarded as a mere reflection of economic conditions. *As soon as an ideology has taken hold of and molded human structure, it beomes a material, social power.* There is no socioeconomic process of historical significance which is not anchored in the psychic structure of the masses and activated in the form of mass behavior. There is no "development of production forces per se," but only a development or an inhibition of the human structure, its feeling and thinking on the basis of economic and social processes. The economic process, i.e., the development of machines, is functionally identical with the process of psychic structure in the men who create it, propel it, inhibit it, and are affected by it. Economy without an active drive structure is unthinkable; conversely, there can be no human feeling, thinking, and acting without an economic foundation and its consequences. The one-sidedness of both views forms the basis of *psychologism* ("The emotional forces of men alone make history") as well as *economism* ("Technology alone makes history"). One ought to talk less about dialectics and, instead, comprehend the living interrelationships among groups of men, nature and machines. They function as a unity while at the same time conditioning one another. Therefore, we will never succeed in mastering the current cultural process if we do not understand that the nucleus of psychic structure is sexual structure and that the cultural process is essentially a process of sexual needs that serve to maintain life.

The small, wretched, allegedly "unpolitical" sexual life of man must be investigated thoroughly and mastered in relation to the problems of authoritarian society. In reality, high politics does not take place at diplomatic dinners but in ordinary life. Therefore, the politicization of man's so-called personal life can no longer be postponed. If the 1,800 million people on this earth understood the activities of the hundred leading diplomats, everything would be all right; there would be no regulation of society and no ordering of the gratification of human needs on the basis of armament interests and on-the-agenda principles. But these 1,800 million people will not be able to control their destinies so long as they are not conscious of their own modest, personal lives. The inner forces which prevent this are called *sexual moralism* and *religious mysticism*.

The economic order of the last two hundred years has greatly changed human structure; but this change is minimal when compared to the all-pervading human impoverishment that has existed ever since natural life, particularly sexual life, began to be suppressed thousands of years ago. It took millennia of suppressing instinctual life to create the mass-psychological basis for the fear of authority, the slavishness, the incredible humbleness on the one hand, and the sadistic brutality on the other. On this base the capitalistic profit economy was able to run rampant and maintain itself for two hundred years. But we should not forget that it was social and economic processes which brought about the changes in human structure thousands of years ago. Hence, we are no longer concerned with a two-hundred-year-old machine age but with a six-thousand-year-old human structure which so far has been incapable of putting the machines to beneficial use. No matter how splendid and revolutionizing the discovery of the laws of capitalist economy was, it alone is insufficient to solve the problem of human bondage and self-subjugation. Although groups of people everywhere, including members of the oppressed classes, are battling for "bread and freedom," the overwhelming majority of the masses stand passively aside and pray, or else they are fighting for freedom on the side of their oppressors. That

these masses suffer incredible hardship is something
they themselves experience daily and hourly. That
someone is willing to give them bread alone, without
all the pleasures of life, reinforces their humbleness.
And in reality, what freedom is, can, or will be, has
not been presented to the masses in concrete and
intelligible form. The potential for general happiness
in life has not been tangibly described to them. Whenever someone attempted to do so in order to win
them over, they were presented with the sick, wretched,
guilt-ridden pleasures that can be found in the philistine lower-middle-class dives and honky-tonk joints.
The core of happiness in life is *sexual* happiness.
No one with political power has dared touch upon
this. The general view was, and still is, that sexuality
was a private matter and had nothing to do with
politics. But political reaction knows better.

The French translator of my book *Geschlechtsreife,
Enthaltsamkeit, Ehemoral*[1] contrasts Freudo-Marxism
with authentic Marxism and says that the specific psychoanalytic thought pattern has changed the Marxist
postulate. "With him [Reich] the sexual crisis does
not result primarily from the conflict between morality
and the conditions of declining capitalism on the one
hand, and the new social relationships, the new proletarian morality, on the other; it results from the
contradiction between the natural, eternal, sexual needs
and the capitalist order of society." Such reflections
are always instructive and productive, leading invariably to a sharpening and amplification of the
original formulation.

In this instance, the critic contrasts class distinctions
with differences between need and society. Yet all
these differences have *one* origin and should not be
viewed merely as antitheses. It is correct that, objectively and from the viewpoint of class, the sexual
crisis is a manifestation of the conflict between capitalist decline and revolutionary ascendancy. But it
is also correct that it expresses the contradiction

---

[1] *La Crise Sexuelle* (Paris, 1934).

between sexual needs and mechanistic society. How can this be reconciled? Very simply. The critic cannot find the solution because the sharp distinction between the subjective and the objective sides of social processes is unfamiliar to him, although it is self-evident. Objectively, the sexual crisis is a phenomenon of class distinctions; but how is it represented subjectively? What does it mean: a new proletarian morality? Capitalist class morality is *opposed* to sexuality, i.e., it creates the contradiction and the resulting misery. The revolutionary movement eliminates this contradiction by its ideological endorsement of sexual gratification, which is then strengthened by laws and a new ordering of sexual life. Thus, capitalism and sexual suppression go together as do revolutionary "morality" and sexual gratification. To speak of a "new revolutionary morality" is meaningless. This new morality derives only its specific content from the orderly gratification of needs, and not just those in the realm of sexuality. Unless revolutionary ideology recognizes that this, among other things, is its real content, it merely *speaks* of a new morality but actually remains stuck in the old. This is clearly demonstrated in the contradiction between ideology and reality in the Soviet Union. The new morality consists precisely in making moral regulation superfluous and in establishing the self-regulation of social life. An obvious example can be found in stealing, or in the moral law against theft: someone who is not starving has no need to steal and therefore does not need a moral code to prevent him from stealing. The same basic law applies to sexuality: someone who is leading a gratifying sexual life has no need to rape and requires no moral law against rape. The "sex-economic regulation" of sexual life replaces authoritarian regulation. Owing to confusion about the laws of sexuality, Communism has tried to retain the form of bourgeois morality while changing its content; thus a "new morality" is produced in the Soviet Union, displacing the old one. This is erroneous. Just as the state does not merely change its form but "withers away" completely (Lenin,) so compulsory morality, too, does not merely change but withers away.

A second error of the aforementioned critic consists in believing that we postulate an *absolute* sexuality which comes into conflict with contemporary society. For example, a basic error of psychoanalysis is to comprehend the drives as absolute biological facts; but this is not rooted in the heart of psychoanalysis, which is specifically dialectical, but in the mechanistic thinking of psychoanalysts, which, as usual, is supplemented by metaphysical theses. Drives emerge, change, and disappear. But the time intervals between biological changes are so vast, and those of social processes relatively so small, that the former impress us as absolute events, while the latter are regarded as relative and in flux. To investigate specific social processes which are very limited in time, it is sufficient to establish the conflict between a given biological drive and the manner in which the social order understands and deals with it. But for biological laws of the sexual process which are measured in terms of centuries, it is in no way sufficient; here, the relativity and change-ability of the instinctual organization must be clearly elaborated. If we recognize the life process of individuals as the *first* prerequisite of *every* social event, it is sufficient to assume that life, with its basic needs, exists. But life itself is not absolute; it emerges and disappears in changing generations, while, at the same time, it is preserved unchanged in the form of genes which continue to live from generation to generation. Considered in terms of cosmic time, all life has emerged from the inorganic and, just as in the case of the rise and decline of stars, will disappear, i.e., return to the inorganic state. This is a necessary assumption of dialectical thinking. Perhaps no other point of view is better suited for comparing the infinitesimal smallness and insignificance of human illusions and their "spiritual," "transcendental" mission with the overriding affinity of human vegetative life and nature in general. This might be interpreted to mean that social struggles also appear futile when compared to the cosmic processes of which man and society are only a small part. How ridiculous, one might say, that people slaughter one another "to end unemployment" or to carry to power someone like Hitler and then organize nationalistic consecration processions, while the stars are moving in the cosmos and one would be better off enjoying nature. Such an interpretation would be erroneous because it is precisely the natural scientific viewpoint which argues *against* political reaction and for work democracy.[2] The former tries fruitlessly to press the infinite cosmos and man's reflected feeling for nature into the framework of the infinitesimal idea of sexual asceticism and patriotic self-sacrifice. Work democracy, on the other hand, tries to integrate the insignificant individual and all social life into the immensity of natural occurrences, to eliminate the contradiction caused by a "faulty development" of nature in society—six thousand years of exploitation, mysticism, and sexual suppression—even though this development may have been "necessary." In brief, it supports sexuality and opposes the unnatural sexual ethic; it supports international planned economy and opposes exploitation and national boundaries.

Nazi ideology contains a rational core which gives this reactionary movement its driving force. It is expressed in the phrase "unity of blood and soil." National Socialist practice, however, retains all those social forces which run counter to the basic trend of the revolutionary movement, i.e., unity of society, nature, and technology. It retains class distinctions, which cannot be eliminated by any illusion about the unity of the people; it retains private ownership of the means of production, which no amount of

---

2 Work democracy. The functioning of the natural and intrinsically rational work relationships between human beings. The concept of work democracy represents the established reality (not the ideology) of these relationships, which, though usually distorted because of prevailing armoring and irrational political ideologies, are nevertheless at the basis of all social achievement.

"community ideas" can obscure. Nazi ideology expresses mystically what is inherent in the revolutionary movement as a rational nucleus—a classless society and a life oriented in natural processes. The revolutionary movement, however, while it is not yet entirely aware of its ideological content, is completely clear about the economic and social preconditions for realizing its rational philosophy, *the realization of happiness on earth.*

The critique of the prevailing sexual conditions and concepts which is summarized in this book was formed over a period of years from the sex-economic insights gained in my medical practice. Its first part ("The Fiasco of Compulsory Sexual Morality") was published about six years ago under the title *Geschlechtsreife, Enthaltsamkeit, Ehemoral.* Although it has been enlarged in a few places, it is essentially unchanged. The second part ("The Struggle for a 'New Life' in the Soviet Union") has been added; it is based on material gathered in ten years of research. The description of the retarding of the sexual revolution in Soviet Russia will show why I referred time and again to the Soviet Union in my first sex-political writings. During the last three or four years, there have been significant changes in that country and much is no longer in keeping with previously correct trends. The general retrogression to authoritarian principles in the social order has accompanied the erosion of Soviet sexual revolutionary accomplishments.

This volume does not pretend to examine all pertinent problems, let alone solve them. A critique of prevalent theories of psychic illnesses would have belonged here, as would an extensive treatment of religion. But this was not possible; the problems are inexhaustible and the book would have become unmanageable. My book *The Mass Psychology of Fascism* dealt with the sexual politics of Fascism and with the Church as a sex-political organization of patriarchy. This book is neither a sexological textbook nor a history of the current sexual crisis. It is deliberately restricted to showing the basic contradictions in present-day sexual life through typical examples. The sex-economic views presented here are not the result of armchair research. Without decades of close contact with youth, without constantly verifying my experiences with youth in my medical work with patients, I could not have set down a single sentence of this book. I am stating this in anticipation of a certain type of criticism. As fruitful and indispensable as critical debate is, it is a waste of time and energy unless the critics personally investigate those areas of social life where the source of sexological knowledge is to be found: in the lives of the broad, uncultured or faultily cultured, suffering, and sometimes struggling masses, whom the "Godsent" leaders of nations call "subhuman." On the basis of my practical experiences in Germany and Austria and my clinical practice, I have ventured to form an opinion on the course of the Soviet sexual revolution without having constant personal contact with the sex-political conditions in that country. It is quite possible that one thing or another has been overdrawn in describing the sexual conditions in Soviet Russia. However, it was not my intention to pronounce absolute truths but to present a basic picture of general trends and contradictions. Needless to say, I will take into account any pertinent corrections of facts in future printings of this book.

Finally, I would like to say to my worried friends who admonish me to leave "dangerous politics" alone and to devote myself solely to my work. In natural science; sex-economy, insofar as it deserves the name, is neither left nor right but forward-directed, *nolens volens* toward a rational revolutionary orientation. Who, in a house that is on fire, would leisurely write aesthetic treatises on the color sense of crickets?

November 1935   WILHELM REICH

PART ONE

The Fiasco of Compulsory Sexual Morality

The editor of *The Yarn Roll*, who posed the question "Why are we alive?", apparently likes to move around in the tangled shrubbery of philosophy. But, on the other hand, he may be in the throes of great fear and trembling as he contemplates the futility of human life. If the first is the case, it's good; if the second is the case, it's bad. And for this reason the only answer to that question is: "Man must live for the sake of living," even if this sounds strange and single-minded. For man, the whole purpose, the whole meaning of life, lies in life itself, in the process of living. To comprehend the purpose and meaning of life, one must above all love life and become totally submerged in the turmoil of living; it is only then that one can grasp the meaning of life and understand why one is alive. Unlike everything that man has created, life requires no theory; he who understands the sheer experience of living will by the same token understand the theory of life.

—FROM THE DIARY OF THE STUDENT
KOSTYA RYABTSEV

I

The Clinical Foundation of the Sex-Economic Critique

1. FROM THE MORALISTIC TO THE SEX-ECONOMIC PRINCIPLE

The sex-economic views presented here rest on clinical observations and experience with patients who undergo a change in their psychic structure in the course of a successful character analysis. The question will be raised, and rightly so, whether what we have learned about restructuring a neurotic person can be applied forthwith to the problems of restructuring and reeducating large groups, or masses, of individuals. Rather than offering theoretical reflections, we shall let the facts speak for themselves. For the irrational, unconscious, purposeless phenomena of instinctual life can in no way be understood unless we are guided by our experience with the individual neurotic. This is basically no different from the procedure used in fighting an infection of epidemic proportions—that is, we closely examine the individual victims and investigate the bacillus as well as its effects, which are the same for all victims of the epidemic. The comparison may be carried further. In an epidemic, an external factor damages a previously healthy organism. With cholera, for instance, we would not be content with healing the individual victim but at the same time would isolate and destroy the source of the epidemic-causing bacillus. In the unhealthy emotional behavior of the average person, we can see similarities with our patient's symptoms: general sexual timidity, the force of moralistic demands, which are at times transformed into undisguised brutality (e.g., storm troopers); the inability to imagine that the gratification of drives can be reconciled with constructive work achievement; the belief, which is considered natural, that the sexuality of children and adolescents is a morbid aberration; the inconceivability of any form of sexual life other than lifelong monogamy; the distrust of one's own strength and judgment and the concomitant longing for an omniscient, all-guiding father figure, etc. Average individuals experience basically the same conflicts, although the details may differ according to each person's unique development. If we would apply what we learn from the individual to the masses, we can use only those insights which relate to conflicts that are typical and generally valid. It is then quite correct to apply conclusions drawn from the processes involved in the restructuring of individual patients to the restructuring of the masses.

The emotionally sick come to us with typical symptoms of emotional disorder. The patient's capacity for work is always more or less impaired, and his actual accomplisments correspond neither to the demands he makes on himself nor to those society makes on him, nor even to the abilities he feels he possesses. Without exception, sexual gratification is sharply diminished, if not absent entirely. In the place of natural genital gratification we invariably find nongenital (pregenital) forms of gratification; e.g., sadistic fantasies about the sexual act, rape fantasies, etc. One becomes unequivocally convinced that the development of the patient's character and sexual behavior is always clearly outlined by the fourth or fifth year of life. The emotional disturbance in social or sexual achievement is sooner or later evident to any observer. Under the condition of neurotic, sexual repression, every patient carries within himself the insoluble contradiction between instinctual drive and moralistic compulsion. The moral demands that, under the constant pressure of social influence, he places on himself intensify the blocking of his sexual and general vegetative needs. The greater the damage to his genital potency, the wider the discrepancy between the *need* for gratification and the *capacity* for it. This, in turn, increases the moral pressure necessary to suppress the dammed-up drives. Since the essential parts of the entire conflict are unconscious and therefore cannot be understood by the affected person, he is also completely unable to solve them by himself.

In the conflict between instinct and morals, ego and outside world, the organism is forced to armor itself against both the instinct and the outside world, to restrict itself. This "armoring" results in a more or less reduced capacity for living. It is relevant to emphasize that the majority of people suffer from this rigidity. It is by far the most important source of loneliness in so many people, despite community living.

Character-analytic treatment is intended to free the vegetative energies from their bindings in the armor. At first, this strengthens the asocial, perverse, cruel impulses and, along with them, social anxiety and moral inhibition. But if childhood ties to the parental home, with its early traumatic associations and sexual prohibitions, are simultaneously dissolved, then more and more vegetative energy will flow toward the genitals. In other words, the natural genital needs acquire new life or appear for the first time. If, as a result, genital inhibitions and anxieties are removed, if the patient thereby attains the capacity for full orgastic gratification, and if he is fortunate enough to find a suitable partner, we can regularly observe a far-reaching and, in many instances, astonishing change in his overall behavior. The most important aspects of this are the following.

If the actions and thoughts of the patients were formerly conditioned by the more or less acute and disturbing effects of unconscious, irrational motives, now his reactions are in tune with reality and irrational motives recede. Thus, in this process, the tendency toward mysticism, religiosity, infantile dependence, superstitions, etc. disappears spontaneously, without any attempt on the part of the physician to "educate" the patient.

It the patient had been severely armored, devoid of contact with himself and his environment, or capable merely of substitute, unnatural contacts, he now achieves an increasing capacity for immediate contact with both his impulses and his surroundings. The result of this process is the subsidence of the former unnatural behavior and the appearance of natural, spontaneous functioning.

In most patients we observe a double state. Outwardly, they appear somewhat odd, but we can sense a healthy quality through the sickness. Today the so-called individual differences among people represent basically a stifling neurotic behavior. But these differences disappear in the process of getting well, to give way to a *simplification* of overall behavior. As a result of this simplification, these persons become similar in their basic traits, without losing their individuality. For example, every patient conceals his work disturbance in a very specific way. If he loses this disturbance, if he gains self-confidence, he also loses all those character traits which compensated for his sense of worthlessness. Self confidence based on free-flowing work accomplishment is similar among all men.

A person's attitude toward sexual life is influenced in the same manner. For example, someone who represses his sexuality develops his own particular forms of moral and aesthetic self-protection. If the patient regains contact with his sexual needs, his

neurotic differences vanish. The attitude toward a
natural sexual life becomes more or less the same
among all individuals—particularly in the affirmation
of pleasure and the loss of sexual guilt feelings. The
formerly insoluble conflict between instinctual needs
and moral inhibitions resulted in a sickness in which
the person had to act according to the criteria of
an established norm outside himself. Everything he
did and thought was measured by the moral standard
that had been created for him; at the same time he
protested against it. If, in the course of restructuring,
he recognizes not only the necessity but also the in-
dispensability of genital gratification, the moral straitjacket drops off along with the damming up of his
instinctual needs. If previously the pressure of morality had strengthened the drive or made it antisocial,
and this had, in turn, required a stronger moral inhibition, now the equalizing of the capactiy for gratification
with the strong drives destroys the moralistic regulation in the patient. The formerly indispensable
mechanism of self-control also disappears because
vital energies are withdrawn from the antisocial impulses. There is scarcely anything left to be controlled.
The healthy person is virtually without compulsive
morality, but neither does he have any impulses that
would require a restraining morality. Any residual
antisocial impulses are easily controlled if the basic
genital needs are gratified. This is evident in the daily
conduct of the orgastically potent individual. Sexual
intercourse with prostitutes becomes offensive; any
existing fantasies of murder or rape lose their force
and significance. To force a partner into a love affair
or to rape her becomes bizarre and unthinkable, just
as do any impulses to seduce children that may have
existed previously. By the same token, former anal,
exhibitionistic, or other perversions also recede, along
with social anxiety and guilt feelings. The incestuous
ties to parents and siblings lose their interest, freeing
energies hitherto repressed. In brief, the processes

mentioned here are all to be regarded as a sign that
the organism *regulates itself*.

It has been shown that people with the capacity
for orgastic gratification are considerably better adjusted to monogamous relationships than those
whose orgastic function is disturbed. However, their
monogamous attitude rests not on inhibited polygamous impulses or moralistic considerations but on
the sex-economic ability to experience pleasure
repeatedly with the same partner. The prerequisite
is sexual harmony with the partner. (In this respect,
no difference between men and women could be
clinically established.) But if no suitable partner is
available, as seems to be the rule under the prevailing
conditions of sexual life, the tendency toward
monogamy turns into its opposite, namely, into the
uncontrollable search for the right partner. If that
partner is found, the monogamous behavior is spontaneously restored and is maintained as long as sexual
harmony and gratification last. Fantasies and wishes
for other partners are either very weak or else ignored
because of the interest in the current partner. However,
the relationship collapses irretrievably if it becomes
stale and if another companion promises greater
pleasure. This unshakable fact is the insoluble contradiction in the sexual organization of modern society, encumbered with economic obligations and considerations of children, which oppose the principle
of sex-economy. For this reason, it is the healthiest
people who suffer most severely under the conditions
of the sex-negating social order.

The behavior of orgastically disturbed people, i.e.,
the majority, is different. Since they feel less pleasure
in the sexual act or can do without a sexual partner
for greater periods of time, they are less selective:
the act does not mean very much to them. Here
promiscuity in sexual relationships results from sexual
disturbance. Such sexually disturbed people are more
capable of adapting to a lifelong marriage; however,

their fidelity rests not on sexual gratification but on moral inhibitions.

If a patient regaining his health succeeds in finding a suitable partner, all nervous symptoms disappear and he can order his life with an astonishing ease previously unknown to him. He can resolve his conflicts without neurosis and develop self-confidence in regulating his impulses and social relationships. He follows the pleasure principle. The simplifying of his attitude toward life, in action, thought, and feeling, removes many sources of conflict. At the same time, he acquires a critical attitude toward the prevailing moral order, thus demonstrating that the principle of sex-economic self-regulation opposes that of compulsory moral regulation.

In today's sexually depraved society, the healing process frequently runs into almost insurmountable obstacles—particularly the paucity of sexually healthy people who might become partners for patients who are approaching health. Beyond that, there are the general impediments of a compulsive sexual morality. One might say that the genitally healthy person turns from an unconscious into a conscious hypocrite toward those institutions and social conditions which impede his healthy, natural sexuality. On the other hand, some develop the faculty of changing their environment to such an extent that the effects of today's social order are diminished or removed altogether.

I have to limit myself here to the briefest of descriptions and I refer the reader to my extensive investigations in *The Function of the Orgasm* and *Character Analysis*. Clinical experience has permitted me to draw basic conclusions about the social order. The wide scope of these conclusions for the prophylaxis of neuroses, the fight against mysticism and superstition, the old problem of the apparent contradiction between nature and culture, instinct and morals, was at first surprising and confusing; but, after years of reexamination on the basis of ethnological and sociological material, I became convinced that the conclusions based on the structural change from the moralistic principle to that of sex-economic self-regulation are correct; they were confirmed everywhere. If a social movement were to succeed in changing social conditions in such a manner that today's sex negation would be replaced by general sex affirmation (with all its economic concomitants), then the principle of restructuring the human masses would become reality. Of course, we do not mean to treat every member of society. The fundamental idea of sex-economy has often been misconstrued in this way. The experiences gleaned from the restructuring of individuals will serve merely to establish general principles for a new form of education of infants and adolescents in which nature and culture, individual and society, sexuality and sociality, would no longer contradict each other.

But the therapeutic experiences and their theoretical results through which it was possible to make the orgasm theory accessible to psychotherapy contradicted, and still contradict, virtually all approaches which have been developed in all relevant scientific fields. The absolute contradiction between sexuality and culture governs all morality, philosophy, culture, science, psychology, and psychotherapy as an inviolable dogma. Here the most significant position is no doubt held by Freud's psychoanalysis, which adheres to these contradictions, in spite of its clinical discoveries rooted in natural science. It is essential to describe briefly the contradictions which produced the psychoanalytic theory of culture and led to the deterioration of scientific psychoanalysis into meta physics. This cultural theory has caused only confusion.

2. A CONTRADICTION IN FREUD'S THEORY OF CULTURE

SEXUAL REPRESSION AND INSTINCT RENUNCIATION

A serious discussion of the sociological consequences of psychoanalysis must first of all clarify whether the so-called psychoanalytic sociology and world view, as reflected in Freud's later writings, and then obscured to the point of grotesqueness in the works of several of his students such as Roheim, Pfister, Müller-Braunschweig, Kolnai, Laforgue, and others, are the logical outcome of analytic psychology or whether this sociology and world view stem from a break with the analytic principles of clinical observation, due to a misconstrued or incomplete conceptualization of clinical facts. If such a rift or break could be demonstrated in the clinical theory itself, if furthermore we could show the relationship between the divergent clinical concept and the basic sociological viewpoint, we would have found the most important source of error. (Another source lies in equating the individual and society.)

Freud endorsed the cultural-philosophical viewpoint that culture owes its existence to the repression or renunciation of instinctual drives. The basic idea is that cultural achievements result from sublimated sexual energy, indicating that sexual suppression, or repression, is an indispensable factor in establishing any culture. Now there is already historical proof that this concept is erroneous, for there are highly cultured societies in which sexual suppression is non-existent and whose members enjoy completely free sexual lives.[1]

This theory is accurate only insofar as sexual sup-

---

[1] Cf. Reich: *The Invasion of Compulsory Sex-Morality* (New York: Farrar, Straus and Giroux, 1971).

pression forms the mass-psychological basis for a
specific culture in all its forms, namely, the *patriarchal*
culture, but it does not apply to the basis of culture
and its formation in general. How did Freud arrive
at this concept? It was certainly not from *conscious*
political and philosophical motives. On the contrary,
early writings such as his essay on "cultural sexual
morality" point in the direction of a revolutionary
sexual critique of culture. But Freud never again pro-
ceeded along that path; instead, he struggled against
any efforts in that direction and once described them,
in a conversation, as being "outside the middle line
of psychoanalysis." It was precisely my attempts at
a sex-political criticism of culture that gave weight
to our first differences of opinion.

In analyzing the psychic mechanisms and contents
of unconscious emotional life, Freud found that the
unconscious was filled with asocial and antisocial
impulses. Anyone using the corresponding analytic
method can confirm this discovery. Ideas of murdering
the father and possessing the mother are of central
importance in the fantasy life of every man. Cruel
impulses are inhibited in everyone by more or less
conscious guilt feelings. The majority of women are
seized by violent urges to castrate the man and acquire
his penis or incorporate it in one form or another,
as, for instance, by swallowing it. If these impulses
are retained in the subconscious, their inhibition
creates not only social adaptation but also a number
of emotional disturbances, e.g., hysterical vomiting.
Cruel fantasies in the man, such as injuring, stabbing,
or piercing the woman in the sexual act, give rise
to various forms of impotence if they are blocked
by feelings of anxiety and guilt; and they are at the
root of perverse actions, including sex murder, if
the inhibiting mechanism is disturbed. Analysis shows
that impulses to eat their own or others feces fill
the unconscious of a large number of people in our
culture, regardless of their social class. The psychoanalytic discovery that the overaffectionate mother

or wife acts in direct ratio to the force of her unconscious murderous fantasies were anything but agree-
able to the ideologues of "sacred mother love" and the
"marital communion." We might list countless other
examples, but let us return to our subject. These contents of the unconscious largely proved to be residues
of infantile attitudes toward the immediate environment, toward parents, siblings, etc. The child had
to master these impulses in order to exist in our culture.
Most people, however, pay for this mastery with a
more or less severe neurosis, even at an early age,
i.e., with a serious impairment of their capacity for
work and their sexual potency.

The discovery of the antisocial nature of the unconscious was correct, as was the finding that instinct
renunciation is necessary for adaptation to social
life. The latter, however, results in two contradictory
facts: on the one hand, the child must suppress his
instinctual drives so that he can become capable of
adapting to culture; on the other hand, this suppression
of instinctual gratification usually leads to a neurosis,
which in turn restricts his capacity for cultural adaptation, sooner or later makes it completely impossible,
and again turns him into an asocial person. In order
to restore the individual to the conditions of his true
nature, however, his repressions must be eliminated
and his instinctual drives set free. This is the prerequisite for recovery but not the cure itself, as Freud's
early therapeutic formulations suggested. But what
is supposed to replace the repression? Certainly not
these impulses which have been freed from repression,
for then the individual would be unable to exist in
this culture.

In various passages of analytic literature we find
the statement (which, incidentally, has already
become part of the psychoanalytic viewpoint) that
the discovery and liberation of the unconscious, i.e.,
the affirmation of its existence, should on no account
signify an affirmation of corresponding action. Here
the analyst establishes the rule of conduct for life

as well as for the analytic situation: "You must and should *say* whatever you want; but this does not mean that you can *do* what you want." However, the question of what should happen to the drives that had been liberated from repression still confronted, and continues to confront, the responsible analyst with its vast implications. The answer given was: condemn and sublimate. But since only a small number of patients proved capable of the sublimation required by the recovery process, the demand for instinct renunciation by means of condemnation took precedence. Repression should now be replaced by censure. To justify this demand, it was argued that the instincts which in infancy faced a weak, undeveloped ego that could merely repress were now confronted by a strong, adult ego that could resist by "voluntary renunciation of the instincts." Although this therapeutic formulation is largely at odds with clinical experience, it has been—and still is—the dominant formulation in psychoanalysis. It also governs analytic pedagogy and is advocated, for instance, by Anna Freud.

In this view, the individual becomes capable of culture and a bearer of culture through instinct renunciation instead of repression; and since, according to the other basic psychoanalytic concept, society behaves like the individual and can be analyzed as such, it follows logically that the culture of society is predicated and based on instinct renunciation.

The whole construct seems flawless and enjoys the approval of the vast majority of analysts as well as the exponents of an abstract concept of culture in general. For the substitution of repression by condemnation and renunciation seems to ward off a threatening specter which caused grave uneasiness when Freud disclosed his first unequivocal findings that sexual repression not only causes sickness but also renders people incapable of work and culture. The world was up in arms because his theory seemed to threaten morality and ethics, and it accused Freud of preaching, *nolens volens,* a form of "living out" which was a menace to culture, and so on. Freud's alleged antimoralism was one of the strongest weapons of his early opponents. His original assurances that he affirmed "culture" and that his discoveries did not endanger it had left little impression, as was shown by the countless references to Freud's "pansexualism." The specter receded only when the theory of renunciation was established. Then hostility was partly replaced by acceptance; for as long as the instinctual drives were not acted out, it did not matter, from the cultural viewpoint, whether the mechanism of instinctual renunciation or that of repression played the role of Cerberus who would not allow the shadows of the netherworld to rise to the surface. One could even register progress, namely, from the unconscious repression of evil to the voluntary relinquishment of instinctual gratification. Since ethics is not asexual but fights off sexual temptations, all parties arrived at a meeting of minds, and the proscribed psychoanalysis itself became culturally acceptable—unfortunately, by "instinct renunciation," i.e., by renouncing its own theory of the instincts.

I regret that I must destroy the illusions of all concerned, for this formulation contains a demonstrable error which proves it wrong. It is not wrong in the sense that the findings of psychoanalysis, on which the conclusions are based, are incorrect. On the contrary, they are entirely accurate; it is only that they are partly incomplete and they partly obscure the true consequences by their abstract terminology.

INSTINCT GRATIFICATION AND RENUNCIATION

To justify their unscientific conduct, the German psychoanalysts who, because of their middle-class background or under the severe pressure of conditions in Germany, tried to carry out the political adjustment of psychoanalysis, invariably quoted from those writ-

ings by Freud in which they felt they found a justification for their actions. Freud's works do contain some
formulations which deprive psychoanalytic clinical
discoveries of their cultural and revolutionary mo-
mentum and effect and demonstrate the contradiction
between the natural scientist and the bourgeois cultural philosopher. One such passage reads as follows:

> It is a sinister misunderstanding, justified solely
> by ignorance, to believe that psychoanalysis ex-
> pects recovery from neurotic complaints by means
> of "free living out" of sexuality. Rather, in making
> the repressed sexual desires conscious in analy-
> sis, we are able to achieve a *control* [emphasis
> added] which was unattainable by previous re-
> pression. One might be better entitled to say that
> analysis frees the neurotic from the chains of his
> sexuality.[3]

If the seventeen-year-old daughter of a National
Socialist dignitary falls ill with hysteria—say, with
hysterical seizures caused by repressed coital desires—the coital desires are recognized as incestuous
and condemned as such in psychoanalytic treatment.
But what happens to the sexual needs? According
to the formulation just described, the girl is "freed"
from the chains of her sexuality. But clinically the
matter looks different: if the girl frees herself from
her father by means of analysis, she frees herself
merely from the chains of her incestuous desire, but
not from sexuality itself. Freud's formulation neglects
this central fact; we may say that the scientific contro-
versy about the role of genitality is kindled precisely
in this area of clinical postulation and forms the core
of the difference between the theses of sex-economy
and "adjusted" psychoanalysis. Freud's formulation
postulates the girl's renunciation of all sexual life.
In this form, psychoanalysis is acceptable even to
a Nazi dignitary and furnishes Müller-Braunschweig

2 Freud: *Gesammelte Schriften*, Vol. XI (Vienna: Internationaler
Psychoanalytischer Verlag, 1928), pp. 217–18.

with a tool for "breeding heroic man." But this formulation has nothing to do with the psychoanalytic writings burned by Hitler. They represented a psychoanalysis which, disregarding reactionary prejudices, establishes unequivocally that the girl can recover only if she transfers her genital desires from the father to a friend with whom she finds gratification. But this is precisely what contradicts the whole Nazi ideology and inexorably involves the question of society's sexual order. For, in order to satisfy sex-economic requirements, the girl does not merely need to be free genitally; she also needs privacy, a means of contraception, a sexually potent friend who is capable of love (i.e., *not* a National Socialist with his negative sexual structure) understanding parents, and a sex-affirmative social atmosphere—all the more so if her financial means of breaking through the social barriers against adolescent sexual activity are minimal.

The problem of replacing the mechanism of sexual repression with the mechanism of instinct renunciation or, in analytic work, with condemnation would be solved simply—and in the context of Freud's formulations—if the condemnation of instinctual needs and the instinct renunciation were not themselves tied to the economy of instinctual life. The psychic apparatus can tolerate instinct renunciation only under very specific sex-economic conditions, just as the sublimation of drives is governed by specific preconditions. Character-analytic clinical experience teaches us that permanent renunciation of pathogenic or anti-social impulses is possible only if the sexual economy is regulated, i.e., if there are no sexual blocks which invest the impulse to be condemned with additional force. *The sex-economic regulation of biological energy requires the possibility of sexual gratification corresponding to each age group*. This means that one can give up infantile and pathogenic desires in adulthood only if the road to normal genital gratification is open and if such gratification can be experienced. Since the perverse and neurotic gratifica-

tions, from which social life must be protected, are
themselves substitutes for genitality and develop only
if genitality is disturbed or impeded, it is obvious
that we cannot speak generally and abstractly of the
gratification and renunciation of instincts but must
ask concretely *which* instincts are being gratified and
which renounced. If analytic therapy seeks only to
eliminate repressions and not to preach morality,
it can only achieve the renunciation of a need that
does not correspond to the patient's age and stage
of development. Thus, treatment will enable a sexually
maturing girl, who produces neurotic symptoms
because of her infantile fixation to her father, to censure
her infantile incest demands by making them conscious. But this does not mean that these wishes are
eliminated, for the constant sexual stimulation continues to press for discharge. Only moralistic arguments will bring about a renunciation of sexual gratification in a person of her age, but this cannot be
done without seriously violating therapeutic principles
and intentions. Actually, the girl can resolve the fixation to her father only if she finds a satisfactory sexual
partner and experiences real gratification. If this does
not happen, the infantile fixation either is not resolved
or else regresses to other infantile instinctual goals,
while the problem remains.

The same is true for every case of neurotic illness.
The woman who is unsatisfied in her marriage will
unconsciously reactivate infantile sexual needs which
she will give up only if her sexuality is gratified in
an extramarital relationship or in a new marriage.
Just as the condemnation of infantile impulses is itself
a precondition for establishing a healthy sexual life,
so this new sexuality and its effective gratification
are indispensable prerequisites for a definitive solution of the pathological striving. A sex murderer will
relinquish his pathological sexual goals only if a biologically normal sexual life is opened to him. Therefore, the alternative is not instinct renunciation or the

living out of impulses, but which impulses are renounced and which are gratified.

In speaking abstractly of the infernal nature of
the repressed unconscious, we obscure the most crucial facts not only for the therapy and prophylaxis of
neuroses but also for the whole field of pedagogy.
Freud discovered that the content of the unconscious
in neurotics—and in our culture this means the overwhelming majority of people—essentially consists of
infantile, cruel, antisocial impulses. This is correct.
But one fact has been overlooked: the unconscious
also contains demands which completely accord with
natural biological requirements—for instance, the sexual needs of the adolescent or those of the person
trapped in an unhappy marriage. Historically and
economically, the subsequent intensity of asocial and
infantile drives stems from the nongratification of
these natural needs insofar as the ungratified libido
either strengthens primitive infantile impulses or else
creates new, mostly antisocial impulses such as exhibitionism or the impulse toward sex murder. Ethnology teaches us that up to a certain point of economic
development such impulses are absent in primitive
cultures and appear only as a substitute when that
society suppresses normal love life.

These impulses, which resulted from the social
development of sexual forms, and had to become unconscious because society justifiably prohibits their gratification, are invariably understood in
psychoanalysis as biological facts. This viewpoint
is not far removed from that of Magnus Hirschfeld,
e.g., that exhibitionism is based on specific exhibitionistic hormones. Such fatuous mechanistic bi-
ologism is so hard to unmask because it fulfills
a certain function in modern society. It shifts the
problem from the social to the biological realm, render-
ing it for all practical purposes inaccessible. Hence
there is a sociology of the unconscious and of asocial
sexuality, which means a sociological history of unconscious impulses, in terms of both the quantity

and the quality of the repressed impulses. Not only
is repression itself a social phenomenon but what
causes repression is also a social phenomenon. The
investigation of the origin of partial drives will have
to be oriented in ethnological findings. For example,
in certain matriarchal tribes, an anal phase of libidinal
development—which in our own society is generally
placed between the oral and genital phases—is rarely
seen, because the children are suckled up to their
third or fourth year and then immediately and actively
engage in genital games.

The psychoanalytic concept of antisocial impulses
is absolute and therefore leads to conclusions which
clash with the facts. If these impulses were understood
in context, however, basically different conclusions
would result, not only for the concept of analytic
therapy but also, and in a particularly important
way, for sociology and sex-economy. The anal activity
of a child in his first or second year has nothing
whatsoever to do with being "social" or "asocial."
The abstract view of the asocial nature of anal impulses
in the child favors the often applied rule to make
the child "capable of culture," if possible even in
the first six months of life. Later this approach results
in the exact opposite, severe inhibitions of anal
sublimations and anal-neurotic disturbances. The
mechanistic view of the absolute contradiction
between sexual gratification and culture caused even
analytically oriented parents to resort to measures
against childhood masturbation, or at least to "mild
diversions." Unless I am mistaken, there is no reference in Anna Freud's writings to what she pri
vately considers to be in accord with psychoanalysis,
namely, that the child's masturbation must be regarded as a physiological development and should *not*
be curtailed. If unconscious, repressed material is
also considered inimical to culture, the genital
demands of adolescents must be condemned. This
is usually done with the well-intentioned comment
that the reality principle requires a postponement

of instinct gratifiction. That this reality principle is itself relative and that it serves, and is determined by, today's authoritarian society, is excluded from the discussion as mere politics which has nothing to do with science. That this exclusion also constitutes politics is not recognized. The most ominous fact is that such postulates have gravely threatened analytic investigation, not only by impeding the discovery of certain facts but also by paralyzing the practical application of confirmed results by connecting them with reactionary cultural concepts, and sometimes even by falsifying them. Since psychoanalytic research constantly operates with the effects of society on the individual as well as with judgments about health and sickness, sociality and asociality, but is unaware of the revolutionary character of its method and results, it moves in a tragic circle between the finding that sexual repression is inimical to culture and that it is a cultural necessity.

To summarize the facts overlooked by analytic research and contradicting its concept of culture:

Qualitatively and quantitatively, the unconscious is itself conditioned by culture.

The condemnation of infantile and antisocial impulses is predicated on the gratification of the physiological sexual needs at a given time.

Sublimation, as the most important cultural achievement of the psychic apparatus, requires the elimination of sexual repression and in adulthood is applicable only to the gratification of pregential, not genital, needs.

Genital gratification as the decisive sex-economic factor in the prophylaxis of neuroses and in the restoration of the capacity for social achievement is in flagrant contradiction to today's laws and to every patriarchal religion.

The elimination of sexual repression which was introduced by psychoanalysis as an essential element of the therapeutic process and as a factor of sociological significance stands in sharp opposition to those aspects of cuture which are based on this repression.

Insofar as psychoanalysis maintains its theory of culture, it does so at the expense of the factual results of its research because it tries to resolve, in favor of its cultural philosophy, the contradictions between the cultural views of analytic scientists and those scientific data that are directed against this culture. Wherever it does not dare to draw the conclusions from the results of its own research, it takes shelter behind the allegedly unpolitical (nonpragmatic) character of science, while every step of analytic theory and practice deals with political (pragmatic) facts.

If we examine the unconscious psychic content of clerical, Fascistic, and other reactionary ideologies, we find that they are essentially defense mechanisms arising from the fear of the unconscious inferno which every individual carries inside himself. This might justify ascetic morality and the concept of God as opposed to the "satanic" element, but only if the antisocial unconscious impulses constitute a biologically given, absolute factor; then political reaction would be correct, but by the same token any attempt to eliminate the sexual plight would be senseless. The conservative world would then rightly appeal to the fact that the deterioration of the "higher," "divine," and "moral" qualities in man would lead to chaos in his social and ethical conduct. This is precisely what is meant unconsciously by the term "cultural Bolshevism." Apart from its sex-political wing, the revolutionary movement often does not know this interconnection and frequently makes common front with political reaction when basic questions of sex-economy are at issue. To be sure, it opposes the concept of sex-economy for other reasons than does political reaction (it does not know this concept and its historical modifications). However, it, too, believes in the biological and absolute nature of evil sexual drives and in the necessity of moral inhibition and regulation. Like its opponents, it ignores the fact that the moralistic regulation of instinctual life creates precisely what it alleges to keep in check: the antisocial drives.

However, sex-economy teaches us that the antisocial unconscious instinctual life of modern man—insofar as it is indeed antisocial and not merely regarded as such by moralists—is a product of moralistic regulation and can be abolished only with its elimination. Sex-economy alone can resolve the contradiction between culture and nature because in eliminating repression of the instincts it also eliminates the perverse and antisocial drives.

3. SECONDARY DRIVES AND MORAL REGULATION

In the struggle between so-called "cultural Bolshevism" and Fascistic "anti-Bolshevism," the assertion that social revolution completely destroys morality and leads social life into sexual chaos has played an enormous role. So far, attempts have been made to invalidate this argument by claiming that, on the contrary, a shattered capitalism has created the social chaos and that the social revolution is entirely capable of restoring the security of social life. Here, one contention faced another. And in the Soviet Union the substitution of the authoritarian moral principle with non-authoritarian self-regulation did not succeed.

The confrontation of the two claims is just as unconvincing as the attempt to compete with political reaction by insisting on one's own "morality." It must first be understood why the average person is so bound to the concept of morality and why he invariably connects the words "social revolution" with the image of sexual and cultural chaos. Part of the answer to this question has already been given by our investigation of Fascist ideology: to the unconscious, affective

life of the average man, structured in terms of sex
negation, being a cultural Bolshevist meant the "living
out of sexual sensuality." Now, if someone believed
that in the social revolution sex-economic insights
which eliminate moral regulation could be immediately applied in practice, this would merely furnish
evidence that the concept of sex-economy was misunderstood.

As soon as a society assumes ownership of the
means of production, it is inevitably confronted by
the question of how human communal life should
be regulated: morally or "freely." Even superficial
reflection shows that there can be no question of
immediately freeing sexuality or suspending moral
norms and regulations. We have frequently encountered the fact that man, with his present character
structure, cannot regulate himself, that although he
can immediately establish an economic democracy
he cannot create a political one. This is, after all,
the whole point of Lenin's thesis that the state would
only gradually wither away. Therefore, if we want
to suspend moralistic regulation and replace it with
self-regulation, we must know to what extent the
old moralistic regulation was necessary and to what
extent, in terms of both individuals and society, it
was a calamity and caused further calamities.

The compulsory moral viewpoint of political reaction regards biological drives and social interests in
terms of an absolute contradiction. As a result, it
is said, if "morals were suspended," the "animal instincts" would take over and "cause chaos." It is
clear that the evocation of social chaos, which plays
such a tremendously important role in politics, is
nothing but the fear of human drives. Therefore, is
compulsory morality necessary? Yes, insofar as antisocial drives do threaten the social community. How,
then, is it possible to eliminate compulsory moral
regulation?

This question is answered immediately if we take
into account the following sex-economic findings:

moral regulation of the natural, biological needs by means of repression, nongratification, etc., creates secondary, pathological, antisocial drives that must, of necessity, be inhibited. Thus, moralism did not arise from the need to suppress socially disturbing drives, because it existed *prior* to the formation of these drives. It originated in primitive society when a developing upper class, which was becoming economically powerful, had certain interests in suppressing the natural needs, which in themselves did not disturb society.[3] Compulsory moral regulation acquired justification for its existence at the moment when social life *actually* became threatened by the conditions that moral regulation had produced. Correspondingly, suppression of the gratification of the need for food produced the tendency to steal, which in turn necessitated the moral regulation against stealing. Hence, if we discuss the question of whether compulsory morality is necessary or not, whether one form of morality should be replaced by another, or whether moral regulation per se should be replaced by self-regulation, we can make no progress whatever unless we distinguish between *natural* biological drives and the *secondary,* antisocial drives created by a compulsory morality. The unconscious psychic life of man in a patriarchal society is filled with both kinds of drives. Therefore, if the antisocial drives are suppressed—and justifiably so—natural biological drives will also be sacrificed, because it is impossible to separate them. However, while political reaction *a priori* associates the concept of drives with the idea of antisociality, the distinction we have made above offers us a way out.

As long as the restructuring of man has not succeeded to the extent that the sex-economic regulation of his biological energy precludes any tendency toward antisocial acts, moral regulation will not be eliminated. Since the process of restructuring will presumably

---

3 Cf. *The Invasion of Compulsory Sex-Morality.*

take a very long time, we can say that the elimination
of compulsory moral regulation and its displacement
by sex-economic regulation will be possible only to
the extent to which the realm of the secondary, antisocial drives is reduced in favor of natural biological
drives. We are justified in making this prediction
on the basis of the processes observed in the character-
analytic treatment of individuals. There, too, we
see that the patient relinquishes his moralistic form
of regulation only to the extent to which he regains
his natural sexuality. Along with the moral regulation
by his conscience, the patient also loses his antisocial
tendencies and becomes "moral" to the same extent
that he becomes genitally healthy.

Hence social development will not do away with
moral regulation overnight; it will first of all restruc-
ture people in such a way as to enable them to live
and work in a social community with independence
and truly voluntary self-discipline, which cannot be
imposed by authority and moral pressure. Moral inhibition will apply only to antisocial drives; e.g., the
seduction of children by adults will be severely punished. Moral regulation will not be abolished as long
as the impulse to seduce children is structurally present
in the masses of adults. In this respect, conditions
after the revolution will still be the same as in an
authoritarian society. The crucial difference is that
the free society will provide ample room and security
for the gratification of natural needs. Thus, it will
not only not prohibit a love relationship between
two adolescents of the opposite sex but will give it
all manner of social support. Such a society will not
only not prohibit the child's masturbation but, on
the contrary, will probably conclude that any adult
who hinders the development of the child's sexuality
should be severely dealt with.

We should not now regard the concept of "sexual
drives" as absolute and rigid, for the secondary drive
is conditioned not merely by what it wants but also
by the point of time at which it develops and by the

circumstances under which it seeks to obtain its graitification. One and the same drive in one situation and at a given time may be natural, while in another situation and at another time it may be asocial. To clarify this point: If a child in his first and second years urinates in bed and plays with his feces, this is a natural phase in the pregenital development of his sexuality. At that age, the impulse to play with feces is natural and biologically conditioned, and punishing the child for this natural activity itself calls for the severest punishment. But if the same person wanted to eat or play with his feces at the age of fourteen, this would be a secondary, antisocial, pathological impulse. Such an adolescent should not be punished; he should be hospitalized. Even so, a free society should not be content with this. Rather, its most important task should be to transform education in such a way that the impulse toward such actions would no longer exist.

To mention another example: If a boy of fifteen wanted to start a love relationship with a thirteen-year-old maturing girl, a free society would not only not oppose it but would support and protect it. On the other hand, if the same boy of fifteen were to induce three-year-old girls into sexual games or if he tried to seduce a girl of his own age against her will, such conduct would be antisocial. It would indicate that he is neurotically inhibited in his capacity to choose a partner his own age. To summarize, we may say that during the period of transition from an authoritarian to a free society the following principle would be valid: moral regulation for secondary, asocial drives and sex-economic self-regulation for natural biological needs. The goal of social development is progessively to eliminate secondary drives and the moral compulsion that accompanies them, and to replace them completely with sex-economic self-regulation.

Moralists or even persons who function in abnormal ways might easily interpret what we have said about the secondary drives as serving their own purposes. But it will doubtless be possible to clarify the distinction between natural and secondary drives to such an extent that the moral superman of patriarchy can no longer slip through the back door into the life of the community. The existence of strict moral principles has invariably signified that the biological, and specifically the sexual, needs of man were not being satisfied. Every moral regulation is in itself sex-negating, and all compulsory morality is life-negating. The social revolution has no more important task than finally to enable human beings to realize their full potentialities and find gratification in life.

Sex-economy aspires to "moral conduct" just as much as does moral regulation. But sex-economy wants to establish it differently and it has also a totally different understanding of morality—not as something antithetical to nature but in full harmony with nature and civilization. Sex-economy opposes compulsory moral regulation, but not a morality that is life-affirming.

4. SEX-ECONOMIC "MORALITY"

All over the world people are fighting for a new order of social life, sometimes under favorable but often under the most adverse circumstances. Not only do they wage their fight under the worst social and economic conditions, but they are also inhibited, confused, and threatened by their own psychic structures, which are basically the same as the psychic structures of those who oppose them. The goal of a cultural revolution is to create human character structures capable of self-regulation. Today's fighters who are struggling to reach this goal frequently live by principles formed by this goal, but they are no more than "principles." It is important to make clear that today there are no people with a fully developed, integrated, sex-affirmative structure, because all of us have been influenced by the authoritarian, religious, sex-negating machinery of education. Nevertheless, in shaping our personal lives we struggle for an attitude which might be described as sex-economic. One person may succeed to a degree, another may have great trouble in restructuring himself. Whoever has participated for years, even decades, in the workers' movement knows from experience that something of a future sex-economic life has been anticipated here and there in the personal lives of these people.

A few examples will show what "sex-economic morality" means even today and how it has anticipated the morality of the future. It should be emphasized that we are by no means alone in advocating this kind of life and its aspirations; rather, we can hold such views and lead such a life because these modes of conduct, embodying new "moral principles," have already begun to penetrate the total process of human society, entirely independent of and unrelated to an individual's will imposed upon it from outside or to party slogans.

Fifteen or twenty years ago, it was a disgrace for an unmarried girl *not* to be a virgin. Today, girls of all social strata are developing the attitude, more or less clearly, that it is a disgrace *still* to be a virgin at the age of eighteen, twenty, or twenty-two.

Not too long ago it was a rigorously punishable offense if a couple who wanted to marry had physical knowledge of each other prior to marriage. Today, quite spontaneously and in spite of an opposing church, conventional medicine, philosophy, etc., the view has penetrated wide circles of the population that it is unhygienic, imprudent, and perhaps destructive for the future if a man and a woman who wish to establish a permanent relationship are tied to each other without previously being convinced that they are sexually compatible.

Extramarital sexual intercourse, which only a few

years ago was still a disgrace, and even branded by the law as an "offense against nature," has today become a matter of course and a vital necessity.

Not long ago, the idea that a sexually mature girl of fifteen or sixteen could have a boyfriend seemed absurd, even unthinkable. Today the question is under discussion, and in a few years it will have become just as self-evident as is now the right of the unmarried woman to have a partner. In a hundred years, the insistence that woman teachers should not have any sexual life will evoke the same surprised smile that is reserved today for the time when men forced women to wear chastity belts. The idea still generally prevails that a woman must be seduced and should not herself be the seducer. But who today does not find this ludicrous?

At one time the woman could not be sure that sexual intercourse would not take place if she was unwilling. The concept of marital duty, which is dictated by law and has serious consequences, proves this. But in our sexual counseling and our medical practice we learn every day that it is becoming increasingly a matter of course that, all social ideologies notwithstanding, a man does not have sexual intercourse with his partner if she is unwilling; even more, he does not embrace her unless she is genitally aroused. A number of years ago (and even today) it was well known that women tolerated the sexual act without participating in it. It is part of the new morality not to have sexual intercourse unless it is mutually desired; this eliminates the rape ideology and the attitude that the woman should be seduced or at least gently subdued.

A few years ago (and even today) the opinion prevailed that one had to watch jealously over the fidelity of the partner, and the statistics on sex murders convince us at first glance that social depravity in this area is widespread. But gradually, and more or less clearly, the insight gains ground that no individual has the right to forbid the partner either a temporary or a permanent sexual relationship with another. He (or she) is only entitled to withdraw or to regain the affections of the partner, or perhaps to tolerate infidelity. This attitude, which is in complete accord with sex-economic findings, has nothing to do with the hyper-radical ideology that one should not be jealous at all, that it "makes no difference" if the partner establishes another relationship. The pain in envisioning a beloved partner in another's embrace is natural. This natural jealousy must be strictly distinguished from possessive jealousy. Just as it is natural not to want to know that a beloved partner is in the arms of someone else, so it is unnatural, and tantamount to a secondary drive, to forbid a partner to establish another relationship when there is no longer any sexual intimacy in a marriage or long-lasting relationship.

We are satisfied with citing these few examples and contend that the complicated personal and in particular sexual life of people today would be very simply regulated if human character structure were capable of drawing all those conclusions that result from taking pleasure in life. It is the essence of sex-economic regulation to avoid absolute rules or norms and to accept the interests of life affirmation and life enjoyment as the regulators of human society. That, owing to the ruined structure of human beings, this awareness is extremely restricted today, argues only against the moralistic regulation which has created this structure, but not against the principle of self-regulation itself.

Thus, there are *two* kinds of "morality" but only one kind of moral self-regulation. That "morality" which all people affirm to be self-evident (not to rape, not to murder, etc.) can be established only if natural needs are fully gratified. But the other "morality" which we reject (abstinence for children and adolescents, absolute and eternal marital fidelity, compulsory marriage, etc.) is itself pathological and causes the very chaos it feels called upon to master. It is this morality which we inexorably oppose.

It is said that sex-economy intends to destroy the family. People prattle about the "sexual chaos" that would follow in the wake of a freeing of the capacity to love, and the masses listen to their words and trust them because these people wear morning coats and gold-rimmed glasses and talk as if they were in command. Whether or not what they say is true, however, depends on what is meant here. The economic subjugation of women and children must be eliminated; and also their subjugation to authority. Only if this is accomplished will the man love his wife, the woman her husband, the children their parents, and the parents their children. They will no longer have any reason to hate one another. Thus what we want to destroy is the hatred which the family breeds, and the violation it causes under the guise of love. If familial love is the great human blessing, it will have to prove itself. If a dog on a leash does not run off, no one will regard him as a loyal companion on the basis of this fact alone. No reasonable individual will speak of love if a man sleeps with a defenseless woman who is virtually chained hand and feet. No one, unless he is a real scoundrel, will be proud of a woman's love gained by financial support or by power. No decent person will accept love that is not given voluntarily. The compulsory morality of marital obligations and familial authority is a morality of cowards and impotent people who are afraid of life, people who are incapable of experiencing through the power of natural love, what they try to procure for themselves with the help of marital laws and the police.

These people want to put the whole human race into their own straitjacket because they are unable to tolerate the sight of natural sexuality. It irritates them and turns them green with envy because they themselves woul like to live in this manner but cannot. We do not want to force anyone to give up family life, but we also do not want anyone who does not want it to be forced into it. Those who can and want to live their lives monogamously should do so; but those who cannot, those whom it will destroy, should have the possibility of making other arrangements. After all, the establishment of a "new life" is predicated on recognizing the contradictions in the old one.

II

The Failure of Sexual Reform

Sexual reform seeks to remedy abuses in social and sexual life which, in the final analysis, are rooted in the economy and are expressed in the emotional suffering of the members of society. Within the context of economic and ideological conflicts in authoritarian society, the contradictions between the prevalent morality, as imposed by the ruling classes in the interest of maintaining and strengthening their hold over society, and the natural sexual needs of particular individuals have intensified, producing a crisis that is insoluble within the framework of existing society. Never before in the history of mankind have these contradictions resulted in such sharp, objectively cruel, even murderous consequences as in the past thirty years. Therefore, no other era has produced so much discussion and printed matter on sexual questions as the present era; nor has there been an era in which all aspirations failed so acutely as in the "age of technology and science"—which is only an apparent paradox. The contradiction between the corrosive sexual plight of men and women and the enormous progress in sexology is the counterpart to that between the economic plight of the working masses and the tremendous technical achievements of our time. It is only an apparent contradition that, at a time of aseptic operations and highly sophisticated surgical skills, about 20,000 women per year died in Germany from abortions between 1920 and 1932, while 75,000 women per year became seriously ill with sepsis due to abortions. Likewise, with the progressive simplification of production between 1930 and 1933, more and more industrial workers became unemployed and, with their families, were ruined physically and morally. Far from being paradoxical, this contradiction makes good sense if it is not regarded as independent of the economic and social structure which produced it. We will have to show that the facts of social misery as well as the insolubility of the sexual problem are part of the social order from which they stem.

Sexual reformist aspirations fall into the category of cultural-political struggles. The liberal, for instance Norman Haire, fights only one flaw in society with his sexual reform but he does not want to touch upon society as a whole. The pacifistic socialist, the "reformist," believes that with sexual reform a part of socialism makes its way into our society. He tries to reverse the course of development by attempting to reach the goal before changing the economic structure.

No matter how factual our argumentation, the moralist will never understand that sexual misery is one of the inevitable symptoms of the compulsory morality he defends. He sees the causes of this misery either in human wickedness or in a mysterious *ananke* (supernatural compulsion) or in a no less mysterious will to suffer, particularly if he is really convinced that sexual misery is so great only because his ascetic and monogamous demands are not met. And although we are willing to accept in good faith his merciful intentions of eliminating by reform the harm that has been done, it is too much to expect him to admit his own responsibility and his own role as a mere tool. Under certain circumstances, the consequences of such an admission could undermine the economic basis from which he launches his reform. For he has not yet learned that Fascists do not joke in serious matters and will liquidate the liberal pacifist by the hangman, without much ado, if their existence is at stake.

For decades, sexual reform has tried to alleviate sexual misery. The questions of prostitution and venereal disease, of sexual suffering, interrupted pregnancy, and sex murder as well as the problem of the neuroses are constantly in the center of public debate. None of the measures taken so far has been able to mitigate sexual suffering. To go further, the proposals of sexual reform invariably lag behind the actual changes in the relationships between the sexes. The decrease in marriages, the increase in divorces and adultery, cry out for a discussion of marital reform. Extramarital sexual intercourse is gaining more and more acceptance, the view of ethically oriented exponents of sexology notwithstanding. Sexual intercourse among large segments of youth between the ages of fifteen and eighteen is becoming a general fact, while sex reformers are still debating the question of whether abstinence among adolescents should not go beyond the twentieth year or whether masturbation should be regarded as a natural phenomenon. "Criminal" abortion and the use of contraceptives are constantly gaining ground, while sexual reform is still beleaguered by the question of whether social criteria as well as medical indications should be taken into account in interrupting pregnancy.

This lag in reformist endeavors and the fact that concrete changes in sexual life are running far ahead of the nominal efforts of sex reformers clearly show that there is something inherently wrong with these efforts, that an innate contradiction acs like a brake and renders them futile.

Thus, we face the task of finding the hidden meaning of the fiasco of authoritarian sexual reform and to tracing the relationships which organically connect authoritarian sexual reform and its failure with the authoritarian order of society. These relationships are by no means simple, and the problem of the formation of sexual ideology required a special, comprehensive investigation of its own.[1] This book will deal only with a single aspect in which the following factors will intersect:

1. The institution of marriage as a brake on sexual reform.
2. The compulsory family as the educational apparatus.
3. The insistence on asceticism for youth as the logical measure, from the authoritarian point of view, for fostering monogamous, lifelong marriages and the patriarchal family.
4. The contradiction between conservative marriage reform and conservative marital ideology.

Up to now, many of these factors have remained unnoticed, because the critique of sexual reform emphasized the external aspects of sexual life (housing, abortion, marital laws, etc.) instead of sexual needs, processes, and experiences. Little can be added to that critique; it has been thoroughly confirmed, sociologically in Europe by Hodann, Hirschfeld, Brupbacher, Wolff, and others and especially by the revolution in sexual legislation carried out in the Soviet Union in 1918–1921.[2]

But a critique of the psychic and cultural consequences which the authoritarian social order imposes on the sex-economy of the individual and of society is predicated on a knowledge of sexual processes, both psychic and somatic.

---

[1] Cf. Reich: *The Invasion of Compulsory Sex-Morality* and *The Mass Psychology of Fascism*.

[2] Cf. the writings of Genss on the abortion question in Soviet Russia. Also Wolfson: *Soziologie der Ehe und Familie* [Sociology of Marriage and Family]; and Batkis: *The Sexual Revolution in the Soviet Union*, among others.

Insofar as medical criticism is added here to sociology, it rests entirely on the experiences of character-analytic clinical practice and on orgasm research.

III

The Institution of Compulsory Marriage as the Basis of Contradictions in Sexual Life

Sexual reform is pursued from the vantage point of the interests of compulsory marital morality. Behind it stands the institution of marriage, which in turn is firmly anchored in economic interests. Marital morality is the supreme exponent of these economic interests in the ideological superstructure of society and as such permeates the thoughts and actions of every conservative sex reformer. It also makes sexual reform impossible.

The demand for premarital chastity and marital fidelity of the wife is an immediate consequence of economic interests. The German sexual hygienist Gruber correctly recognized this fact:

> We must value the chastity of the woman as the highest national good, for the chastity of the woman offers the sole guarantee that we are truly the fathers of our children, that we work and toil for our own flesh and blood. Without this guarantee there is no possibility of a secure, intimate family life, this indispensable foundation for the prosperity of people and state. It is this, and not egotistical arbitrariness on the part of the man, that causes law and ethics to make greater claims on the woman with regard to her premarital chastity

and marital fidelity. Her lack of ties offers far
greater dangers than do his.[1]

Through the connection of the right of succession
with procreation, the accursed marital problem is
firmly rooted in sexual life; the sexual union between
two people ceases to be a matter of sexuality. In
the long run, the wife's extramarital chastity and
marital fidelity cannot be maintained without a high
degree of sexual repression on her part. This, in turn,
results in the demand that girls remain chaste.
Originally, and even today in some primitive societies,
a girl could live sexually as she pleased until she
married. Only when the marriage is contracted does
extra-marital chastity become mandatory.[2] In our
society, particularly around the turn of the century,
the demand for virginity prior to marriage has been
strictly upheld. The rigid fidelity of the wife and the
premarital chastity of the girl form the two pillars
of reactionary sexual morality which support patriarchal marriage and family by creating a human
structure characterized by sexual anxiety.

Up to this point, the ideology logically expresses
economic interests. But now the contradiction of this
process sets in. Because of the demand of the girl's
chastity, the young males are deprived of love objects.
This, all at once, produces several conditions which
were not intended by the social order but which necessarily derive from the form of its sexual system:
adultery becomes the counterpart of monogamous
marriage and the chaste young women are supplemented by prostitutes. Thus adultery and prostitu
tion are an integral part of a double-standard sexual
morality which permits the men, before as well as
during marriage, what, for economic reasons, it *must*

1 *Hygiene des Geschlechtslebens* [Hygiene of Social Life], 53rd to
54th ed., pp. 146-47.

2 Cf. Bryk: *Negereros*, p. 77; Ploss-Bartels: *Das Weib* [The Woman]
(Leipzig, 1902), Vol. I, p. 449; and especially Malinowski: *The Sexual
Life of Savages* (London, 1929).

deny the women. But the natural demands of sexuality bring about the opposite of what a strict sexual morality intended. Immorality, in the reactionary sense of adultery and extramarital relationships, evolves into two grotesque social phenomena: sexual perversion and venal sexuality outside as well as inside of marriage. Since sensual activity generally takes place outside of marriage in the marketplace, a tender relationship with the sexual partner naturally suffers. The young man splits his sexuality by gratifying his sensual needs with a woman of the "lower classes" while bestowing his tender feelings on a girl of his own social circle. This split, together with the linking of sensuality and monetary gain, results in a complete degradation and brutalization of love life, its most important repercussion being widespread venereal diseases, which, also unintentionally, become an essential part of the conservative sexual order. The struggle against prostitution, sexual intercourse outside of marriage, and venereal disease is pursued under the watchword "asceticism," in accord with the view that sexual intercourse is moral only within marriage. The ostensible dangers of extramarital sexual activities are used as apparent proof of its perniciousness.

The reactionary authors themselves affirm the impossibility of asceticism as an effective protection against venereal disease, but they do not draw the right conclusions from the dead end of marital morality. Even though venereal diseases are caused by bacilli, they owe their dissemination to the debased extramarital sexual life, which is established as a moral contrast to the sanctioned marital relationship. The reactionary sexologist, whether he wants to or not, must give ideological support to this contrast, if he wishes to remain in his social milieu.

The question of abortion also shows the contradictions between factual evidence and the demands which support marital morality. One of the arguments against the repeal of the abortion law is that of "morality."

Where would it lead us if abortion were legalized? The specific passage in the law was intended as a brake on "unbridled sex life." One wants the population to increase (and achieves the opposite: a constant decrease in the birth rate). Yet it is known that the liberalization of abortion laws did not hinder the population increase in Soviet Russia. On the contrary, legal abortion combined with the necessary social prerequisites caused a significant increase in the population.[3] Furthermore, why is "morality" so concerned about an increased population? Is it because one needs national hegemony and cannon fodder?

It is erroneous to believe that the desire for an industrial reserve army is an incentive here. Presumably this used to be the case when unemployment of a specific small percentage of workers was an extraordinarily effective means of maintaining low wages. But times have changed. The mass unemployment in Western countries, which has become an integral part of our economy, has invalidated this incentive. The direct economic motives for the prohibition of birth control are minimal when compared to the ideological, philosophical ones, which in the final analysis are also rooted in economic interests. The essential motive for the punishment of abortion is the consideration for "morality." If abortions were legal, they would have to be permitted not only for married women but also for unmarried women. This would imply approval of extramarital relationships and would eliminate the moral compulsion of marriage after pregnancy. The institution of marriage would be damaged. Ideologically, marital morality must be kept intact, in spite of the contradictory facts of sexual life, because marriage is the backbone of the authoritarian family, which in turn is the breeding ground for authoritarian ideologies and character structure.

3 Cf. Genss: *Was lehrt die Freigabe der Abtreibung in Sowjetrussland?* [What does the liberalization of abortion in Soviet Russia teach us?] (Agis Verlag, 1926).

Until now, this factor has been too often neglected in the discussion of abortion. One might adopt halfway measures, e.g., abortion might be permitted for married women but not for unmarried women. Respect for marriage would then be preserved. This argument would be valid if a factor in the sex-ideological machinery did not militate against it. It is a basic element of compulsory sexual morality that the sexual act must not be divorced from procreation and become an act of need and pleasure. Official recognition of sexual gratification—irrespective of procreation— would suddenly overthrow all official and ecclesiastical conceptions of sexual life. Thus, for example, Max Marcuse writes in his collected work *Die Ehe* [Marriage] (the chapter on "Preventive Measures in Marriage," p. 339):

> If internal medication of women would actually succeed in sterilizing them temporarily, as desired, it will be the most urgent task to find a method of distributing this medication which will safeguard its advantages for . . . hygienic purposes but avert the tremendous danger it poses for the sexual order and morality, even for life and culture [i.e., authoritarian life and culture.]

German Fascism took into account this grave moral concern which was expressed by the liberal sex reformer Marcuse in 1927. About 1,500 sterilizations in the Third Reich did not safeguard any hygienic purposes but "averted the tremendous danger [the separation of sexuality and procreation] it posed for the sexual order and morality, even for life and culture"—in the interests of staving off "sexual Bolshevism."

We can demonstrate by a simple calculation what these statements really mean. No patriotic sexologist, concerned about the perpetuation of humanity, can ask a worker's wife to bear more than, say, five children. This means having sexual intercourse five times in one's life, if the act is regarded merely as a means to procreation. However, human nature, probably to cause precisely such headaches for our sex reformers, has arranged it so that man feels sexual excitation and wants to have sexual intercourse even when he has no marriage license. Furthermore, he feels this urge roughly every third day. That means that if he is unconcerned about conventional morality, he has sexual intercourse three thousand to four thousand times from his fourteenth to his fiftieth year. Therefore, if Marcuse merely meant to safeguard the increase of the race, he would have to propose that the woman be allowed to use safe contraceptives all but five times or as often as necessary to produce five children.

But in reality the sex reformer is distressed not by the "five" acts of procreation but by the fear that man might indeed, with the consent of the authorities, not only desire three thousand acts of pleasure but even experience them. Why does this idea frighten him?

1. Because the institution of marriage is not organized for this natural state of affairs but nevertheless must be preserved as the basic element in the factory of authoritarian ideology—the family.

2. Because he would be unable to escape the problem of adolescent sexuality, which today he thinks he can brush off with the catchword "asceticism" or "sexual enlightenment."

3. Because his theory of the monogamous nature of women, indeed of mankind in general, would collapse, shaken by biological and physiological facts.

4. Because he would get into serious conflict with the Church, with which he is on good terms only as long as he, like Van de Velde in his book *Ideal Marriage,* propagates the idea of various erotic activities within the framework of marriage, while pointing out at some length that his aspirations do not contradict the dogma of the Church.

The ideology of conventional morality is a supportive part of the authoritarian institution of marriage.

It conflicts with a realization of the importance of sexual gratification and is predicated on sexual negation. Thus the really inhibiting influence in the question of abortion emanates from the institution of marriage.

IV

The Influence of Conservative
Sexual Morality

1. "OBJECTIVE, NONPOLITICAL" SCIENCE

The specific characteristic of prevailing sexual ideology consists in the negation and debasement of sexuality which operates in every individual within authoritarian society through the process of sexual repression. It does not matter which sexual needs are affected by this repression, to what extent this happens, and what consequences ensue for the individual. For the moment, it is important to note the means that are used by "public opinion," which includes conservative sexology, and the general results that are achieved.

Conservative sexology is the most significant exponent of the ideological climate. In discussing marriage problems and adolescent sexuality we will explain this in detail; for now we wish to show typical examples of the moralistic prejudice of allegedly objective sexology.

Timerding, in his thesis on "sexual ethics" in Marcuse's *Handwörterbuch der Sexualwissenschaft* [Handbook of Sexology], a work which certainly represents the opinion of official sexology, writes:

> The general ethical attitude has invariably proved to be significant for the whole concept of sexual

46

life; reform proposals in the field of sexuality are almost always justified by ethical principles. [2nd ed., p. 710]

The real importance of the ethical view of sexual life is that it teaches one to perceive the manifestations of sexual life within the broad context of total personality development and the social order. [p. 712]

We know that the social order means the authoritarian order, and that the development of a personality means a personality that can be integrated into the authoritarian order. But all official sexual morality is neccessarily sex-negating, even if it makes some concessions to sexual gratification in its battle with the realities of sexual life, and even if the ruling class lives and promotes a sexual life which violates this official morality. Owing to their inner contradictions, many investigators arrive at formulations which are incompatible with the social atmosphere. But in practice this natural-scientific opposition is always ineffectual; it never reaches any concrete action that would transcend the framework set by a reactionary society. This, of course, must lead to inconsistencies, even absurdities. Thus, Wiese writes:

. . . Beyond religious asceticism (especially in attenuated forms) we find much asceticism in modern life, i.e., abstinence based on principle, the motives of which stem from philosophy, ethics, considerations of social purposefulness, weak psychic or physical eroticism, a tendency toward spiritualism, or a mixture of all these impulses that originate in traditional religious instincts. It is often believed that the spiritualization . . . of human intercourse can be achieved only by virtue of (greater or lesser) asceticism. This is rooted in the disdain of the body and the idea that emotions and body are separate and in competition with each

other. This modern asceticism, often existing only in
theory and making a virtue of necessity, can be
equated with genuine religious asceticism only in
rare cases. It is often the feeble result of satiety or
of an insufficient vitality which cannot tolerate the
fervor or the lively reciprocity of sensuality.

In judging any form and degree of asceticism, it
is valid to observe that a strong, natural drive cannot be eliminated but merely rechanneled and transformed. Asceticism "represses" the sexual drive.
While we must be strongly aware of some exag-
gerations of Freud's school, the doctrine of re-
pressing the sexual drive into the unconscious
through asceticism must be basically acknowledged. Much fanaticism, eccentricity, hatred of
mankind, unchaste fantasies originate from asceticism. [p. 40]

And further on:

A natural instinct of abstinence (not to be confused with a temporarily diminished drive or with
its cooling off in advancing age) does not exist in
a healthy man; asceticism is primarily of social
and not biological origin. Sometimes it appears as
an adaptation to unnatural conditions of life; at
other times, as an unhealthy ideology. [p.40]

All in all, these statements are correct; but even
Wiese precludes any practical consequences by distin-
guishing religious ascetism from other forms of
asceticism, a distinction which overlooks the fact
that religious asceticism, too, springs from a "tendency
toward spiritualism," and not from any "inherited
religious instincts." By making allowance for religious
instincts in an asceticism that is primarily conditioned
by society, he leaves open a religious back door
through which asceticism can again sneak into the
ideology from which it had been excluded by his cor-

rect scientific statement that a "natural instinct for abstinence" does not exist in the healthy person.

Another moralistic back door of official sexology is the manner of speaking about the "civilizing" and "spiritualizing" of sexual relationships. Originally, sensuality was condemned; but it always returned with a vengeance to hound every individaul who approved this condemnation. So what is to be done with a phenomenon which is in such sharp contradiction to the "moral," i.e., ascetic and chaste, way of life? There is only one thing left: to "spiritualize" and "civilize" the sensuality. Even if it uses general phraseology, the "ennobling of the sexual drive," the slogan of a wide sector of sex reform, means something quite concrete, namely, the repression or paralysis of the sexual drive. If this interpretation is inaccurate, the moralists owe us an explanation of exactly what they do mean.

For the observer of these contradictions, the absurdities that result from the mixture of established facts and sexual morality are interesting. Thus, Timerding writes:

If the unmarried woman is denied the right to love, we must also demand sexual abstinence from the man prior to marriage. It must be admitted that *complete chastity prior to marriage is a condition which, if it can be realized, would furnish the best safeguard for human society and would spare the individual many struggles and much suffering. But if the requirement remains only an ideal that is seldom reached* [emphasis added], and is used for censuring others but not as a guideline for oneself, little has been gained. The ideal of chastity would first have to be generally accepted as an individual ethical norm. But this seems all the less probable the more the simple life conditions of former times recede and, with them, the possibility of entering into marriage immediately

after sexual maturity. The mere social ethical demand, which is meant to serve as a far-reaching
protection of the family, will be shaken off by the
individual only too easily as an unwelcome coercion. [p. 721]

It is significant how this viewpoint has failed in
the face of the actual circumstances shaped by
life conditions and how it has become almost a
farce in the application of the law. [p. 714]

We have the following inconsistencies in this logical
argumentation: if the woman must live chastely prior
to marriage, why not the man, too? Correct! The
possibility of achieving the ideal of chastity as an
individual ethical norm is dwindling more and more.
Correct! But this ideal of chastity would have to assert
itself although "this viewpoint . . . has failed and
. . . has become . . . a farce." We also learn that
the realization of "chastity prior to marriage . . .
would furnish the best safeguard for human society."
The proof of this assertion is invariably missing. As
a typical phrase, however, it makes sense insofar
as the continuance of authoritarian society is meant.
We have already tried to demonstrate this.

Further on:

The hygienic critique of sexual life splits in two
different directions. One side is cognizant of the
damages to health, both psychic and physical,
which are connected with the violent suppression
of the sexual drive, and it therefore demands the
safeguarding of healthy sexual intercourse for
man corresponding to his individual capacity, but
independent of his economic circumstances. The
other side firmly endorses the harmlessness of
complete sexual abstinence and points to the dangers to health that are connected with an unregu-
lated sexual intercourse. We are indeed faced with
widespread and ruinous venereal disease. . . . The
only safe protection against them is, in fact, com-

plete sexual abstinence. But since this can be required only in exceptional cases, we return to the ideal of sexual intercourse conducted solely within the *rigorously monogamous marriage. The complete realization of this ideal would attain the desired goal in a practical way.* Venereal disease would decline rapidly. *However, this ideal will almost never be realized* [emphasis added], and the purity of the marriage is scarcely helpful because the greatest dangers of infection occur prior to marriage. Therefore, only a general strengthening of conscience with regard to sexual matters can be useful, if only to avoid careless and frequently changing sexual relationships. One might even think that the freeing of sexual intercourse, based on strong personal affection, from the coercions of bourgeois society and, in part, from its legal regulations, might favor long-lasting, perhaps even permanent relationships, eliminate overt and secret prostitution, and thereby considerably decrease not only venereal disease but also other physical and emotional dangers. In any case, it is undeniable that persons of both sexes who are inclined toward sexual activity have never been deterred from following their drives by the demands of morality and that these drives were followed all the more excessively if, for the sake of appearances, they had to practice strictest secrecy. On the other hand, the ideal of finding permanent physical and emotional gratification with only one partner may very well be maintained, for there is no question that those who succeed must be regarded as fortunate indeed. [pp. 714, 715]

We see that the conservative sex reformer himself comes close to the practical solution of sexual misery, but he cannot free himself of the ideology of monogamous marriage which distorts his judgment and forces him into a dead end: "On the other hand, the ideal may very well be maintained," because "those

who succeed must be regarded as fortunate indeed."
That may be so, but who succeeds? And has not
the sexual moralist himself proclaimed the fiasco of
this ideal? Here, too, the contradiction is explained
by the economic basis of this ideal and the impossibility
of realizing it sex-economically.

So we swing back and forth between the ideologies
of chastity and marriage, for in between gapes the
monster "venereal disease," which we cannot cope
with because it is the practical counterpoint of marital
morality and the ideology of chastity. It has been
established that "the freeing of sexual intercourse"
from coercions, reactionary views, and legislation
"might favor . . . permanent relationships" and
decrease venereal disease, but the moral order and
the compulsion cannot be given up—and we mean
this quite seriously—so all that remains is a "general
strengthening of conscience." This was supplied in
the following way by Gruber, the master of sexual
hygiene himself:

> "The sensual pleasure of creatures is mingled
> with bitterness." The reader of these pages has
> seen many times before how the truth of this
> adage was confirmed by Master Eckhart. And yet
> we have not even spoken in any detail about the
> worst evils which sexual intercourse can bring.[1]

"The sensual pleasure of creatures is mingled with
bitterness." This is correct. But no one has ever asked
himself whether this bitterness is of social or biological
origin. The phrase *"omne animal post coitum triste"*
(all creatures are sad after the sexual act) has become
a veritable scientific dogma. Such phrases, when
spoken by authorities, make a deep impression on
the emotional life of those who reverently follow the
words of a man like Gruber—so deep an impression
that not only do they falsify their own perceptions
which contradict these words but, with their minds

---

[1] *Hygiene des Geschlechtslebens*, p. 121.

befogged and numbed by the high-flown phrase, they also renounce every independent thought which would infallibly bring them to question a social situation in which sensual pleasure *must* be mingled with bitterness.

We have only to put ourselves inside the mind of an adolescent who reads, say, the following words of a sexologist of the reputation of Fürbringer:

> New problems arise in adolescence, above all the medical attitude toward sexual intercourse, with its dangers of infection and injury to general health. It is no longer a secret that the large majority of young men in our culture have sexual intercourse prior to marriage. We do not have to deal with the question of whether and to what extent these customs are tolerated if not approved[!] by society.[2]

From this the adolescent absorbs the following suggestion:

1. The medical viewpoint—for which the layman has the greatest respect—is that sexual intercourse harms "general health." Anyone who has seen how adolescents react to such statements, how they plunge into the horrors of sexual conflict, and how such pronouncements combine with childhood experiences to produce hypochondria or neurosis in general, will agree with us that such authoritative statements should be not only protested against but opposed with practical measures.

2. The physician finds that sexual intercourse can lead to infection. Gruber insists that every woman who engages in extra- or premarital intercourse is suspect. The answer would seem to be to have intercourse only with a person one knows well and toward whom one feels tenderness; further, to agree with the partner on fidelity for the duration of the relationship or to have no sexual relations for several weeks after having intercourse with another partner,

2 *Handwörterbuch*, p. 718.

and so on. But where does that leave "morality"?
Since Gruber, Fürbringer, and other scientists of similar convictions regard all extramarital sexual life
through "the eyes of the bordello," as Engels once put
it, they faithfully reflect the reactionary, sex-ideological climate with the following "moralistic" exhortations.

> In view of the revulsion against and the danger
> of prostitution, many will be tempted to seek grati-
> fication in an "affair" until they are able to marry.
> But let them take the following to heart: such an
> affair would fully guarantee against infection only
> if it is conducted with an untouched virgin and if
> fidelity is guaranteed by both partners; for, as
> was stressed before, with today's dissemination of
> venereal diseases *every* act of polygamous inter-
> course is charged with extreme danger. One cannot
> expect fidelity from a girl who enters such an af-
> fair with a light heart and perhaps for financial
> gain, even if its form is concealed. If the girl, as
> is so often the case, has passed from hand to
> hand [!], she is scarcely less dangerous than the
> prostitute. Also, the young man who is aspiring
> to higher things should not stoop to living with a
> girl who is spiritually and emotionally his infe-
> rior, who has no understanding for his goals and
> knows only crass pleasures, for this debases his
> own cultural level. Such a "love affair" is emotion-
> ally far more degrading than the occasional visit
> with a prostitute, which is in the nature of a neces-
> sity, comparable to visiting a public comfort sta-
> tion.[3] [Gruber]

But in order also to eliminate the possibility of
intercourse with an "untouched" girl, Gruber presents
us on the next page with the very epitome of moralistic
conviction:

---

3 Gruber: *Hygiene des Geschlechtslebens*, pp. 142–43.

To seduce an honorable, high-minded girl into a "love affair for a limited time" is an irresponsible undertaking even if both parties are fully aware of the final intentions.

I will not speak of the fact that even defloration itself can harm the girl insofar as it makes a subsequent marriage more difficult, because the man—with completely correct instinct—prefers the untouched woman as his wife [*sic!*].

The main factor is that the woman's spirit and emotions are invariably hurt or deeply wounded. The desire for motherhood is innate in a real woman. Only if sexual intercourse opens to her the hope of becoming a mother does it give her unrestrained pleasure. Anyone who introduces a woman to sexual intercourse by means of wretched manipulations robs her of the hour of highest happiness which she would have experienced with the first uninhibited embraces in a true marriage. [p. 145]

Thus "scientific" facts are "fabricated" in the interests of marriage: the woman experiences pleasure in the sexual act only if it is connected with the possibility of motherhood. We are familiar with the same notion from the analyses of frigid, sex-negating women. And we learn in the treatment of stricken women what the "first uninhibited embraces . . . in a true marriage" are really like.

Who would be more suitable than a famous university professor for influencing the masses in the realm of sexual morality? Authoritarian society is adept at selecting its preachers.

By far the most dangerous use of scientific authority in the service of reactionary ideology is Gruber's claim that abstinence is not harmful, that, on the contrary, it is extremely useful because the semen is reabsorbed, which means "additional protein." "There can be no harm whatever in retaining the semen in the body. Semen is not a harmful excretion; it

is not a metabolic excretion like urine or feces."
However, even Gruber had some reservations about
setting down this nonsense without comment. He
wrote:

> Now one might think that the reabsorption of
> semen is useful only if it does not go beyond a
> certain quantity, that too much might cause dam-
> age. To counter this objection, it should be said
> that nature, with its spontaneous nocturnal emis-
> sions—which are quite normal unless they occur
> too frequently—has taken care that excessive se-
> men accumulations do not occur; furthermore, that
> *the secretion of semen decreases by itself if the*
> *sexual apparatus is not used. In this connection,*
> *the testicles act just like other organs of the body.*
> *If they are not used, they receive less blood sup-*
> *ply, and if they receive less blood supply, their*
> *nourishment diminishes along with their general*
> *vitality* [emphasis added]. This, too, prevents harm.
> [pp. 72–73]

These sentences should be read with the attention
they deserve. What Gruber has written openly and
honestly is concealed in the ethical attitude of all
reactionary sexology: the atrophy of the sexual apparatus is promoted in the interest of morality, culture,
the people, and the state. If we had presumed to
make such a statement without proof we would have
been unworthy of any scientific consideration. What
has been articulated here forms the nucleus of reactionary sexology: *sexual atrophy!* We need no longer
wonder why about 90 percent of all women and 60
percent of all men are sexually disturbed and *neuroses*
have become a problem of the masses.
If one relies on additional protein, nocturnal
emissions, and the atrophy of testicles, all that is
left as an active measure is castration. But then such
"objective" science would put an end to itself, which
must be prevented in the interest of "human progress"

and the "elevation of culture"! In the form of Fascistic sterilization, this flowering of our "culture" has become a reality.

Since Gruber's *Hygiene des Geschlechtslebens* sold 400,000 copies and was read, at a low estimate, by a million people, predominantly adolescents, we can well imagine its social effect: as an external source of restraint, it produced at least as many cases of impotence or neurosis.

Now, someone might object that it is malicious to single out Gruber since the majority of sexologists do not identify with him and many have emphasized the importance of sexuality. But it would be proper to ask who among sexologists allegedly not identified with Gruber has written a paper opposing him in order to counteract his influence. I do not speak here of the theses on masturbation or on the origin and essence of pollutions that are yellowing in scientific periodicals. I mean a consistent practicing of scientific conviction, such as writing popular pamphlets as a countermeasure against the stream of trashy literature put out by unscrupulous doctors who know that the hunger of the ignorant masses for sexual knowledge, for a little clarity in the confusion which ruins them, guarantees a nice income. The bugaboo of "venereal diseases" and the ogre of "masturbation," the lures of alleged cultural interests, cannot be fought with esoteric treatises. Nor can professional considerations and the desire to maintain one's "status" be advanced as an excuse. No, the situation is quite different. Anyone who on the basis of his knowledge must reject the unequivocal dictums of a man like Gruber is bound to hesitate in formulating and offering his own correct views and scientific convictions because it not only takes him beyond the conservative limitations of knowledge but also endangers his position in society; and this risk is not gladly taken.

While there are attempts to fight these views, their halfheartedness betrays the self-consciousness of the

authors, or the argument evaporates into platitudes.
Here is a typical example:

> For the purpose of a fairer judgment and to
> avoid social ostracism, which all too easily re-
> sults from a sexual situation, it would be desir-
> able to have a more widespread knowledge of the
> physiological and psychic rudiments of sexual
> life. Also, for insight into one's own emotions and
> the conduct which is influenced by them, famil-
> iarity with established scientific facts can be of
> great importance. One must have confidence that
> an advancing culture, particularly if it is not lim-
> ited to individual manifestations but unfolds its
> full strength, in the final analysis will not bring a
> brutalization but a refinement and an ennobling of
> sexual mores.[4]

Knowledge of the rudiments of sexual life would
be desirable (not *required*); familiarity with scientific
facts can be of great importance (not *is* of great importance) . . . brutalization of mores, refining and
ennobling . . . etc. Empty phrases!

But this unfortunate situation extends still further:
even facts and theory formation are moralistically
biased, and this reaches deep into groups of authors
who do not have a conservative prejudice in other
areas. No wonder, since reactionary sexual ideology
is the most widespread and most deeply anchored
of all ideologies.

It is known that frigidity is based on an inhibition
of vaginal sensation and that vaginal excitation and
the capacity for orgasm occur once the inhibition
of the general and vaginal eroticism is removed. Yet
Paul Krische wrote a popular booklet called *Neuland
der Liebe, a "Soziologie des Geschlechtslebens"*
[New Domain of Love, a Sociology of Sexual Life],
in which we find a description of vaginal anesthesia:

---

4 Timerding: *Handwörterbuch,* p. 713.

The only stimulator of feminine bliss is the clitoris and not, as even scientists and physicians insist today, also the inside of the vagina and the uterus. For sensations of pleasure require the corpora cavernosa and the Krause end-bodies, and these are found only in the clitoris. Thus neither the uterus nor the inside of the vagina can transmit feelings of sexual pleasure, particularly since they form the birth canal for passing the ripe fruit of life. . . . So that birth will not involve intolerable pain, nature had made the sensitive part of the woman, the clitoris, smaller . . . so that the outlet of the vagina becomes insensitive . . . Thus nature has produced the conflict which it has not been able to resolve in the history of mankind—that, in order to give birth, the outlet of the vagina was made insensitive, thus preventing the desirable pleasure of the woman during intercourse. [p. 10]

The fact that in the German race "at least 60 percent of women never, or seldom, experience sexual pleasure during regular sexual intercourse" [*Sic.* The rest experience it after all, but how, since nature has arranged it differently?] is explained by Krische in terms of the allegedly greater separation between clitoris and vagina in the German race. The sexual function is ultimately explained as a function of the preservation of the species, as so often occurs in official sexology, but one page further the influence of conservative morality appears:

For the woman, the most favorable age for motherhood is in her early twenties. But ovarian maturation in the girl occurs at the age of fourteen. In order to prevent a premature pregnancy, nature has arranged it so that the young girl experiences little sexual excitation, as a distinct protection. [p. 10]

Why nature was so clumsy as not to postpone ovarian maturation until the age of twenty-five remains unfathomable. What is even less comprehensible is that this modern god called "nature" has not granted this protection to a large percentage of girls who suffer gravely from sexual excitation in spite of all. Considering that nature has picked the twenty-fifth year as the right one, it is particularly embarrassing to our sensibilities that girls masturbate not only at fourteen but even at three and four years, play with dolls, and want to have children with their fathers. Is it possible that "nature," upon close scrutiny, stands revealed as the special economic position of the woman in our society, as well as our upright "moral" sensibilities? For what has happened to the fourteen-year-old Negro and Croatian girls? Have they been forgotten by nature?

Objectively, such theory formations are nothing but diversionary methods to turn us away from the true social and psychic causes of sexual disturbance.

The preponderant or exclusive biologistic view that the sexual drive exists for the purpose of preserving the species is one of the repressive methods of conservative sexology. It is a finalistic and thus idealistic view which presupposes a goal for the events that necessarily must be based on supra-individual intervention lest it collapse under its own logic. It reintroduces a metaphysical principle; fundamentally, it has a religious or mystical bias.

2. MARITAL MORALITY AS THE INHIBITOR OF ALL SEXUAL REFORM

HELENE STÖCKER

In the preceding section we have tried to show that the dead end of any kind of conventional sexual reform is the clinging to the alleged biological, in reality economically based, institution of marriage; that sexual misery is derived logically, step by step, from the ideology of marriage through which an authoritarian society directly influences the entire sexual situation. Yet even the best and most progressive sex reformers fail in this one point, whereas elsewhere the theses they advance are sex-economically correct. And it is precisely this one point which condemns them to sterility.

Germany's sexual reform movement has been smashed. But in all other countries this movement presses ahead even though it is afflicted with all the contradictions that result from the rejection of adolescent sexuality. It is not difficult to superimpose the following discussion on every form of progressive liberal sexual reform.

The German Association for the Protection of Mothers and for Sexual Reform (*Deutsche Bund für Mutterschutz und Sexual-reform*), with Helene Stöcker as its guiding spirit, published its *Guidelines*.[5] We now quote the principles with which sex-economy is in basic agreement:

GUIDELINES
of the
German Association for the Protection of Mothers
and for
Sexual Reform

1. Content and Goal of the Movement

The movement for the protection of mothers and for sexual reform grows out of a joyous, life-affirmative world view. It springs from the conviction of the highest value, the sanctity and inviolability of human life.

It is from this basis that our movement seeks to make life between man and woman, between parents and children, among all people, as rich and fruitful as possible.

---

5 Publishing House of the New Generation, Berlin, adopted by the Convention of Delegates of the Association in Berlin, November 25-6, 1922.

Therefore, it is our task to unmask the offensive social conditions and ethical views which tolerate and promote prostitution and venereal diseases, sexual hypocrisy and compulsory abstinence, and to carry this insight to ever-widening circles.

The confusion of prevalent moral judgments and their resulting personal suffering and social evils cry out for help. However, this cry cannot be answered by eliminating symptoms but only by the radical extermination of the real causes.

But our movement should not only eradicate evils but also promote the progress of individual and social life. It will support and improve life and foster joy in living.

To protect life at its source, to let it develop pure and strong: to protect mothers; to recognize the sexuality of man as a powerful instrument, not only for propagation but also for the progressive development of a joy in living, i.e., *sexual reform*, which is the content and final goal of our aspirations.

2. The General Principle of Morality

The first precondition for the improvement of human and sexual relationships is the absolute break with those moral views which base their commandments either on allegedly supernatural arrangements or on arbitrary human laws or simply on tradition. The laws of morality should also be founded on the insights gained by progressive science. What was true in other times and circumstances or served only the interests of the ruling classes must not be allowed to continue thoughtlessly as the moral command of today. The hallmark of our morality should be its stability for enriching human life—the social cooperation among people—of making it more harmonious and freeing it from evils!

Therefore, we reject the idea that man's body and mind oppose each other. We do not want natural sexual attraction to be branded as "sin," "sensuality" fought as something degrading or animalistic, or the "overcoming" of "carnality" raised to a matter of moralistic principle. Rather, to us man is a sensual emotional being whose intellectual and physical traits have the same right to a healthy and progressive development.

The commands of morality are those requirements which necessarily spring from a peaceful social life which guarantees all people equally the best possible education and development of their abilities and strengths. To us, morality serves, under given circumstances and according to our best insights, the development of the individual personality, the guidance of all people toward higher and more perfect forms of living.

3. Sexual Morals

We see that our prevalent moral views, our existing social conditions, provoke and promote hypocrisy and compulsory abstinence, physical diseases, and other infirmities in sexual matters. We therefore consider it our task to create a general awareness of the intolerability of such conditions and to fight such conditions and views vigorously. We do not want "virtue" to be confused with "abstinence"; we do not want a double-standard morality for man and woman.

Sexual intercourse itself is neither moral nor immoral. Born from a strong, natural drive, it becomes one or the other only through opinions and accompanying circumstances. The importance of sexuality is not measured by its obviously important effect: procreation. Rather, for man, a sexual life corresponding to his nature and his needs is the precondition for inner and outer harmony in life. By its nature, it presupposes a second being, similarly oriented, won by the force of attraction. Then the love life offers a multitude of new possibilities of living and experience, ways of deepening and refining one's knowledge of human nature and one's own views of life—ultimately the only way to the full creative development of human existence and nature in motherhood and fatherhood.

We have quoted so extensively because, so far, we are in agreement with these principles, but also because we want to stress more clearly the contradiction that follows.

In the section "Content and Goal of the Movement," the "radical extermination of the real causes" of sexual misery is emphasized; it is properly recognized and stated that "morality" serves the interests of certain classes, that "a sexual life corresponding to [man's] nature and his needs is the precondition for inner and outer harmony in life," which is in complete agreement with sex-economic findings. But with the formulation that this is the only way "to the full creative development of human existence and nature in motherhood and fatherhood," an unproved and unprovable thesis sneaks in which radically reverses everything that has been said before. It is the point where every previous attitude toward sexual life has failed, namely, the problem of youth and marriage.

We think it is necessary that the youth of both sexes be steeled in self-discipline and respect for the other sex and its tasks; that especially *the male youth learn and practice at an early age to consider the woman's dignity and emotional and instinctual life. We therefore demand abstinence until full physical and emotional maturity is reached*. But we recognize the natural claim of the adult and mature person, whether man or woman, to engage in sexual intercourse according to capability and inclination and in free accord with the love partner, provided that intercourse takes place with awareness of the responsibility for the *pos-*

sible consequences and without violation of the rights of other persons [e.g., to sexual fidelity]. [Emphasis added.]

Here we find the following contradictions of what has previously been said:

1. Consideration for the "woman's dignity." The next sentence makes it clear that we are not dealing merely with the old sex-negating phrase about female sexuality:

2. "We *therefore* demand abstinence until full physical and emotional maturity is reached."

There is no specific investigation of why today, in our society, the sexual act means a violation of the woman's dignity. Is this generally valid? Is it an abstract idea? Furthermore, it is not specifically stated *when* young people are physically and emotionally mature, and by which criteria this is determined. For, in our latitudes, the average age at which an adolescent becomes physically mature is between fourteen and fifteen. The development of the emotional maturity of an adolescent depends primarily on his early and later environment. Here we can already see a number of contradictions which can in no way be comprehended by the general formulation of physical and emotional maturity.

3. Recognition of the natural claim of the "adult and mature person" ("Adult"—when? "Mature"—when? Is a sixteen-year-old industrial worker "mature" or "immature"?) . . . "to engage in sexual intercourse according to capability and inclination," etc., provided that such intercourse occurs "without violation of the rights of other persons"; e.g., to sexual fidelity. This means the husband has the right to the body of the wife, and vice versa. What right? The right that is conferred by the legal institution of marriage, and no other. Hence, it is a viewpoint which differs in no way from that of the reactionary one representing immediate economic in-

terests from whose influence the authors of the *Guide-lines* want to liberate sexuality. As for the next contradiction:

> We do not regard the essence of marriage and its "morality" as residing in the fulfillment of certain formalities, as is generally the case today. If only the prescribed form is observed, today's attitude disregards entirely the spirit which led to the marital relationship; neither does it ask whether and how such obligations are to be fulfilled. It declares to be "moral" all formally stamped love relationships, and only these, and ostracizes all others as being "immoral"—without probing into their inner justification, their value, and their voluntary responsibility. Finally, it still maintains a marriage by compulsory law even if this relationship has become a useless and painful tie in the eyes of the participants, even if it has been dissolved inwardly and sometimes *de facto*.

But:

> *We regard legally recognized monogamy as the highest and most desirable form of human sexual relationship*, as best suited to guarantee a permanent regulation of sexual intercourse, the healthy development of the family, the preservation of the human community. But we do not fail to recognize that a lifelong, strictly monogamous marriage has existed, and still exists, only as an ideal attainable by a very few. The larger part of sexual life does occur *before and outside marriage*. For emotional and economic reasons the legal marriage is incapable of absorbing all possibilities of justified love relationships, i.e., of turning them into permanent monogamy in all cases. [Emphasis added.]

Thus, "legally recognized monogamy" is endorsed, but "we do not fail to recognize" that permanent monogamy has existed, and still exists, as an ideal attained by a very few and that the larger part of sexual life occurs *de facto* outside marriage. In endorsing the institution of marriage, it seems not to have even occurred to these reformists to deal with its history and social function. By decree, marriage becomes the best of all sexual forms, although, in one and the same breath, the exact opposite is maintained. Thus, it is only natural that reformist intentions are couched in general, empty phrases, as, for instance, in the following:

Accordingly, we favor:

a) Preservation of the legally recognized monogamous marriage on the basis of real equality of the sexes; the furtherance of the economic possibilities of marriage, but also the emotional possibilities through education for marriage and parenthood as well as through coeducation and other suitable methods for a better and deeper "learning to know each other" of the sexes.

b) Liberalization of divorce laws when the conditions which led to marriage no longer exist; also, if the marriage can no longer fulfill the purpose of a lasting relationship.

c) Moral and legal recognition for relationships in which the partners are aware of their responsibility to fulfill their obligations and have demonstrated their intention to do so—even if the legal formalities are not preserved.

d) The fight against "prostitution" by sanitary measures as well as by intellectual and economic means for eliminating its causes.

1. The "real equality of the sexes" is just a flowery phrase in authoritarian society. In actuality, it presupposes a work-democratic economy as well as the right to one's own body. But with this, marriage ceases to be marriage.

2. The "furtherance of the economic possibilities

of marriage" is an empty phrase under the prevailing conditions of production. Who is to do the furthering? The society whose very structure demands the preservation of an industrial reserve army?

3. Education for marriage. This occurs uninterruptedly from infancy on, and the Association was constituted to fight against the consequences of such education. As we shall demonstrate at length, an institution which requires sexual repression for its preservation is *a priori* opposed to the "common education of the sexes" and to a "deeper" understanding of each other, unless these pronouncements are again to be taken as empty phrases.

4. The "liberalization of divorce laws" in itself does not mean very much, for either the economic position of the woman is such that the divorce is economically impossible, in which case liberalizing the laws is useless to the masses, or the conditions of production are changed in such a manner that the economic independence of the woman and the social care of the children gradually become possible, in which case the dissolution of a sexual relationship generally encounters no external difficulties anyway.

5. Fighting the causes of prostitution. These lie in unemployment and the chastity ideology of the middle-class girl. To fight this requires more than sanitary measures. Who is supposed to carry this out? The same reactionary society that cannot cope with unemployment and cannot do without the ideology of chastity?

Sexual misery cannot be attacked by such means; it is an essential part of the prevailing social structure!

AUGUST FOREL

Among socialist sexual reformers, no one emphasized as clearly as August Forel the hygienic damage caused by the mercenary use of the sexual function. He has correctly seen that all the basic difficulties of sexual life spring from the authoritarian manner of existence, without, however, comprehending the deeper economic roots of sexual misery. Thus, his statements end up as complaints instead of a thorough intellectual elaboration, as well-intentioned advice about what should be done to alleviate sexual suffering, instead of a recognition of the specific connection between this suffering and the prevailing social structure. As was to be expected, his philosophical bias is expressed in contradictions in his own opinions. In a booklet entitled *Sexuelle Ethik* [Sexual Ethic], he endorsed the viewpoint—as long as the formulations remained of a generalized nature—that "the gratification of the sexual drive, in both man and woman, is by and large a matter of indifference to ethics." "Therefore we have the audacity to contend that any intercourse which can damage neither the one nor the other of the participants, nor third parties, nor the quality of a child that might be conceived . . . cannot be immoral" (p. 20). It was pointless to want to prevent the procreation to which ethics is indifferent, Forel said. "As long as intercourse does no harm, it must be tolerated, all the more so as happiness and healthy joyful creativeness frequently depend on normal instinctual gratification" (p. 20). Splendid words, considering the time when Forel wrote them. However, after stating that the man "is mostly polygamous by instinct" (p. 19) (Why men alone? A double standard of sexual morality which beclouds the finding of facts!), he gives the following advice (p. 20):

> The ethical sexual ideal is no doubt a monogamous marriage resting on mutual permanent love and fidelity and blessed with several children. . . . [Emphasis added.] This is not quite the rarity that our modern pessimists think it is; but neither is it very frequent. In order for this marriage to

be entirely what it should be, and can be, it must
be completely free, i.e., both spouses have to be
absolutely equal, and no external coercion can
keep the marriage glued together except for the obligations toward children. Here it is above all separate property rights and the proper evaluation
of every accomplishment of the woman as well as
the man that are necessary.

But, then, marriage destroys itself because the latter
requirement takes away its basis, the sexual and
economic suppression of the women.
And here is how this looks in practice:

Polygamous conflict: "For some time I have
been ruled by a passion for a woman. I try to
fight it, but in vain. Being a married man with a
dearly beloved wife, with whom I have lived peace-
fully for thirty-two years . . . I realize that such a
liaison cannot be justified, let alone excused. Nevertheless, I weaken time and again in resisting
this passion."

"At first, control by suggestion should be tried."
"In these cases not much can be done" [emphasis
added], Forel himself says. Of course, not much can
be done if every member of conservative society is
perpetually told that a relationship with another man
or a woman "cannot be justified, let alone excused."

THE COLLAPSE OF THE WORLD LEAGUE
FOR SEXUAL REFORM

In the second half of the 1920's, the liberal
humanist and socialist Magnus Hirschfeld gave his
research work an organizational shape in the World
League for Sexual Reform. It comprised the world's
most progressive sexologists and reformers and offered
the following program:

1. Political, economic, and sexual equality of women.

2. Liberation of marriage (particularly divorce) from all domination by church and state.

3. Birth control in the sense of responsible conception of children.

4. Eugenic influencing of offspring.

5. Protection for unwed mothers and their children.

6. Accurate evaluation of intersexual variants, particularly as applied to homosexual men and women.

7. Prevention of prostitution and venereal diseases.

8. The interpretation of disturbances of the sexual drive not as a crime, sin, or vice, as heretofore, but as more or less pathological phenomena.

9. A sexual penal code which punishes only real interference in the sexual freedom of another person, but not sexual acts based on mutual consent between adults.

10. Planned sex education and enlightenment.

The Danish sex-politician J. H. Leunbach, who was one of the three presidents of the World League, has critically examined the great merits of the League but also exposed its contradictions.[6] His most significant criticism concerned the attempts of the World League to achieve sexual reform "unpolitically"; its liberalistic generosity which went so far as to permit every country to be guided by its own laws; the omission of infantile and adolescent sexuality; the affirmation of the institution of marriage; etc.

After Hirschfeld's death, Norman Haire and Leunbach published the following declaration:

INFORMATION FOR ALL MEMBERS AND SECTIONS
OF THE WORLD LEAGUE FOR SEXUAL REFORM

6 "Von der bürgerlichen Sexualreform zur revolutionären Sexualpolitik" [From Bourgeois Sexual Reform to Revolutionary Sex Politics], *Zeitschrift für politische Psychologie und Sexualökonomie*, Volume 2, Issue 1/1935.

We, Dr. Norman Haire of London and Dr. Leunbach of Copenhagen, the surviving presidents of
the WLSR, are in the sad position to announce the
death of our president, Magnus Hirschfeld. He
died on May 15, 1935, in Nice.

We would like to convene a congress in order to
determine the future of the WLSR. But for the moment this seems to be impossible, for the same
reasons that have prevented a new international
congress since the last one in Brno in 1932. Political and economic conditions in Europe have
made it impossible not only to hold international
congresses but also to further the work of the
WLSR in many countries. The French section no
longer exists, the Spanish section has given up all
activity since the death of Hildegart, as have sections in most other countries as well. As far as
we have been able to ascertain, the British section
is the only one that still functions actively.

In the absence of an international congress, the
two surviving presidents are obliged to state that
it is no longer possible to maintain the WLSR
as an international organization.

We therefore declare that the World League for
Sexual Reform is dissolved. The national sections
will have to decide for themselves whether they
wish to operate as independent organizations or
whether they wish to dissolve.

There have been vast differences among the
members of the various sections as to how far
the League should maintain its originally nonpolitical character. Several members are of the opinion that it was impossible to carry out the purposes of the WLSR without simultaneously fighting
for a socialist revolution.

Dr. Haire insists that all revolutionary activity
should be removed from the program of the WLSR.
Dr. Leunbach feels that the WLSR can accomplish
nothing because it did not, and could not, join the
revolutionary labor movement. Dr. Leunbach's

point of view has been published in the *Zeitschrift für politische Psychologie und Sexualökonomie,* Volume 2, Issue 1/1935. Dr. Haire's comments on the subject will be published in Issue 2, i.e., in the same issue which contains the information.

After the World League for Sexual Reform has been thus dissolved, the members of the national sections can freely decide these problems for themselves.

NORMAN HAIRE   J. H. LEUNBACH

This was the end of an organization which wanted to liberate sexuality within the framework of reactionary society.

3. THE DEAD END OF SEXUAL ENLIGHTENMENT

The atmosphere of crisis surrounding education in general and sexual education in particular has given emphasis to the question of whether children should be "sexually enlightened" and become accustomed or not to the sight of the naked human body or, more specifically, to the human genitalia. Although there is agreement about the fact—at least in those circles not under the immediate influence of the Church—that sexual secrecy is infinitely more harmful than useful; although there is a decent and energetic will to change the dismal conditions in education, there undoubtedly still exist severe contradictions and obstacles within the group of educational reformers, which can be distinguished on two grounds: those of an individual and those of a social nature. I will confine myself to discussing several basic difficulties which result from establishing the goal of "nude education" and "sexual enlightenment."

Among the sexual drives we know particularly well is the drive to look and to exhibit, whose instinctual goal is the observation or exhibition of erogenous zones, especially the sexual organs. Given educational conditions as they exist almost without exception today, this drive is bound to fall prey to repression very early in the child's life. The child quickly learns that he may neither exhibit his own sexual organs nor look at those of others. As a consequence, he develops two kinds of feelings: first, guilt feelings which develop when he yields to his desire to do something that is strictly forbidden; and second, with the concealment of the genitals and the taboo about them, mystical feelings in connection with everything sexual. Therefore, the original natural pleasure in looking is transformed into lascivious curiosity. In order to escape the conflict between looking and its prohibition, the child must repress the impulse. Depending on the scope and degree of repression, either shyness and shame or lasciviousness will become more pronounced. Usually both coexist, producing a new conflict in place of the old one. With further development, there are two extreme possibilities: either the beginning of a damaged love life and neurotic symptoms if the repression of looking is retained, or the beginning of a perversion, exhibitionism. One can never safely predict which of the two will occur. Given a sex-negating education, the development of a sexual structure that does not disturb either the social existence or the subjective state of the individual is almost always a matter of accident and the interaction of many factors, such as experiences during puberty, liberation from parental authority and, to some extent, the overcoming of social authority, but above all the ability to find the way to a healthy sexual life.

Thus we see that repression of the pleasure in looking and exhibiting produces results which no educator can regard as desirable.

Prevailing sexual education proceeds invariably from negative assessments of sexuality and from ethical, not hygienic, arguments. Its results are neuroses and perversions. To reject an education which approves of nudity means to affirm the customary sexual education, because the one cannot be separated from the other. But to approve of nudity and otherwise leave the sexual educational goals intact means constructing a contradiction which *a priori* would turn every practical attempt into an illusion or else would place the youngster in even more difficult situations. However, a compromise in the area of sexual education is hardly possible because of the inherent lawfulness of the sexual drive. Before posing the question of sexual enlightenment at all, one must first decide unequivocally in favor of sex affirmation or sex negation, against or for the prevailing sexual morality. Without such clarification about one's own position on the sexual question any discussion is futile; it is the prerequisite for understanding in these matters. But where such a clarification leads will be shown presently.

We assume that we reject the sex-negating education because of its hazards to health and choose the opposite, the sex-affirmative upbringing. We will then probably say that this is really not so dangerous and that we recognize the value of sexuality and have only to "further the sublimation of sexuality." But this is not the point here. It is not a matter of sublimation but of the whole concrete question of whether or not the sexes are to lose their shyness in revealing their genitals and other erogenous parts of the body. Still more specifically, it is a question of whether educators and pupils, parents and children should appear naked or in swimsuits before one another when bathing and playing, whether the state of nakedness will be taken for granted. Anyone who unconditionally recognizes the naturalness of being naked during bathing, playing, etc. (a conditional affirmation has its place only in clubs for nudist culture, in which nakedness is practiced as an exercise in sexual abstinence, following which one will have to cope with the stiffening of the body), anyone who strives not for islands in the sea of social morality but for natural sexuality in general and a form of education that accepts nudity, will examine the relationship between nudity and sexual life in general. He will then have to decide whether the consequences of such striving, disregarding the possibility of achieving them for the time being, are in the direction of his intentions.

Medical experience with sexuality teaches us that sexual repression causes disease, perversions, or lasciviousness. Let us try to guess at the condition and consequences of a sex-affirmative education. If we show no shame to the child with respect to the genitals, he will not become shy or lascivious; but after his sexual curiosity is satisfied and therefore reduced, he will certainly want to gratify his desire for sexual experience. It will be hard to deny him this, for otherwise there would be a far greater conflict and the child would have far more trouble suppressing it. Furthermore, the danger of perversion would be greatly increased. Of course, one could also have no objection to masturbation, which has long been recognized as being natural. The process of conceiving would have to be explained to the child too. One might evade the request of the child to observe this process if the relationship is such that one can distract the child. But this undoubtedly would mean a decrease in the attitude of sexual affirmation; for what could we reply to a cynical sexual moralist if he asked us why the child could not actually witness sexual intercourse. Every child, even in the most sophisticated family, has listened to it anyway, as analytic experience teaches us, so why not allow him to see it? Our hypothetical cynic might embarrass us particularly if he asked why seeing the act would be so objectionable from the child's viewpoint, since he has seen dogs copulating in the streets and presumably has been properly enlightened about it. If we had the courage to be honest, we would have to admit that we have no argument against it, unless it were of an ethical nature, which in turn would strengthen the position of our opponent. Or else we might be heroic enough to concede that we are not acting in the interests of the child but are striving for our own undisturbed pleasure. Thus, driven into a corner, we would have the alternative of returning to sexual morality, which, by definition, is always sex-negating, or else facing the most ticklish of all questions, the question of our attitude toward sexual intercourse. But if we decided upon the latter, we ought to make sure that the attorney general hears nothing about it, for otherwise the laws against moral turpitude would automatically be applied.

If anyone thinks we are exaggerating, we would ask him to go a step further in order to convince himself that education which involves nudity and sexual enlightenment in general, factually and deliberately carried out, would at present take educator and pupil right to jail.[7]

Let us make a concession and assume that, in our own sexual interests, we had diverted the child from wanting to observe the sexual act. We would immediately become embroiled in insoluble contradictions and would throw overboard everything we had striven for if we did not give a truthful answer to the child's inevitable question as to when he could do the same. He has learned that children grow in the mother's womb; he has also understood that for this purpose the father has put his "Lulu" or "Wipfi" into the mother's "hole." If the parents are courageous, they have also told him that it was a "good" feeling, just as it was when he played with his own "Lulu." (We should not forget that we act purposefully, i.e., consistently, when we enlighten the child.) If he knows that, we may perhaps console him for a short time with the idea that "adulthood" must be postponed; but when the child reaches puberty, with its sexual excitations, erections, emissions, he will want what

---

7 The editor of a journal who printed this section, which first appeared as an article in 1927 in the *Zeitschrift für psychoanalytische Pädagogik,* was given a forty-day jail sentence by the court of a highly liberal government.

we asked him to postpone during his childhood. If we suggest further postponement, our sexual moralist, who wants to carry us to the point of absurdity and who might very well succeed, would now ask the logical question, as ironic as it may sound, why we objected to sexual intercourse at the time of sexual maturity. He will be justified in recalling that among many industrial workers and peasants the beginning of sexual life with complete sexual maturity is taken for granted at about the fifteenth or sixteenth year. We will no doubt be embarrassed at the thought that our sons and daughters at fifteen or sixteen, perhaps even earlier, might insist on the fulfillment of their natural sexual needs, and after some painful hesitation we might look for arguments to support a position that is not very promising. For example, the argument of "cultural sublimation" might occur to us: asceticism in puberty is necessary for intellectual development. One might endeavor to influence these young people (who up to now have been raised in a free physical environment!) and recommend abstinence for a while, for their own good. But now our malicious and well-informed sexual moralist will bring up two arguments which are unanswerable. First, asceticism does not really exist, for there are sexologists and analysts who seriously claim that almost all adolescents masturbate and he cannot see the basic difference between the sexual act and masturbation. Furthermore, although masturbation discharges sexual tensions under ordinary conditions, just as the sexual act does, it is connected with infinitely more conflicts than the latter and is therefore certainly even more disturbing. Second, he will rightly object that if the claim of the universality of masturbation is correct, the thesis that asceticism is necessary for intellectual development cannot be right. He will have heard the contention that not masturbation but, on the contrary, its absence during childhood and adolescence is a serious pathological symptom; that it has not yet been established that adolescents who live in abstinence are, in the long run, more active intellectually, and that some people insist that the opposite is true. Here we might even recall that Freud once derived women's general intellectual inferiority from their greater sexual inhibitions and claimed that sexual life is the basis of social achievement. Later he contradicted himself when he stressed the cultural necessity of sexual repression. He did not differentiate between gratified and ungratified sexuality; the former advances, the latter inhibits cultural achievement. The few bad poems occasionally produced in abstinence do not matter.

Now intellectually convinced, we will ponder the motives of our flimsy argumentation and will discover all kinds of interesting and, for us, unpleasant tendencies, tendencies which, to our surprise, do not seem to fit properly into our progressive aspirations. Our argument about intellectual development will turn out to be a rationalization of an unconscious timidity about letting sexuality run its natural course. This we will wisely conceal from our moral philosopher. We will admit the futility of our arguments and raise a more serious one. What is to happen to children that may result from these youthful relationships? There is no economic possibility of raising them. Astonished, our opponent will ask why we do not want to enlighten all pubescent school children about contraception. A vision of the law on pandering will bring us back to reality, to social reality. All kinds of things will occcur to us, e.g., that with our efforts for an acceptance of nakedness and for sexual enlightenment (not about the pollination of flowers but of people!) and for other fine things, we are about to pull out one brick after another from the whole structure of conservative morality; that, then, the ideal of virginity for women until marriage collapses just as irretrievably as does that of eternal monogamy and, with it, of marriage itself. For no reasonable person will contend that people who have received a genuine sexual education, i.e., one that is serious, uncompromising, and based on scientific facts, will submit to the compulsion of today's customs and mores.

Our moral philosopher, who has led us to this point, will now ask triumphantly whether we believe that any of the demands which might result from the first serious beginning of a genuine sexual education will, in the framework of present society, be realized automatically within a few years. And he will ask if we have stopped to consider whether all of them are desirable. Once again he will add, quite rightly, that he merely wants to prove that everything must be left as it has been—the sex-negating education, sexual repression, neuroses, perversions, prostitution, and venereal diseases—if one wants to maintain (as he assumed we did) the high quality of marriage, chastity, family, and authoritarian society. Whereupon many a fanatic of enlightenment will take flight, acting more honestly and responsibly and understanding more quickly his own point of view than those who, in order not to lose their sense of progressiveness, will insist that all this is quite exaggerated, that sexual enlightenment cannot possibly have such effects, that it is not all that significant. But now we must ask: why make the effort at all?

Individual parents who would organize the education of their children according to their own tastes and convictions must be aware of the fact that, with a consistent, scientifically established sexual education, they will have to give up many things which other parents greatly value in their children, e.g., attachment to the family far beyond puberty, a "decent" sexual life by today's standards, influence on crucial decisions, "good" marriages of their daughters, and other matters. The few parents who follow their own convictions in educating their children will be inconspicuous and, more importantly, will have no social influence. They will also have to consider that they will expose their children to grave conflicts with the prevailing social order and its morality even if neurotic conflicts are perhaps avoided. But anyone who is discontented with this society and believes that it can be undermined on a large scale, e.g., in schools, will soon learn, either by the loss of his means of subsistence or by stronger measures (institutionalization or imprisonment), that he will have no opportunity to discuss with us whether his methods of changing society are appropriate or not. We do not require proof that the stratum of society which is materially interested in the continued existence of the current social order will tolerate and even endorse reformist endeavors which are mere child's play, but will immediately become brutal and apply all the means of prevention that might undermine its material and ideological values.

It is my conviction that sexual education offers much more serious and far-reaching problems than most sex reformers imagine. This is precisely the reason why there is no progress in this area, in spite of the knowledge and means which sexual research has placed at our disposal. We are faced with a powerful social apparatus which for the moment engages in passive resistance but will turn to active resistance at the first serious effort on our part. And all hesitation and caution, all indecision and tendency toward compromise in questions of sexual education, can be reduced not only to one's own sexual repression but, in spite of the honesty of pedagogic efforts, to a reluctance to enter into a serious conflict with the conservative social order.

To conclude, we offer two typical cases from our clinics for sexual counseling which should demonstrate that medical conscience imposes measures that are diametrically opposed not only to conservative morality but also to the sexual reforms described earlier.

A sixteen-year-old girl and a seventeen-year-old boy, both strong and well developed, had come to the clinic shy and anxious. After much encouragement, the boy asks whether it is really harmful to have sexual intercourse before the twentieth year.

"Why do you think it is harmful?"

"The group leader of the Red Falcons told us that, and they all say the same thing in discussions of sex."

"Do you talk about these things with the Red Falcons?"

"Of course. We all suffer terribly, but no one dares to say so *openly*. A group of boys and girls has just left our section and formed its own group because they couldn't get along with the group leader. He's the one who keeps saying that sexual intercourse is harmful."

"How long have you known each other?"

"Three years."

"Have you had sexual intercourse?"

"No, but we love each other, and we have to separate because we always become terribly excited."

"Over what?"

(Long silence.) "Well, we kiss and do other things. But most of the others do that, too. And now we're both almost crazy. The worst of it is that because of our new jobs we always have to work together. Lately, she's often gone on a crying jag, and I no longer do well in school."

"What do you think would be the best solution?"

"We wanted to separate, but that doesn't work. The whole group that we lead would collapse, and then the same will surely happen with another group."

"Do you go in for sports?"

"Yes, but that doesn't help at all. When we're together we can think of nothing else. Please tell us if this is really harmful."

"No, it is not harmful, but it often leads to great complications at home."

I explained to them the physiology of puberty and sexual intercourse, the social obstacles, the danger of pregnancy, and the use of contraceptives. They left after I had advised them to think things over and then to come back.

Two weeks later I saw them again, joyous, grateful, happy in their work: they had overcome all internal and external difficulties. I followed up the case for several months and am now certain that I saved two young people from illness. My pleasure was clouded only by the knowledge that such success in simple counseling was unusual because the majority of adolescents seeking help have neurotic fixations.

A second example concerns a youthful-looking woman of thirty-five who sought advice in the following matter: she had been married for eighteen years, had a grown son, and her marriage was seemingly peaceful. During the past three years, her husband had been having an affair with another woman. She knew about it and tolerated it, fully understanding that after so many years one might desire another love object. She had remained faithful, although her husband had not had intercourse with her for two years. Over the last few months, she had suffered from this abstinence but was too proud to ask her husband to have intercourse. Palpitations, insomnia, irritability, and episodes of depression had recently become more frequent and more severe. For moral reasons, she could not bring herself to commit adultery with a friend she had met, although she realized that her objections made no sense. Her husband always bragged about her fidelity, and she knew perfectly well that he was not willing to allow her the same right he himself took for granted. What should she do, she asked. She could no longer tolerate the situation.

One should think about this case carefully. Further abstinence meant for her the certainty of neurotic illness. Yet it was impossible to disturb her husband's affair and to win him back for two reasons: first, he would not have tolerated such disturbance or interference and would have acknowledged that she no longer held any erotic interest for him; second, she herself no longer desired her husband. So the only possibility was an adulterous relationship with her friend. But here was the snag: she was economically dependent, and the husband would have asked for an immediate divorce if he had known of such an affair. I explained all these possibilities to the woman, left her time to decide, and learned a few weeks later that she had decided to establish a sexual relationship with her friend and not to let her husband know about it. Her neurotic complaints which were due to sexual stasis disappeared a short time later. She was capable of making this decision because of my successful attempt to eliminate her moral reservations. By law, I had committed an offense: I had enabled a woman on the verge of neurotic illness to commit adultery.

V

The Compulsory Family as Educational Apparatus

The principal breeding ground for the ideological atmosphere of conservatism is the compulsory family, basically the triangle: father, mother, and child. Whereas in the conservative view the family is the basis or, as some say, the "cell" of human society itself, we regard it as the result of specific economic factors, taking into account its changing forms in the course of historical development and its corresponding changing social functions. Thus, we do not view the family as the cornerstone and basis of society but rather as the result of its special economic structure (matriarchal and patriarchal family, Zadruga, polygamous and monogamous patriarchy, etc.) When conservative sexology, reactionary sexual morality, and the legal order continue to speak of the family as *the* basis of "state" and "society," they are correct only to the extent that the compulsory family belongs inseparably to the authoritarian state and to authoritarian society. Its social import is wholly revealed in three basic characteristics:

1. Economic. At the beginning of the capitalist era, it was the economic unit of work, a role it still plays in peasant communities and small businesses.
2. Social. In an authoritarian society, it has the

important function of protecting the economically
and sexually disenfranchised woman and her children.

3. Political. In the precapitalistic times of private
enterprise and in the early stages of capitalism, the
family's immediate economic roots were in the family
small business (as is still the case today among small
landowners. But with the development of productive
forces and the collectivization of the work process,
the family underwent a change in function. Its immediate economic basis became less important with
the increasing integration of women into the productive process. What was lost in economic importance,
however, was replaced by a political function. Its
cardinal task, which is defended mainly by conservative science and conservative law, is to serve
as the factory of authoritarian ideologies and conservative structures. It forms the educational apparatus through which every member of society,
almost without exception, must pass from his first
breath on. Not only as an institution of authority,
but also, as we shall see, by virtue of its own structure,
the family imposes upon the child a conservative
world view. It is the bridge between the economic
structure of society and its ideological superstructure;
it is permeated by a conservative atmosphere which
necessarily makes an ineradicable impression on each
of its members. Through its very form and its direct
influence, it not only transmits general attitudes
towards the existing social order and a conservative
way of thinking, but also, due to the sexual structure
from which it springs and develops, it exercises an
immediate influence, in the conservative sense, on
the sexuality of children. It is no coincidence that
the attitude of youth for or against the prevailing
social order is in direct ratio to their attitude for
or against the family. Neither is it a coincidence that,
by and large, conservative and reactionary youth,
a few divergent individual cases notwithstanding,
is attached to the family and tends to preserve it,

whereas revolutionary youth is hostile and destructive to the family, and tends in varying degrees to dissolve its family ties.

This is intimately connected with the sex-negative atmosphere and structure of the family, and with the relationships among individual family members.

Thus, in examining the educational importance of the family, we must investigate two sets of facts separately: the influence of specific social ideologies which serve family education by influencing the young, and the immediate influence of the family triangle itself.

1. THE INFLUENCE OF SOCIAL IDEOLOGY

The families of the upper classes are different from those of the lower middle classes, and the latter differ from those of industrial workers. However, all are exposed to the same sexually moralistic atmosphere, which does not wipe out the specific class morality but exists side by side with it, as a contradiction and sometimes as a compromise.

The predominant type of family, i.e., the lower middle class, reaches considerably beyond the social stratum of the "lower middle classes"; it reaches far into the upper classes and still further down into the industrial working classes. The basis of the lower-middle-class family is the relationship of the patriarchal father to his wife and children. The father is the exponent, in the family, of the state's authority. Owing to the contradiction between his position in the production process (servant) and his familial function (master), he is logically and typically a drill-sergeant type. He is cowed by his superiors and completely absorbs their views because of his tendency toward imitation; but he steps on those below him.

He transmits the authoritarian viewpoint and reinforces it.

In terms of sexual ideology, the lower-middle-class family's ideology of marriage coincides with the basis of the family itself, with lifelong monogamous marriage. No matter how wretched and dismal, grievous and intolerable, the marriage situation and family constellation are, they still must be defended ideologically, both inwardly and outwardly, by the family members. The social necessity of this form of existence causes the misery to be concealed, and both family and marriage to be ideologically cherished. It also produces the widespread family sentimentality and the slogans of "family happiness," the "cozy home," the "peaceful resting place," and the happiness which the family allegedly signifies for the children. It is a fact that in our society things look even more dismal outside of marriage and the family where sexual life enjoys no protection, whether material, legal, or ideological, and one concludes that the family institution is a necessity of nature. The self-deception and the sentimental slogans which form a significant part of the ideological atmosphere are emotionally necessary because they support the continuance of the psychically uneconomic family situation. This explains why the treatment of neuroses so frequently destroys family and marriage ties; it wipes out illusions, and the truth comes mercilessly to the fore.

From the beginning, education for marriage and the family is the goal of rearing children. Education for a profession is not brought in until much later. Not only is a sex-negating and sex-denying education dictated by the social atmosphere; it also becomes necessary because of the sexual repression of the adults. Without far-reaching sexual resignation, it is not possible to exist in the customary family atmosphere.

In the typical lower-middle-class family, the influence of the sexual drive assumes specific forms which lay the groundwork for the individual's disposition toward "marriage and family feeling." Thus pregenital eroticism is fixated by overemphasizing the functions of eating and excretion, while genital activity is completely inhibited (prohibition of masturbation). Genital inhibition and pregenital fixation cause a shift of the sexual interest into sadism, and the sexual curiosity of the child is actively suppressed. This conflicts with the familial living arrangements, with the general lack of constraint in the sexual behavior of the parents, and with the sexually conditioned milieu that is inevitable in the family. The children perceive everything that goes on anyway, though in distorted form and pervaded by misinterpretations.

The ideological and educational inhibition of sexuality on the one hand, and the witnessing of the most intimate acts among adults on the other, lay the basis for the child's sexual hypocrisy. This is somewhat attenuated in industrial workers' families, where emphasis on the functions of food intake and digestion is less strong and genital activities are more prominent and less forbidden. Hence the contradictions are fewer, the road toward genitality is less blocked. This is invariably connected with the economic level of the worker's family. If an industrial worker is promoted into the ranks of the workers' aristocracy, his convictions change accordingly, and his children come under stronger pressure by conservative morality.

While sexual suppression in the lower-middle-class family is more or less a *fait accompli,* in the industrial worker's milieu it comes into conflict with the necessarily diminished supervision of the children, who are left mostly to their own devices.

2. THE TRIANGULAR STRUCTURE

While the family thus transmits to the child the
ideological atmosphere of society, its triangular structure, moreover, results in a specific configuration for
the child that is totally oriented toward the conservative tendencies of society.

Freud's discovery that, wherever this triangular
structure exists, the child develops specific sexual
relationships of a sensual and tender nature toward
his parents, is basic for the understanding of individual
sexual development. The so-called "Oedipus com-
plex" comprises all these relationships which in their
intensity, but above all in their end results, are further
conditioned by environment and by family structure.
The child directs his first genital love impulses (for
the sake of simplicity, let us disregard the pregenital
impulses) toward those in his environment who are
closest to him, usually the parents. At first, typically,
the parent of the opposite sex is loved while the other
parent is hated. The feelings of jealousy and hatred
that develop are accompanied by feelings of guilt
and fear. The fear is primarily related to the child's
own genital impulses toward the parent of the opposite
sex. This fear, together with the real impossibility
of gratifying the incestuous desire, causes the desire
as well as the genital striving to become repressed.
From this repression most of the sexual disturbances
of later life are derived.

However, two cardinal facts that affect the outcome
of this childhood experience cannot be overlooked.
First, there would be no repression if the boy had
to give up his mother but would be allowed to masturbate and play genital games with children of his age.
Adults do not like to face the fact that such sexual
games ("doctor games," for instance) always take

place when children spend some time together. Admittedly, the children clearly know that such games are forbidden; hence they are charged with guilt feelings and harmful fixations on these games. The child who does not dare indulge in such games when the opportunity arises is more certain to become a candidate for serious inhibitions in his later sexual life, even though he is behaving in accord with the principles of his family upbringing. Future generations will simply regard the attempts to ignore these facts as the products of depraved imaginations. But they cannot be ignored much longer and their consequences will have to be faced. Of course, an official social discussion cannot take place as long as family education is economically and politically anchored in authoritarian society.

The repression of early sexual impulses is determined, both qualitatively and quantitatively, by the sexual attitudes of the parents. Much depends on the severity of the repression and whether it is directed against masturbation, etc.

The fact that the child, at the critical age between the fourth and sixth year, experiences his genitality in his home imposes on him a specific solution in favor of family education. A child who might be raised from the third year on in the company of other children, uninfluenced by ties to his parents, would develop a quite different sexuality (but this is not germane to the present discussion). One also should not underestimate the fact that family education is for all practical purposes individualistic; it precludes the favorable influence of a collective education, even though the child may spend several hours a day in a kindergarten. Family ideology influences the kindergarten far more than the kindergarten influences it.

Thus, the child is pressed into the family and develops a fixation of a sexual and authoritarian nature to his parents. He is crushed by parental authority because he is physically small, regardless of whether or not such authority is strict. The authoritarian tie soon overwhelms the sexual one, represses it into the unconscious, and emerges later, when sexual interests turn to the extrafamilial world, as a powerful block between sexual interest and reality. Precisely because the authoritarian tie becomes largely unconscious, it is not accessible to conscious influence. It does not mean very much if the unconscious tie to parental authority is frequently expressed in terms of its opposite, as a neurotic rebellion; this still does not permit sexual interests to unfold, except in the form of impulsive and uncontrolled sexual acts, as a morbid compromise between sexuality and guilt feelings. The eventual dissolution of parental ties is *the* prerequisite for a healthy sexual life. Today, it occurs only rarely.

The parental ties—both the sexual fixation and the submission to the father's authority—make it more difficult in puberty to take the first step into sexual and social reality, and sometimes make it impossible. The conservative ideal of the good son and the good daughter of the house, both of whom adhere to the infantile situation far into their maturity, is the extreme opposite of a free, independent youth.

It is a further hallmark to family education that the parents, especially the mother—unless she has to go out and earn a living—increasingly seek in their children the meaning of their own lives; that the children are pressed into the role of house pets which can be loved but also tortured at will; that the affective attitude of the parents makes them completely unsuited to the task of educating their children. All these are truisms which need not concern us here any further.

Whatever misery in marriage cannot be acted out in marital discord is directed toward the children. This not only inflicts new injuries to their independence and sexual structure but also creates another contradiction: the contradiction between the witnessing of hostility in the parental marriage, and the later economic compulsion to marry. It is during puberty that tragedies occur when adolescents, fortunate enough to have salvaged themselves from the harm done during their earlier education, now want to free themselves from their family chains.

The sexual restraint which adults had to bear in order to tolerate marital and familial existence is perpetuated in their children. And since the latter, for economic reasons, must eventually sink back into the family situation, sexual inhibition is perpetuated from one generation to the next.

Inasmuch as the compulsory family is economically inseparable from authoritarian society, one would have to be totally blind to the facts and interconnections to expect that its effects can be eradicated within this society. These effects are conditioned by the family situation itself and, through the unconscious mechanisms of the instinctual structure, are inextricably anchored in the individual.

Added to the direct sexual inhibition which results from the relationship with the parents are guilt feelings that spring from the bottomless hatred the children have stored up over the years of family living. If this hatred remains conscious, it may turn into a powerful individual revolutionary drive; it becomes the motor force for dissolving the family ties and can easily be transformed into rational goals in the fight against those conditions which originally caused it.

But if the hatred is repressed, the individual develops the opposite impulses of faithful attachment and childish obedience which severely restrict him if later, on rational grounds, he decides to join the freedom movement. It is here that we meet the type of person who is probably in favor of complete freedom but exposes his children to religious instruction and does not leave the Church, even though it contradicts his convictions, because "he cannot do such a thing to his old parents." We also observe in him traits of faltering and hesitating, indecision, ties for the sake of family consideration, etc. He is certainly not the type who will fight for freedom.

The same family situation can also produce the

"revolutionary neurotic." He is frequently encountered among the intellectuals of the middle class. This, of course, does not say anything about his value as a revolutionary. But the connection with guilt feelings makes a revolutionary personality who is structured in this way an uncertain quantity.

Family sex education, by definition, must injure the sexual life of the individual. If someone succeeds in fighting his way through to a healthy sexual life, he usually does so at the expense of his family ties.

Beyond that, the repression of sexual needs is reflected in a general weakening of intellectual and emotional functions, particularly self-confidence, will power, and critical capacity. The authoritarian social order is not interested in "morality per se." The changes in the psychic organism which must be ascribed to the anchoring of sexual morality create only that particular psychic structure which forms the psychological mass basis of every authoritarian order of society.[1] The structure of the submissive person constitutes a mixture of sexual impotence, helplessness, a need for attachments, a nostalgia for a leader, fear of authority, timidity, and mysticism. It is characterized simultaneously by the tendency to rebellion and bondage. Sexual timidity and sexual hypocrisy form the nucleus of what is called philistinism. People structured in this manner are incapable of democracy. All attempts to build up or maintain genuine democratically directed organizations come to grief when they encounter these character structures. They form the psychological soil of the masses in which dictatorial strivings and bureaucratic tendencies of democratically elected leaders can develop.

Thus, the family has a dual political function:

1. It reproduces itself by crippling people sexually. By maintaining the patriarchal family, it also preserves

[1] Historically proved in *Der Einbruch der Sexualmoral*, 1934 (*The Invasion of Compulsory Sex-Morality*, Farrar, Straus & Giroux, 1971).

sexual repression and its results: sexual disturbances, neuroses, psychoses, sexual crimes.

2. It produces the authority-fearing, life-fearing vassal, and thus constantly creates new possibilities whereby a handful of men in power can rule the masses.

In this way, the family assumes, in the eyes of conservatives, its special importance as a bulwark of the social order they affirm. This is why it is one of the most strongly defended positions in conservative sexology. For it "maintains the state and the people" —in the reactionary sense. Therefore, evaluating the family may serve as a yardstick for judging the general nature of social orders.

VI

The Problem of Puberty[1]

There is probably no other field in which authoritarian
philosophy has managed to influence sexology to such
an extent as in the sexual problem of youth. The
alpha and omega of all investigations is the leap from
stating that puberty is essentially sexual maturity to
the demand that adolescents must or should live in
abstinence. Those who recognize the contradiction
in this remain silent. No matter how the demand
is disguised or rationalized, whether one resorts to
biological arguments such as "incomplete maturity"
before the twenty-fourth year (Gruber) or whether
ethical, cultural, or hygienic reasons are given, it has
occurred to none of the authors known to me that
the sexual plight of youth is basically a purely social
problem, which only begins with the demand for
abstinence. In the attempt to justify this social demand
biologically, culturally, or ethically, its adherents find
themselves trapped in absurd contradictions.

---

1 Cf. Reich: *Der sexuelle Kampf der Jugend* [The Sexual Struggle of
Youth]. [This work will appear in English as part of Reich's early
writings.—Editor.]

1. THE CONFLICT OF PUBERTY

The phenomena of the conflict of puberty and the neurosis of puberty in all their forms can be reduced to the single fact that a contradiction exists between the reality of full sexual maturity at about the age of fifteen, and with it the physiological need to have sexual intercourse and the ability to conceive and bear children, and the economic and structural impossibility of creating for this age group the legal framework for sexual intercourse—marriage. This is the basic difficulty, to which several others must be added, such as the effects of the sex-negating upbringing of the child, which is itself a product of the entire system of the conservative sexual order. In primitive matriarchal societies, sexual misery among youth is unknown. On the contrary, all reports, whether by missionaries or scholars, with or without the proper indignation about the "moral depravity" of "savages," state that the puberty rites of adolescents lead them immediately into a sexual life; that some of these primitive societies lay great emphasis on sexual pleasure; that the puberty rite is an important social event; that some primitive peoples not only do not hinder the sexual life of adolescents but encourage it in every way, as, for instance, by arranging for community houses in which the adolescents settle at the start of puberty in order to be able to enjoy sexual intercourse.[2] Even in those primitive societies in which the

2 "Such people allow their children, with their scarcely awakened drive, to find gratification with a freedom which we would regard as impudent lewdness [!] but which the adults look upon as games . . . Among many primitive peoples boys and girls meet each other with the most innocent devotion." Ploss-Bartels: *Das Weib* [The Woman] (Leipzig, 1902), Vol. I, p. 449. Cf. also Havelock Ellis: *Sex and Society* (1923), pp. 355 and 368; and Mayer: "Das Sexualleben bei den Wahehe und Wossangu" [Sexual Life among the Wahehe and Wossangu], *Geschlecht und Gesellschaft*, XIV ed., issue 10, p. 455. The best description is found in Malinowski's *The Sexual Life of Savages*.

institution of strict monogamous marriage exists, adolescents are given complete freedom to enjoy sexual
intercourse from the beginning of puberty to marriage.
None of these reports contains any indication of sexual
misery or suicide by adolescents suffering from un-
requited love (although the later does of course occur).
The contradiction between sexual maturity and the absence of genital sexual gratification is nonexistent. But
this is only the basic distinction between primitive and
authoritarian society. Although, in the latter, puberty
rites are conducted in the form of various religious
ceremonies (confirmation, etc.), this is done with
a total camouflage of their real nature, even with
the actual intent of influencing youth in the opposite
direction.[3]

The clearest expression of pubertal distress is
masturbation. Except for pathological cases, it is exclusively a substitute for the lack of sexual intercourse.
This statement, simple and self-evident as it is, I
have yet to find in any learned treatise. (If I have
overlooked one, I beg to be excused.) This self-evident
fact is so carefully hidden that it is overlooked altogether. The authors of these treatises derive the
conflict of puberty not from the conflict of "maturity—

---

3 There is a whole science which uses every means of complicated
argumentation to prove that the essence of puberty is not puberty itself,
not the maturing of the genital sexual apparatus, which produces the
well-known emotional changes, but that the essential element of puberty
and its conflicts consists in "new tasks" which the adolescent has to
face, and inferiority feelings because he is unable to solve those tasks.
This science is the individual psychology of Alfred Adler, according to
which the adolescent who spends the most important period of puberty
in a high school, say, where there are no new tasks (or are the Greek
lessons new tasks?) should have no puberty conflicts at all. Individual
psychology does not seem to be concerned that the achievements of
students generally begin to deteriorate around the age of fourteen; nor
is it interested in the fact that a large segment of working-class youth,
who begin to have sexual intercourse at puberty, experience all manner
of things save sexual misery—except for the fact, of course, that they
know little about contraception and do not have the housing facilities in
which hygienic sexual intercourse would be possible. It is precisely the
young worker who at the age of fourteen is confronted with new tasks.
Their deleterious effect, in Adler's sense, is lacking if genitality is
gratified.

no sexual intercourse," but from the conflict of "maturity—no possibility of marriage." Masturbation continues to be opposed by the Church and by sexologically untrained and morally prejudiced physicians. That the prohibition of masturbation only increases the misery because it reinforces the pathology of guilt feelings has lately been discussed more frequently, but —except for the popular writings of Max Hodann—enlightenment is tucked away in obscure scientific treatises. The masses of adolescents know nothing about it.

Briefly summarized, psychoanalytic investigation of the unconscious motives of the conflict of puberty has shown a reactivation of early infantile incestuous desires and sexual guilt feelings which in reality correspond to unconscious fantasies and not to the act of masturbation. Orgasm research, however, has found that masturbation is caused not by incestuous desires but by sexual excitation which corresponds to the heightened activity of the sexual apparatus. It is only the sexual stasis that revives the old incest fantasy, which in turn is caused not by masturbation but by the form and content of the psychic experience during the act of masturbation. Otherwise, why does the incest fantasy return precisely at the moment of sexual maturity, neither earlier nor later?

The conflict of puberty corresponds to a regression to more primitive, childhood forms and contents of sexual life. Unless this regression has been conditioned earlier by a pathological fixation in childhood, it is exclusively a consequence of the social denial of genital gratification in the sexual act at the time of maturity. Thus, in principle, there are two possibilities: either the adolescent, as a result of his previous sexual development, enters puberty incapable of finding a sexual partner, or society's denial of sexual gratification during puberty impels him into masturbatory fantasies and with them into the pathogenic situation of infantile conflicts. It is clear, however, that these two possibilities are not basically different, for the former is merely the result of the child's pathogenic sexual education, of a rigorously sex-suppressive situation in childhood. In this case, the social restriction of sexuality has taken full effect in childhood, while in the latter it becomes effective only in puberty. We are even more correct when we say that the two inhibitions of sexual development, the infantile and the adolescent, coincide insofar as the infantile inhibition of sexual development creates the fixation to which the later social inhibition during puberty makes sexuality regress. To the degree that the infantile injury to sexuality predominates, the ability of the adolescent to enter a normal sexual life is diminished, and all the more easily can the social barrier to adolescent intercourse take effect.

Thus, the sexual guilt feeling during masturbation is considerably stronger than it is during sexual intercourse because masturbation is overburdened with incestuous fantasies, while satisfactory sexual intercourse under normal circumstances renders these fantasies superfluous. If the fixation to childhood objects predominates, however, the sexual act is also disturbed and the guilt feelings are no less severe than during masturbation. It has been frequently shown that a gratifying sexual experience will also diminish sexual guilt feelings. Since masturbation is never as gratifying as sexual intercourse, its accompanying guilt feelings are experienced more strongly.

From the adolescent who is completely incapable of severing his infantile ties to his parents and entering into sexual reality to the adolescent who takes this step without qualms and thus saves his sexuality from infantilism, there are numerous transitions. Certainly, the first type comes close to the ideal of the "good" adolescent, clinging to the family, submitting to the demands of his parents, who after all represent conservative society. By conservative standards, he is the good student: he makes no claims, is modest and submissive. Later this type forms the elite of the "good" marital partners and uncritical citizens. But it also produces the majority of neurotics.

The other type, who is generally described as antisocial, rebellious, arrogant, basically opposed to the parental home, hostile to the demands of his lower-middle-class milieu, comprises the revolutionary contingent among workers and employess. In certain strata of the middle and upper classes, this type produces many psychopaths, impulsive characters who will deteriorate socially unless they join a social movement in time, because otherwise they will be trapped in an insoluble conflict with their own class. Since their intelligence is above average and they are capable of intense experience, their teachers, who are geared to the "good" students and those of average and below-average intelligence, do not know what to do with them. They are described as "morally insane" (morally is used here in the sense of a reactionary attitude toward life), even if they do nothing worse than fulfill the natural function of their sexual drive. But since, in conservative society with its attendant restrictions of sexual existence, this activity all too often borders on the criminal, such adolescents are, for purely social reasons, exposed to delinquency. In the area of adolescent sexuality, we find ourselves in complete agreement with Judge Lindsey, who discusses the difficulties of adolescents in his book

The Revolt of Modern Youth*:

> In general I find that there are several types of youth who are unlikely to get into trouble. First, there is the type that lacks energy, self confidence, and initiative. One characteristic of most of the boys and girls who get into difficulties is that they have just those qualities, and are all the more worth saving on that account. It is not always true that the boy or girl who never is willful or trouble-

---

4 Judge Ben B. Lindsey and Wainwright Evans: *The Revolt of Modern Youth* (New York: Boni and Liveright, 1925). (Hereafter cited as *Revolt*.)

some lacks energy and character, but it is quite likely to be so. Consistently high marks in deportment in school, especially for a boy, may merely mean that he lacks courage and energy, and perhaps health, and is restrained, not by morality but by *fear,* for "morality" doesn't play much part in the reactions of the normal lad—not if he is the healthy young animal he should be. He ought to be about as unconscious of his soul as he is of his breathing, or any other vital thing about him. [p. 94]

2. SOCIAL DEMAND AND SEXUAL REALITY

Three questions on adolescent sexuality must be answered here:

1. What demands does authoritarian society make on adolescents, and why does it do so?

2. What is the sexual life of adolescents between their fourteenth and eighteenth years really like?

3. What facts have been established about the consequences of (a) masturbation, (b) abstinence, and (c) sexual intercourse among adolescents?

Reactionary society, by establishing "ethical norms" for sexual intercourse, demands from the adolescent complete chastity before marriage. It condemns both sexual intercourse and masturbation. (We do not speak here of individual researchers but of the overall ideological atmosphere.) Scientists, insofar as they are influenced by authoritarian ideology—without of course being aware of it—establish theses which are intended to provide a solid basis for that ideology. Usually, they do not even do that but are content to invoke the famous "moral nature" of man. Thus, they forget their own viewpoint, with which they so often confront their ideological opponents, i.e., that the only legitimate task of science is to describe facts and their origins, without value assessment. Wherever science goes beyond a justification of social demands by ethical arguments, without having really freed itself from those demands, it uses a method which, objectively, is far more dangerous, namely, the concealment of the ethical viewpoint by pseudo-scientific theses. Morality is thus rationalized scientifically.

It is claimed, for instance, that abstinence in adolescence is necessary for the sake of social and cultural achievements. Quoted in support of this is Freud's theory that the energy for man's social and cultural achievements derives from sexual energies which are diverted from their original goal and channeled into "higher" goals. We know this concept as "sublimation." The theory is correct and rests on a great deal of clinical experience. However, sexual gratification and sublimation have been interpreted in such a way that they have become a rigid and absolute contradiction. The question should be: *which* kind of sexual gratification and activity; sublimation of *which* sexual drives?

The argument that an ascetic life is necessary for social development is incorrect even in terms of simple observation. It is contended that sexual intercourse among adolescents would diminish their achievements. The fact is—and on this all modern sexologists are in agreement—that virtually one hundred percent of adolescents masturbate. This completely invalidates the argument. For are we to believe that sexual intercourse is detrimental to social accomplishment, but masturbation is not? What is the principal difference between masturbation and sexual intercourse? Is not the conflict-ridden masturbation far more disturbing than an ordered sexual life could ever be? A hopeless dead end of argumentation! Since no distinction is made between gratifying and ungratifying sexuality, it is not possible to see its diverse connections with social accomplishment and sublimation. And why is there such a clearly visible gap in the theory? Because filling the gap would lead to practical consequences—as does any consistent

thinking about facts—that would take out every nut
and bolt from the complicated and refined structure
of reactionary ideology.

If the principal argument for the chastity of youth
were officially invalidated, adolescents might get ideas
and translate them into actions which would not endanger their health and their sociality but might well
threaten the structure of compulsory marriage and
even the existence of the institution of marriage. Later
the facts will clearly show this interconnection between
the demand for adolescent chastity and marital morality.

What is the sexual life of youth in reality? Certainly
not as morality demands it. Unfortunately there are
no actual statistics. Thanks to questionnaires, knowledge gained from sexual counseling, and questions
asked during lectures for adolescents, as well as wide
spread socioeconomic investigations, we are able to
make these general statements: Among adolescent
boys, complete abstinence, i.e., no sexual activity,
scarcely exists and, if at all, only among those who
are severely neurotic and inhibited. It exists a little
more frequently among girls, but the data are too
unreliable. One thing is clear: sexual conduct which
might rightly be described as abstinence is so rare
that for all practical purposes it is nonexistent.

In reality, under the guise of abstinence, all sorts
of sexual activities are practiced. We meet women
and even men who have masturbated for years without
knowing it. Among women, disguised masturbation
often takes form of pressing the thighs together; bicycle
and motorcycle are useful instruments for unconscious masturbation. Sexual daydreaming, even if it
is not accompanied by sexual activity, has the full
psychic value of masturbation, at least in its harmful
aspects. Sexual daydreamers will absolutely insist
that they practice abstinence. To a certain extent
we concur; they are abstinent in terms of gratification
but not in terms of stimulation.

Working-Class Youth

Without exception, there is great reluctance on the part of adolescents to discuss sexual matters with their leaders. It is significant that they also do not dare discuss them seriously among themselves. However, sex is much talked about in the form of obscenity or jokes, and the daily life of adolescents is pervaded with sexual questions. Very frequently, four-letter words are used to express sexual thoughts and feelings.

Nevertheless, adolescents often engage in sexual intercourse; among peasant youth from about the thirteenth year, among industrial youth from about the fifteenth year.

Among rural youth, it is customary for the girl to wait in front of the dance hall until a boy asks her for a dance and takes her inside. After the dance, which is overtly sensual, the boy takes the girl behind a hedge, where they have sexual intercourse. Contraception is virtually unknown; coitus is most always interrupted and abortion flourishes (performed by charlatans, of course).

The urban working-class youth are generally informed about contraception, but, strangely enough, they make little use of this knowledge. Before the rule of Fascism, youth organizations and parties in Germany and Austria did not concern themselves with the problem of contraception. Many of the younger youth leaders and low-ranking party functionaries showed great understanding for the difficulties of youth. However, the attitude of the presiding leadership was completely negative.

The customary evening classes on sexual enlightenment in workers' organizations were all too often intended to reinforce abstinence among youth. Only seldom did one meet responsible sexologists who correctly presented the central problem to the young people. (The method of broaching the sexual question is particularly important. First, one must be free of shame or negative attitudes; second, one must speak in a straightforward manner without hedging; and third, the adolescents' burning interest is revealed only if their questions are allowed to be presented in writing. This spares their personal feelings of shame, and consequently, after such a lecture few adolescents will hesitate to ask questions.)

Many young people and vigorous youth leaders, therefore, took matters into their own hands and tried to organize lectures on the subject. Here they ran into the greatest obstacle, the parents of the adolescents. It was typical even for parents who belonged to political organizations to forbid their adolescent children to join the youth organizations as soon as they heard that "such things" were discussed there. This applied to those who joined merely to find friends, even to eighteen-year-olds. But experience teaches us that the strictest parents cannot maintain their harsh position in the face of closed ranks of adolescents.

Jealousy, which occasionally degenerated into violence, often splintered the organizations. Among the youth functionaries one could distinguish two types: those who lived in complete abstinence, and those who were sexually mature and had an uninhibited sexual relationship. As for the first type, it was known to those around them that party work served as a diversion from sexual intercourse; typically, their party activity diminished once they had found a girl. Many adolescents joined organizations only to find a sexual partner and vanished after they had found one.

Very often a boy and a girl "go out together" for a long time without intercourse, because there are "no opportunities." Inner inhibitions (fear of impotence) play a role in this, as well as the lack of opportunity. Among girls, the fear of sexual intercourse is common. The boys frequently press for it, but the girls will permit all forms of sex play except intercourse. As a consequence, hysterical outbursts and weeping are everyday occurrences.

Nervous disturbances are a central problem of youth, particularly among girls. Sexual repression is stronger in youth who engage in sports than in those who do not, and often the sport is consciously used to master sexuality.

In summer camps, student homes, and colonies of high school graduates two typical phenomena are found: on the one hand, far-reaching sexual freedom; on the other, the gravest conflicts of irresolute youth which sometimes lead to explosions that undermine the life in the colony.

Occasionally, girls will confide that, when they are sitting at home, they have the most intense longing for a boy friend or *the boy friend*; but when they have occasion to enter a love relationship they unfortunately respond negatively. They cannot cross over from fantasy life to sexual reality.

The boys masturbate alone or together, at times to the point of collective excesses. Young boys masturbate more than young girls do.

Dances and collective festivities raise the sexual tension without resulting in a corresponding relaxation.

Those adolescents who have mastered the problem insofar as they have decided on sexual intercourse complain about the grievous lack of housing facilities. In the spring and summer sexual intercourse takes place outdoors, but in the winter the young suffer terribly. They do not have the money to visit the relatively expensive hotels, and an adolescent seldom has a room to himself. In any event, the parents always refuse to allow them to be together in the home. This produces serious conflicts and unhygienic forms of intercourse (in doorways, on dark street corners, etc.).

The main difficulty of the whole problem is that

the atmosphere in which the young workers live is permeated with sexual tension, while most of them, inwardly inhibited and surrounded by external obstacles, are too beaten down to find a way out. Parents, party leadership, and the whole social ideology are against them, while at the same time their communal life only furthers the breakdown of existing sexual barriers.

A typical picture was presented by a working-class youth group in Berlin with which I was in close contact. The group consisted of about sixty young workers between the age of fourteen and eighteen. The majority were boys. Here, too, there was a great deal of talk about sex, but in the form of jokes, mainly about intercourse and less about masturbation. The young people teased one another, for instance when a young man was "dating" a girl. Almost all had had sexual intercourse, and the partners changed rather frequently. The intimacy was not taken very seriously, but there also was a lack of serious conflicts, with the exception of a few dramatic incidents of jealousy which degenerated into violent brawling. There were never any excesses or so-called public orgies. Sexual intercourse occurred mostly at night parties but also at outdoor gatherings in the daytime. No one seemed to think anything of it when a boy and a girl occasionally "disappeared." Masturbation was scarcely mentioned, any more than homosexual acts. But the boys enjoyed talking about their experiences, and at times the girls did, too. In answer to my question as to why the matter was not taken seriously and treated only as a joke, a young girl who had worked for a while as the functionary of a group said, "How can it be otherwise? Our education tells us that everything is bad, but we must talk about it, and so it comes out as a joke."

Pessaries were hardly known or used; sexual intercourse was interrupted or a condom was used. *Coitus condomatus,* however, was generally regarded as expensive (a condom cost between 30 and 50 pfennig).

Party work was often disturbed by sexual conflicts. Boys and girls were reproached for having joined the party only to find a sexual partner. Frequently, girls stayed on only because of certain boys. A woman functionary thought that things had reached this state of affairs only because the adolescents were not clear in their own minds about their sexuality. To repress it, she felt, would be even worse, but the matter would not take on such importance if their education had been different and dealt openly and seriously with these problems.

In 1934, Germany's National Socialist government forbade all communal hiking and overnight trips of male and female youth. No political party dared to oppose this order and fight for the interests of youth.

I am familiar with only Austrian and German workers' youth. But I contend on the basis of many years of medical and sex-political work among the young that, with minor differences, conditions are equally dismal and detrimental to health in all countries. My view is strengthened by reports from England, especially London, from Hungary, America, and elsewhere.

The most horrible and pernicious sexual misery of the working-class and middle-class youth is caused by gossip-mongering old spinsters and ungratified men and women in small towns and in the country; this happens everywhere. Here young people, even if they were capable, cannot possibly develop a love relationship. The boredom of the population creates much lasciviousness and malice which cause many suicides. The picture presented by the youth is dismal. When I had to live in Malmö in exile I had many opportunities to confirm the accuracy of my viewpoint. Between eight and eleven at night, young people between the ages of seventeen and thirty promenaded up and down the city's main street. Boys and girls

were separate, each walking in groups of three or
four. The boys made stupid jokes, looked insolent,
but their shyness was transparent; the girls giggled
bashfully with each other, aware, without knowing.
Occasional necking in doorways. Culture? Breeding
places for Fascistic convictions when boredom and
sexual depravity encounter the National Socialist
hoopla. And the socialist organizations were not prepared to organize life differently.

UPPER-MIDDLE-CLASS YOUTH

Let us consider Lindsey's report about the sexual
life of America's upper-middle-class youth.

The breakthrough of genital sexuality in the schools
took such forms that the authorities were forced to
intervene:

> Likewise, at Phillips Academy, another boys'
> school of the first rank, it was found necessary a
> few years back to forbid dancing at the school be-
> cause of the license that went with it. This incident
> likewise received wide newspaper publicty. Al-
> fred E. Stearns, Principal of Phillips Academy, said
> in an article in the *Boston Globe* that measures
> which had previously been taken had included the
> appointment of student and faculty committees
> charged with the following duties:
> "1. To serve as police and to remonstrate with,
> if not actually eject from the floor, couples who
> dance in an indecent manner.
> 2. To prevent the admission of girls of ques-
> tionable character.
> 3. To prevent drinking, by boys and girls alike,
> on the floor and elsewhere.
> 4. To eject those found to be under the influence
> of liquor and to prevent the admission of those in
> like condition.
> 5. To supervise the girls' dressing room for the

purpose of preventing extravagant dress and indecent exposure, drinking, and loose talk.

6. To insist that visiting girls should be accompanied by chaperones; to prevent auto 'joy rides' during the dancing.

7. To prevent the parking of automobiles in close proximity to the dance hall.

8. To prevent other and outside gatherings exempt from the control and supervision of the main dance.

9. To see that girls are promptly and properly returned to their rooms at the close of the dance."

I give this list at length because it leaves no doubt of the sort of conditions that existed in a school second to none in this country for the quality of its students. They are for the most part boys drawn from eastern homes of considerable wealth and culture. They have behind them first-rate traditions and training. [*Revolt,* p. 52]

Let us try to overcome the moral astonishment that such conditions can be found among youth "from eastern homes of considerable wealth and culture," and recognize that such conditions exist in spite of external puritanism and antisexual education; only their forms impress us as the dialectical opposite of antisexual morality. What interests us is not that suppressed sexuality becomes manifest in the teeth of moral demands but what influence sexual morality has on the forms of sexual activity. We shall see right away that these sexual activities correspond neither to sexual morality nor to sex-economy but represent a compromise which is disadvantageous to both.

The first item in the testimony of these high-school students is that of all the youth who go to parties, attend dances, and ride together in automobiles, more than 90 percent indulge in hugging and kissing. This does not mean that every girl lets *any* boy hug and kiss her, but that she *is* hugged and kissed. And evidently this 90 percent estimate does not apply to those of our young people who lack the biological energy and the social urge which leads the most worthwhile portion of our youth to express their natural instincts in these social diversions. Another way of putting it would be to say that what leads these youngsters into trouble is an overflowing of high spirits and abounding energy which only needs more wise direction.

The testimony I receive regarding this estimated 90 percent is practically unanimous. If it be true, it means that these young people have more or less definitely come to the conclusion that this minor form of sex experience may be legitimately indulged in. Also that a very large number do indulge in it, without permitting the diversion to exceed certain rather clearly defined limits.

Some girls insist on this kind of thing from boys they go with, and are as aggressive, in a subtle way, in their search for such thrills as are the boys themselves.

I recall one very beautiful and spirited girl who told me that she had refused to go out with a certain boy because he lacked pep, and didn't know how, as she put it, to "love me up."

"Do all the boys do such things nowadays?" I asked.

"Of course they do," she retorted. "If they don't there is something wrong with them." [pp. 56f.]

If Lindsey speaks of an "overflowing of high spirits," he is right only insofar as the "over" corresponds in part to the livelier sexuality of adolescents and in part results from the contradictory character of their sexual activity. We have heard that the young regard kissing and hugging, i.e., the forepleasure acts, as legitimate, but they did not "exceed certain rather clearly defined limits." We can express ourselves less cautiously. What has been revealed here is that adolescents practice all forms of sexual stimulation, but most do not progress to the sexul act. Why, we must ask, do they permit everything except this? If we ponder this question, the answer appears: morality expressly depicts the sexual act as the worst thing one can do sexually. (And it is also the most important culmination of erotic excitation.) The kissing and hugging are already a form of emancipation, but in rejecting the sexual act one still clings to compulsory morality. Here the marriageability of the girls becomes a consideration, for virginity means a greater chance of marriage. Nevertheless, as Lindsey writes, "at least 50 percent of those who begin with hugging and kissing do not restrict themselves to that, but go further, and indulge in other sex liberties which, by all conventions, are outrageously improper." (p. 59). Only 15 percent indulge in sexual intercourse. In 1920 and 1921, Lindsey had to deal with 769 girls, aged fourteen to seventeen, because of "sexual delinquencies." "That this figure was not higher," Lindsey says, "has to do with the physical impossibility of supervising all cases." According to Lindsey, 90 percent of the boys have "sexual experiences" before leaving school, i.e., before the eighteenth year. The girls have also become less reluctant.

One high-school boy with whom I recently talked admitted that he had had relations with fifteen girls of high-school age, about half of them still in school. He had chosen them in preference to "chippies," or common street girls. I verified this confession, talked with practically all of these girls, and found that they were good, average girls. His experience with each of them had been on only one or two occasions. The girls, with one or two exceptions, were not given to promiscuity, and I believe most of them have turned out well.

A Red Light District in Denver might have saved those girls from these experiences, but it

would not have saved the boy—nor the prostitutes,
who have as good a right to be saved as anybody
else.

There can be no doubt, I think, that since the
Red Light Districts were abolished far more
"good" girls than formerly have had sex experiences. But, curious as it may seem, fewer girls
have been "ruined" and "lost." [p. 70]

Here Lindsey, perhaps unwittingly, expresses the
basic secret of prostitution and the solution which
the sexual crisis provides: the decrease in prostitution
by admitting female youth sexual life.

This active and aggressively inquiring attitude
of mind on the part of girls has of late years become general rather than exceptional. Also, it is
more and more unconcealed. The reason is that social and economic conditions have placed these
girls more on a level with men. Many of them, when
they leave school, take positions in which they make
more money than the boys they go with. The result
is that many a youth finds himself subject to rather
contemptuous inspection by the young woman of his
choice. [p. 21]

Furthermore:

I have at hand certain figures which indicate with
certainty that for every case of sex deliquency
discovered, a very large number completely escape
detection. For instance, out of 495 girls of high-
school age—though not all of them were in high
school—who admitted to me that they had had sex
experiences with boys, only about 25 became
pregnant. That is about 5 percent, a ratio of one in
twenty. The others avoided pregnancy, some by
luck, others because they had a knowledge of more
or less effective contraceptive methods—a knowledge, by the way, which I find to be more common among them than is generally supposed.

Now the point is this: First, that three-fourths of that list of nearly 500 girls came to me of their own accord for one reason or another. Some were pregnant, some were diseased, some were remorseful, some wanted counsel, and so on. Second, the thing that always brought them to me was their acute need for help of some kind. Had they not felt that need, they would not have come. For every girl who came for help, there must have been a great many, a majority, who did *not* come because they did not want help, and therefore kept their own counsel.

In other words, that 500—covering a period of less than two years—represented a small group, drawn from all levels of society, that didn't know the ropes, and got into trouble of one kind or another; but there was as certainly a much larger group that did know the ropes, and never came around at all. My own opinion is that for every girl who comes to me for help because she is pregnant, or diseased, or in need of comfort, there are many more who do not come because they escape scot free of consequences, or else because circumstances are such that they can meet the situation themselves. Hundreds, for instance, resort to the abortionist. I don't guess this, I know it. [pp. 64f.]

What conclusions does Lindsey draw from data which from the standpoint of compulsory morality are shattering?

I need not say that this is a difficult and dangerous problem. It is one which cannot be met by denunciation or watchfulness on the part of adults. It can be met only by a voluntarily adopted code of manners—by genuine internal restraints approved and adopted by the young people themselves. Such a code can be called into free and

spontaneous action only by education of the frank-
est and most thorough-going sort. [pp. 59f.]

Just what is this "code of manners"? What concrete
solution does Lindsey suggest? How are "genuine
internal restraints" to be attained? No inhibitions
can be more "genuine" than those experienced by
adolescents through restrictions and suppression of
sexuality as practiced everywhere, at home, school,
and church, and for a very simple reason: there are
no inhibitions except those imposed from the outside,
because nature does not know any "ethical law."
And what is the result of centuries of sexual suppression of youth? Just what Lindsey has described.

Lindsey is caught up in contradictions which, from
the standpoint of his view of life, become completely
insoluble. He confirms facts which signify the decline
of compulsory morality among youth. Then he draws
conclusions which mean nothing but the restoration
of the same morality whose decline he has just confirmed and even in part expressly approves. In the
final analysis, he cannot free himself from the ideology
of compulsory, monogamous marriage and premarital chastity for the girl. He writes:

> Years ago I had in my charge a girl of 17 who,
> when I became acquainted with her five years be-
> fore, had already had relations with several school
> boys. Immoral? Bad? Poppycock! She was igno-
> rant. One talk with me ended it; she became one of
> the finest young women in Denver. No casual male
> would dare cross her path. She is very beautiful,
> has a remarkable mind, and some time ago was
> married to a youth who, I trust, deserves her.
> [p. 116]

Thus, he only alleviates the compulsory moral judgment; he does not oppose it; he does not draw the
conclusion of its fiasco and decline from his observed
facts. The older generation said the girl was stupid

and wicked; Lindsey thinks she was only ignorant. I doubt if she was ignorant. She knew exactly what she was doing, but she eventually landed, and *had* to land, in marriage as it is prescribed for girls. Thereby, she did not become more aware in the sense of sexual orientation but, at most, "aware," under Lindsey's influence, about the consequences that threatened her unless she bowed to the standard form of sexual life. Thus Lindsey contends:

1. That social yardsticks change:

> To say that that happened when this kind of folly was at its height and that the hysteria has since died down—that it was therefore just a passing brain storm on the part of youth after the war, is nonsense. Concealment today is more skillful and more general, because the thing isn't new any longer; but if the adult population of this country think the relative calm on the surface means that there is nothing happening any more beneath the surface, they are living in a fool's paradise. Youth is shrewder, more sophisticated, more contemptuous of its elders, and more coldly bent on following its own path than it ever was before. Nor does that necessarily imply that it is wholly an evil path, nor that they are all, as the saying goes, hell bent for destruction. It does mean that they are changing our social code; and in my judgment they are going to win through, if not with us, then without us. [pp. 53f.]

2. That economic restraints have been removed, primarily among young women:

> The external restraints, economic restraints that were once so potent, have gone never to return; *and the sole question now is how soon and how effectively will the internal restraints of a voluntarily accepted code, which alone can keep young people straight, take their place.* I think this is

already happening. I don't think this younger generation is just a blindfolded bull in a china shop.
[p. 54]

3. That today's youth is "relatively the most moral
and the most sane generation the world has ever seen"
[p. 54]

4. That the replacement of the bordello by girls
of one's own class is better and more moral:

> For in the past, notwithstanding the Red Light
> District and its ruined women, the boys who
> helped by their patronage to make that District
> possible stood excellent chances of becoming
> good citizens, husbands and fathers; but the girl
> denizens of that world did not. Thus these new
> conditions, in spite of the increase of sex experi-
> ences among girls, as compared with the days
> of the Red Light District, would seem to have
> brought with them less that is destructive to
> womanhood than did the old order with its stricter
> conventions, its savage punishments, and its
> hypocritical double standard of "morality." I
> don't say, mind you, that the new order needs no
> mending; I merely insist that it contains more
> essential morality than did the old; and that, all
> calamity howlers to the contrary notwithstanding,
> we have *not* gone backward. [p. 72]   -

5 That today's girls are knowledgeable about the
"male animal."

> Once a "nice" girl would have considered such
> advances an insult. Now, though she may refuse,
> she is not so likely to be offended. She is too
> sophisticated for that, and knows enough about the
> male animal to understand that his impulse is a
> normal one. Whether such frankness between
> boys and girls is a gain or the reverse I shall not
> try to consider at this point. It is, however, quite
> in keeping with the very evident determination of

these young people to call a spade a spade; and we adults have it to reckon with, whether we like it or not. [p. 67]

6. "Sex is simply a biological fact. It is as much so as the appetite for food. Like the appetite for food it is neither legal nor illegal, moral nor immoral." [p. 127]

But in his conclusions Lindsey does not examine the causes of the failure of youth's sexual revolt; he simple assesses it from the moralistic point of view.

By its departures, *en masse*, from ancient standards, it has doubtless achieved some real progress; but its individual members have simply jumped from one form of slavery into another. License is bondage; liberty, on the contrary, is a free obedience to laws more compelling and difficult than human law, and far more exacting. Youth, unhelped by any wisdom but its own, often confuses the two. [pp. 102f.]

In the "more exacting" laws we recognize the existential necessities and conditions of authoritarian society, in their compulsion a reflection of the lack of a social basis for the sex-economic life of youth, the stern determination of society not to let youth escape the trap of the vassal factory called family. And youth itself cannot, and must not, develop a saving insight, because they are themselves materially interested in the social order which causes such great difficulties in their sexual life.

But how does it happen that even Lindsey, the admired and courageous fighter for youth, is not impelled to the inevitable conclusions? How is it that he, too, appears to be moralistically prejudiced and hence an inhibited fighter for the rights of youth?[5]

---

5 Despite his self-restraint, Lindsey was rendered innocuous in America. He lost his judgeship.

Perhaps it is here that we will find the secret of why people insist so sternly on abstinence, despite the obvious fiasco that it is.

Lindsey continues:

> She could live with him "in sin" later, after the marriage ceremony, and it would be all right. Where do they get their logic? *Did that relationship really smirch and defile her, or was she at fault simply because she was violating the social code?* The distinction is extremely important. We may admit that she was at fault in her pre-nuptial intimacy; but the fault lay in her violation of a social convention, and not in a mysterious "defilement" conjured up by our tribal superstitions. [p. 118; emphasis added]

Thus she is not "defiled" by premarital intercourse, but she has transgressed the "mores." The demand for chastity in girls cannot be described more clearly: she was wrong in having intercourse prior to marriage. Absolutely wrong? No, but with regard to the mores insofar as conservative society cannot, for ideological and economic reasons, approve premarital intercourse, for then the ideology of marriage and the family would fall in ruins. Says Lindsey in the case of a rebellious girl:

> And yet this is by no means to say that marriage is a failure and should go into the discard to make way for Free Love or any other social Ism. However imperfect the institution may be *we can't do without it.* It must be preserved by means of sane and cautious alterations in its code . . . [p. 140]

Thus, it is completely clear that *sexual freedom of youth means the decline of marriage (that is, compulsory marriage), and sexual suppression is supposed to make youth capable of marriage.* In the final analysis, the much discussed "cultural" importance of marriage and "the morality" of youth is reduced to this, and this is the sole reason why the question of marriage cannot be discussed separately from that of adolescent sexuality, and vice versa. If this interrelation is disturbed, the young are caught in insoluble conflicts, for their sexual problem cannot be solved without solving the problem of marriage, which in turn depends upon finding solutions to the problem of women's economic dependence and to the difficult problems of education and economic conditions.

These passages were set down in the summer of 1928, two years before their first publication. They formulated a conclusion based on a study of the sociological relationships between marital morality and the demand for abstinence among the young. In the fall of 1929, I chanced upon statistical proof for my conclusions, which up to then had been merely guesswork. In Moscow, M. Barash, a physician of the Venerological Institute, published a thesis, "Sex Life of the Workers of Moscow," in the *Journal of Social Hygiene* (Vol. XII, No. 5, May 1926), which also contained statistics on the relationship between marital infidelity and sexual intercourse prior to marriage. Of those who engaged in sexual intercouse before the seventeenth year, 61.6 percent were unfaithful in their marriage; of those whose sexual life began between the seventeenth and the twenty-first year, 47.6 percent were unfaithful, and among those who did not have sexual intercouse until after their twenty-first year, only 17.2 percent were unfaithful. The author notes:

> The earlier anyone from the investigated groups engaged in sexual intercourse, the less faithful he proved to be later in the marriage; he inclined toward frequent incidental sexual relations. . . . Those who engaged in sexual intercourse at an early age later developed an irregular sex life.

If it is correct that the demand that youth live in abstinence is sociologically conditioned by the institution of marriage, and indirectly by the same economic interests that determine official sexual reform, if it is furthermore statistically proved that early sexual intercourse makes one incapable of marriage in terms of compulsory marriage morality ("a lifelong partner"), then it is clear that the demand for abstinence serves to create a sexual structure in individuals which corresponds to a strict marital sexual life and creates submissive subjects for the state.

What this sexual structure looks like, how it affects the young, and what contradictions it creates for marriage will be the subject of the following investigation.

3. A MEDICAL, NON-ETHICAL CONSIDERATION OF SEXUAL INTERCOURSE AMONG YOUTH

The adolescent has only three choices: abstinence, masturbation (including homosexual activity and heterosexual stimulation), and sexual intercourse. We must be clear from which point of view the question is approached. There are three viewpoints: the ethical, the sex-economic, and the social. Ethically, the question is inaccessible and insoluble. In reality, it merges with that of the sexual economy of the individual and with the interest of society in its members.

We have seen that authoritarian society has the greatest interest in suppressing adolescent sexuality. This suppression is essential for maintaining compulsory marriage and family as well as for producing submissive citizens. The sexual moralist, by confusing authoritarian society with human society, also says that the existence of human society itself is imperiled if the young, as he typically puts it, "live out" their sexuality. But this is precisely what must be investigated. Specifically, we must ask which social interests contradict those of sex-economy and whether one will have to be sacrificed if the other is to be preserved. We may also take into account the interest of the adolescents themselves and ask which hygienic advantages, or disadvantages for them lie in abstinence, masturbation, or sexual intercourse.

SEXUAL ABSTINENCE DURING PUBERTY

We must of course investigate the phenomena of complete abstinence, for everything else comes under the expanded concept of masturbation. Thus we face the unshakable fact that normally around the fourteenth year sexuality, because of increased activity of the endocrine glands and the maturing of the genital apparatus, enters a highly active phase. By nature, the sexual impulse is oriented toward sexual intercourse. If so many adolescents are not consciously ready for sexual intercourse, this is not, as is erroneously assumed, an expression of biological immaturity but a consequence of an education which suppresses all thoughts of such activity. It is important to establish this fact if one wants to see things as they are, and not as authoritarian society and the Church would like us to see them. Adolescents who have overcome the repression of the idea of the sexual act are very much aware of its existence and know it is what they yearn for. A prerequisite for abstinence is therefore the repression of sexual ideas, particularly those of the sexual act.

The more widespread possibility is perhaps that the idea of the sexual act is, though not consciously, so far removed from psychic interest or even so connected with feelings of revulsion and anxiety that it has no practical significance. To effect abstinence, however, it is also necessary that sexual excitation be repressed. That provides a period of peace. It also has the advantage of sparing youth the tormenting masturbation conflict and the dangerous battle with the social environment which is unavoidable if the adolescent has a conscious and therefore insurmountable longing for sexual intercourse.

Most adolescents show a distinct change in their attitude toward sexual pleasure once they have progressed beyond the first stages of puberty. They disavow their sexuality much more sharply after the sixteenth and seventeenth year than before. Analysis has proved that the striving for pleasure has been replaced by the fear of pleasure.

We may call this pleasure anxiety. It is different basically from the fear of punishment for sexual activities, which usually culminates in an unconscious fear of castration. The sexual shyness which becomes increasingly prominent is anchored in this pleasure anxiety, for the following reason: as a result of unrelenting sexual prohibitions, the character of sexual excitation itself is changed. Clinical experience teaches us that inhibited pleasure becomes unpleasure, frequently even resulting in painful excitation in the genitals. Thus pleasureable excitation becomes a source of unpleasure and thereby the actual motive which impels the adolescent to fight against his sexuality and to suppress it. The trained sexological physician is familiar with the adolescent's peculiar practice of deliberately holding back erections, because they become unpleasurable if gratification is lacking. Among girls during puberty, the anxiety is not so much a fear of punishment as it is a fear of the strong excitation, which they experience as a danger. The fear of punishment for sexual activities, which is acquired from the social environment, has its real anchor in this pleasure anxiety. In this way, the adolescent himself often becomes the proponent of sexual prohibitions.

Sexual excitation without gratification cannot be tolerated for long. There are only two solutions: suppression of the sexual excitation or gratification. The first regularly leads to psychic and physical disturbances; the second, to conflicts with today's society.

Abstinence is dangerous and absolutely deleterious to health. First, there is the fact that suppressed sexual excitation produces various effects. Either a nervous disturbance soon appears or else the adolescent lapses into sexual daydreams which severely impede his work. Those who do not wish to see the connection between sexual excitation and nervous disturbances in all their forms can easily say that abstinence is not damaging, or even that it can be practiced in most cases. They find only that some adolescents live in abstinence and that therefore abstinence is possible. But that in exchange such adolescents acquire neuroses and other difficulties escapes the untrained observer. He thinks the neurosis is an expression of a "degenerative trait" or of the "will to power." He spares himself more than he does the adolescents; he spares himself thinking about the difficult problem of adolescent sexuality itself as well as about the problem of social order.

It will be said that not all adolescents who live in abstinence immediately become neurotic. Certainly, but then how are we to explain the fact that the neurosis shows itself later, when the individual is faced with the demands of "legal" sexual activity? Sex-economic clinical experience teaches us that those who never had the courage to masturbate have the most unfavorable prognosis. Sexual feelings have been suppressed (perhaps even for a while successfully), the sexual apparatus has not been used, and then when authoritarian society finally permits gratification, the apparatus fails; it has become "rusty." The numerical predominance of feminine sexual disturbances vis-à-vis masculine impotence reveals an intimate connection between the more severe sexual suppression and the less frequent masturbation of girls and their later inability to experience sexual pleasure. Great care is taken not to reveal such facts to adolescents, even if one is aware of them, for what justification would then remain for preaching abstinence? One could not even point to sports as a way out of the sexual misery.

The possibility of using sports as a means to divert the sexual drive was repeatedly raised by those who opposed me when I discussed the problem of masturbation. All I could answer, unless I wanted to falsify the facts in the interest of our morality, was that sports is certainly the best way to diminish the sexual drive, but that athletes who want to kill their sexual drive completely often succeed so well that, later, they can no longer function sexually. We are continually astounded at the many strong, athletically trained people who are disturbed sexually. They have resorted to sports in a struggle against their sexuality. But since, in the long run, they could not discharge all their sexual excitation in athletics, they finally had to resort to repression, with all its consequences. Thus, sports are a means of diminishing sexual excitation but they are just as unsuited to solve the sexual problem of adolescents as any other means whose aim is to stifle sexual excitation.

Whoever wishes to live in abstinence, with the risk of emotional illness or a decreased capacity to work and enjoy life, is free to do so. We do not want to force anyone into a gratifying sexual life. But anyone who is unwilling to make this sacrifice should try to lead a well-ordered, satisfying sexual life as soon as the sexual urge can no longer be ignored. It is our duty to stress the corrosion of sexuality, its regression into infantile and perverse activities, and the emotional illness which results from adolescent abstinence. The most tragic cases we see in our counseling office and medical practice are those people in advancing years—thirty-five, forty, fifty, and even sixty years old—who are severely disturbed, neurotic, troubled, lonely, tired of living, and asking for help. Most of them boast of the fact that they have not lived "excessively," meaning that they avoided masturbation and early sexual intercourse.

Nor are the dangers of sexual abstinence properly assessed by otherwise clear-minded writers, for two reasons: first, they are not aware of the connection between a later sexual disturbance and an abstinence that lasted too long; second, unlike the practicing psychotherapist or sex counselor, they have not had the opportunity to see this intimate connection. Fritz Brupbacher writes in an otherwise excellent pamphlet, *Kindersegen, Fruchtverhutung, Fruchtabtreibung* [The Blessing of Children, Contraception, Abortion] (Neuer Deutscher Verlag, 1925):

> In all sorts of writings people philosophize about the harm or benefit of abstinence. Those who prefer it should practice it. It is not harmful. . . . In any event, abstinence is healthier than venereal disease.

Brupbacher later revealed in conversations that he had given up this view. He had overlooked the fact that the tendency toward prolonged abstinence is itself a pathological symptom, the sign of an almost complete repression of conscious sexual desire. Sooner or later, it invariably does harm to an individual's sexual life and capacity for work. This is a proven fact. To recommend abstinence to youth means to set the stage for a neurosis. And, from the standpoint of psychic economy, it is doubtful whether abstinence is healthier than veneral disease. One can get rid of the disease if it is properly treated. But the pathological character changes brought about by a life of abstinence can only seldom be removed, and, besides, we do not have a sufficient number of psychotherapists to cure the evils caused by prolonged abstinence. This does not mean that we underestimate venereal disease. But it is used as a bogey man, a convenient means of bringing about sexual repression. Furthermore, the alternative is not abstinence or venereal disease, because the disease can be avoided if one has intercourse only with a beloved partner and has no recourse to prostitutes.

We are speaking here of the abstinence of adolescents, by which we mean those aged fifteen through eighteen. This abstinence is demanded by the authoritarians "until the closing of the epiphyses," that is, up to about the twenty-fourth year. At one time in Vienna a Socialist social worker gave lectures to adolescents in which this harmful "theory" was drummed into them in the guise of scientific doctrine. But she did not discuss what the closing of the epiphysis had to do with the maturing of the sexual apparatus that had occurred almost ten years earlier. In the newspaper *Morgen,* a youth counselor oriented in individual psychology published a question-and-answer column. On March 18, 1929, we found the following pretty piece of advice:

> G. Sch. Your question touches upon the problem of the onset of "sexual practices" often discussed in biological circles. The Roman writer Tacitus praises the ancient German tribes for never touching a woman before the twenty-fourth year, and this rule should also be valid for us. The sexual drive, among the most powerful in human life, should not be given release prematurely, and you are quite right to seek in athletics a discharge to which you are not yet entitled in the sexual realm [!]. If your friends, even those who are younger, act differently, they do so against the precepts of sexual hygiene [!]. The famous leader in the field of hygiene, Professor Max von Gruber, in his lively manner, has never ceased to preach that sexual abstinence can never be harmful.

The reference to Gruber and the ancient Germanic tribes is certainly an impressive argument! But the same Professor Gruber also contended that abstinence was not only not harmful but even useful: the unejaculated semen would be reabsorbed, thereby providing an additional supply of protein. . . . I know of a better and more pleasant way of adding protein: eat meat. But in loyal obedience to the order of the state and the law of morality—both, of course, against all things carnal—it never occurred to Gruber, who was concerned about the authoritarian order of society, that there were means of adding protein other than reabsorption.

I mention these examples not only because they are historically interesting but also because they show how much effort is required to free ourselves of this ideology. In 1930, the Viennese Social Democratic gynecologist Dr. Karl Kautsky launched a strong attack against me, accusing me of robbing the workers of their "ideals." It is extremely important to remember that sexual timidity does not stop at the borders of the working-class movement.

My investigation of the sexual revolution in the Soviet Union proved that one does not help the workers' movement by concealing such things. We must finally reach the point where sexologists and youth counselors stop competing with the Church in the "service of morality." The following example will show how unscrupulously people in this field have acted.

Among the Viennese youth counselors there was a pastor who gave a twenty-two-year-old young woman the following advice (a written report by the young woman):

> By way of introduction I mentioned that I had read about a counseling service in the papers and that I, too, was most unhappy and at the end of my wits.
>
> Dr. P. encouraged me to confide in him.
>
> I told him that I had a boy friend, that we were both very fond of each other, and that lately there was tension between us and I could no longer help myself. I added that I had tried religion but could not find any satisfaction in it.

Now Dr. P. began to question me.

How old was I? Twenty-two years old.

How long had I known my boy friend? For four years.

How old was he? Twenty-four years old.

His general answer was that he knew young people who had been seeing each other for eight and nine years and were still *pure*.

He did not define what he meant by being pure, but he commented that he could well imagine two people being very fond of each other without having a sensual thought about each other.

He also asked me how my fiancé felt about the matter. I said that he, too, was suffering terribly under these conditions and that I could not bear any longer to see him so tormented. Thereupon Dr. P. asked about our financial circumstances. I told him that I made little money and that my friend's position was insecure.

He also asked about the conditions at home and I said that I could not count on any support from my parents.

Dr. P. thought I should talk to my mother and try to get married as soon as possible. In this connection he said, among other things, that the commandments of the Church have deeper reasons, for example, the commandment: thou shalt not be unchaste. For there might be dire consequences if there were a child to take care of.

When I objected that it would take several years before I could afford to get married and that my strength in tolerating this condition would not hold out that long, Dr. P. thought that I should not think in terms of years but should be strong and persevere from day to day. In this connection, he inquired if my friend and I met alone together and if my parents were aware of it. I replied in the affirmative. He then advised me to avoid meeting my friend alone and not to get myself into an unpleasant situation so we wouldn't torture each other.

Dr. P. encouraged me, assuring me that I only needed to believe it would be possible to hold out to accomplish it. Then, with the advice to marry as soon as possible, I was dismissed with a "God bless you."

Nature healers, too, engage in sexual counseling. After a lecture, I was given the following note for comment, a prescription which a nature healer had given an abstinent young man of seventeen who suffered from daily seminal emissions:

Three times a day a pinch of gentian in the form of wafers. Also, boil 30 grams of crushed hemp in 1/2 liter of milk and take a tablespoon of this three or four times a day. Also, take a sitz-bath of an infusion of calamus every other day for about twenty minutes. At night, have your spinal column massaged with the following mixture: arnica spirits, 90 grams; spirit of lavender and balm mint, 4 grams each; spirit of peppermint and field thyme, 1 gram each. Mix well.

This and similar ludicrous "advice" is the product of complete helplessness in the difficult task of counseling youth. Whether or not the counselor believes in the efficacy of his "medication" or is convinced of the futility of the demand for abstinence is a matter of indifference. Aside from his own inhibitions, he is after all only an unconscious tool of a life-negating sexual order, a preparer of "marriageability," of "goodness," or vassalage. We will soon see that awareness of the truth does not in the least ease his situation but only aggravates it.

MASTURBATION

Masturbation presents a means of avoiding the harm of abstinence, but only within narrow limits. It can regulate the sexual energy only if it occurs without overly strong guilt feelings and disturbances in the course of stimulation; furthermore, only as long as the absence of a real partner is not felt as too upsetting. It certainly can help healthy adolescents to weather the first storms of puberty. But under the conditions which have influenced the sexual development of youth from infancy on, it can fulfill this function only in the minority of cases. Very few adolescents have become sufficiently emancipated from the moralistic influences of their upbringing to be able to masturbate without qualms. Most young people fight against the impulse to masturbate more or less successfully. If they do not succeed in conquering masturbatory activities, they masturbate under the most severe inhibitions, often indulging in the most damaging practices, for instance, withholding ejaculation. This contributes at least to a neurasthenic disturbance. If they do succeed in fighting off the impulse to masturbate, they fall back into abstinence; but this time the situation is much worse because the fantasies and sexual excitation that have been activated in the process of masturbation make abstinence still more unbearable. Only very few find their way to the sex-economic alternative, sexual intercourse.

Just a few years ago, masturbation was generally considered a horrible practice. Lately, to protect the moral order and in light of the realization that the demand for abstinence is not feasible anyway, it has become fashionable to present masturbation as totally harmless and completely natural. This is only conditionally correct. Masturbation is certainly better than abstinence, but in the long run it is unsatisfactory and quite disturbing because the lack of a love object will soon make itself felt; and when masturbation is no longer satisfying, it engenders disgust and guilt feelings, and due to the pressing sexual excitation which is subject to the contradictions of the ego, it becomes a compulsion. Furthermore, even under the best circumstances it has the disadvantage that it increasingly forces fantasy activity into neurotic and previously relinquished infantile sexual positions, which in turn makes more repression necessary. The danger of a neurosis grows with the duration of masturbatory forms of gratification. In the long run, masturbation also weakens the relationship with reality. The ease of obtaining gratification often renders the adolescent incapable of struggling for a suitable partner.

If we observe our adolescents closely and understand the relationship between their behavior and their sexual life, we immediately notice that most of them are shy and awkward. Invariably, those who have taken the step from masturbation to sexual intercourse strike us as alert, proficient, and lively.

We have reached the conclusion that just as the specter of "adolescent sexual intercourse," formerly and even today, caused people to consider abstinence harmless and even useful, it has now produced the unjustified attitude that masturbation during puberty is natural and quite harmless and constitutes the solution to the problem of puberty. This attitude, like the preceding one, is only an evasion of the most ticklish problem.

SEXUAL INTERCOURSE AMONG ADOLESCENTS

We must ponder this question in principle as well as in practice by considering the current economic and educational circumstances. In all the literature on the subject so far, it seems to have been almost intentionally avoided.

We have shown that the interests of authoritarian society indirectly (via the family and marriage) bring about the restriction of adolescent sexuality with all its resultant suffering. Although the misery it produces is an unintended by-product, this restriction is intrinsic to authoritarian society. Therefore, a sex-economic solution within this society is a logical impossibility. This immediately becomes apparent when we examine the conditions under which our adolescents enter the phase of sexual maturity. In doing so, we shall disregard the effects of specific class distinctions and examine only the influence of the ideological climate and its social institutions.

1. First of all, the adolescent has to overcome a mountain of inner inhibitions, which is the work of a sex-negating education. His genitality is ordinarily not free (this is particularly true for girls) or it is disturbed or, consciously or unconsciously, homosexually diverted. Under such destructive circumstances, he is emotionally unable to participate in a heterosexual relationship.

2. Either his biological sexual maturity is psychically blocked or there is a disparity between his physical and psychic maturity, as can often be seen among lower-middle-class youth, with their psychic infantilism, their holding on to an infantile position in the family and in their relationship with their parents.

3. In certain social strata which are particularly exposed to material deprivation, the adolescents are also physically retarded. Here we find physical as well as psychic underdevelopment accompanying physiological sexual maturity.

4. On top of the sexual taboo which weighs heavily on adolescent sexuality there is not only the lack of social support; in addition, there are the various means employed to prevent the adolescent actively from engaging in sexual intercourse. For example:

a) The active prevention of factual education for adolescents regarding their sexuality. Today's fashionable "enlightenment" is insufficient and only increases the confusion, because it takes a path which leads inevitably to certain consequences, without arriving at these consequences. Thus, fourteen-year-old girls are taught about menstruation, but there is dead silence about the nature of their sexual excitation. This is a clear example of what we said previously, namely, that the merely biological viewpoint is a diversionary maneuver. For the adolescent, it is less important to know about how egg and sperm cell form the "mystery" of a new living creature; he is more interested in the "mystery" of sexual excitation with which he wrestles in desperation. But what logical argument would there be to keep the adolescent from sexual intercourse if he were truthfully taught that he is now ready for sexual intercourse and that his troubles and difficulties spring from ungratified sexuality? Without this knowledge, "enlightenment" only increases his woes. He must admit that ignorance and sexual negation are in full accordance with the social situation. The sexual crippling of adolescents is the logical continuation of the interference with childhood sexuality.

b) The problems of housing and contraception. If the possibility of being alone and undisturbed is almost nonexistent for the adults of the working population, the misery of adolescents who have no place to stay is increased to a mute but terrible martyrdom. It is characteristic of our otherwise so easily moved sex reformers not to mention this fact. For what could they answer if a bold boy or a lusty girl asked why society did not take care of them in that respect, too? It is to be expected that many a social worker takes flight when confronted with this question, even if he lectures adolescents on the "sexual question" and does not exactly demand abstinence up to "complete emotional and physical maturity" but "humanely" evades the question of sexual intercourse. He will preach a "sense of responsibility" until he succeeds in no longer feeling responsible when adolescents with the necessary "sense of responsibility" have intercourse in doorways, behind fences, in barns, constantly in fear of being discovered.

And now to the question of the means of contraception! High-spirited adolescents might ask naïvely about the interest society has in *not* informing them about the best methods of preventing pregnancy and in *not* supplying physicians to step in if a contraceptive fails.

It is clear that in a social order which does not recognize sexual intercourse outside of marriage, which does not even take care of a hygienic sexual life for adults, such questions can be neither answered nor solved.

It is equally clear that without a basic solution to the problem of the sexual education of children and without solving the problems of contraception and housing, an uncritical invitation to adolescents to have sexual intercourse would be just as irresponsible and harmful as the demand for abstinence. My objective has been to expose the contradictions and to prove their insolubility under existing conditions. I can only hope that I have succeeded. But, in principle, unless we are charlatans or cowards, we must affirm the sexuality of adolescents, help them wherever we can, and do everything to prepare the final liberation of adolescent sexuality. This is a gigantic and responsible task.

But now we can better understand the superficiality, the self-consciousness, and the inconsistency of sexual enlightenment as practiced today. Characteristically, it always comes too late, it is cloaked in secrecy, and it evades the heart of the matter—sexual pleasure. It is inherent in the contradictions of the situation that those who are *against* enlightenment act more consistently. They must be fought because they are enemies of scientific consistency, but they are somehow clearer in their minds than the bliss-spreading reformers who seriously believe they can change the situation with their enlightenment. The reformers only becloud the true situation and the necessity of transforming our whole existence.

Of course, none of this means that we can proceed as did the earlier-quoted Pastor P. In the individual case, after a thorough investigation of the social, psychic, and economic situation, the sex counselor will not forbid sexual intercourse to the mature adolescent; on the contrary, he will recommend it. Individual help and comprehensive social measures are two different matters.

For the moment. small children continue to be educated toward asceticism, adolescents continue to be taught that culture demands abstinence or that masturbation might comfort them until they marry. One has no reason to be proud of such attitudes; they are among the many shames of our time. They certainly protect us from drawing consequences from science and applying them practically.

The contradiction between the growing collectivization of life and the sex-negating social atmosphere must lead to an increasing crisis in the sexuality of the young, for which there is no solution in conservative society. As long as adolescents were trapped in family ties—the girls completely repressed sexually and exposed to minimal sexual excitation, waiting for husbands to take care of them, the boys also staying in the parental home, either living in abstinence, masturbating, or going to prostitutes—there was only silent suffering, neuroses, or sexual brutality. Under today's conditions, however, the sexual needs striving for freedom must degenerate into painful individual struggles with inculcated inhibitions on the one hand and with the opposition of authoritarian society on the other. Sexual reforms consisting of general appeasement, good advice à la "intellectual diversions," a "hard mattress," and "eating little meat," will be powerless against these forces.

I maintain that today's adolescents carry an infinitely heavier burden than did the youth at the turn of the century. The latter could still be completely re-

pressed; but today all the forces of adolescence are
erupting. It is only that youth lack both social support
and structural capacity to deal with these forces. It
will no longer be possible to bury them, and this is
also not at all our intention.

*The sexual crisis of youth is part of the crisis of
authoritarian social order itself. In this framework,
in terms of the masses, it remains insoluble.*

VII

Compulsory Marriage and the Enduring Sexual Relationship

[*Addition, 1945:* The confusion about the concepts of "marriage" and "family" is so great that, as a physician giving counsel on questions of personal life, one always comes into conflict with the idea of *formal* marriage. The general impression is that, to the unconscious of sexually timid people, the legal marriage license is nothing but a permit to indulge in sexual intercourse. This becomes particularly clear in "war marriages": loving couples, who quickly want to experience the genital embrace before the man goes away, rush to city hall to obtain permission in the form of a marriage license. The separation lasts for several years and gradually blots out the partners' memory of each other. If the couples are young, they meet other love partners, for which no reasonable person would condemn them. But the marriage license continues to exercise its purely formal ties, devoid of content. Young people who wanted to make each other happy before the long separation and did not dare to do so without legal permission now find themselves caught in a net. Much has been written about the suffering involved in such "marriages," particularly in the United States. But no author exposed the heart of the problem, the demand for legalizing a love experience. Yet everyone knows that "We want to get married" in reality means "We want to embrace each other genitally."

Another source of confusion and unhappiness is the contradiction between the legal (clerical) and the factual content of the "marriage" concept. For the formal jurist, it seems to be quite different from what it is for the objective psychiatrist. For the jurist, it is an alliance between two people of the opposite sex based on a document. For the psychiatrist, it is an emotional bond based on sexual attraction, frequently accompanied by the desire for children. For the psychiatrist, there is *no* marriage if the parties concerned have a marriage license but otherwise no communion. The license itself does not constitute a marriage. For the psychiatrst, a marriage exists when two people of the opposite sex are in love, take care of each other, live together, and extend the relationship into a family with children. For the psychiatrist, marriage is a sexual relationship, regardless of the presence or absence of a marriage license. For him, the license is merely the official confirmation of that relationship, concurred in, arranged, and consummated by the partners. They are the ones who decide whether or not there is a marriage, not the legal official. Since human sexual structure has degenerated as a result of compulsory morality, the marriage license protects the woman from any irresponsibilities on the part of the man. In that respect, the marriage license fulfills a function, but *in that respect* only. Awareness of the factual quality of *natural* marriage without a license is deeply rooted in people's consciousness. "Common-law marriage" exists in most of the United States, in France, in Scandinavia, and in many other countries. It is only where Catholicism still exercises power that common-law marriage is "not recognized" by the law. There are no laws against factual marriages without a marriage license. But this does not mean that there are not many guilt-ridden people who believe that the factual marriage without a license is forbidden.

In terms of rational mental hygiene, of course, the factual, and not the formal, marriage is the prototype of an enduring sexual relationship. This is self-evident. Mental hygiene aims for inner responsibility, not for responsibility enforced by an external source. The latter serves only as an expedient to control antisocial acts. It is not a desirable end in itself.

In the interest of moral self-regulation the most severe struggle and strict laws are necessary in the fight against the effects of the emotional plague: against defamation of unlicensed marriage partners and their children by emotionally sick persons who themselves can neither understand nor experience this highly moral type of social conduct; against the deeply immoral blackmail and extortions which the laws of compulsory morality make possible; against the sexual lewdness and lasciviousness provoked in divorce proceedings of formal unhappy "marriages"; against the senselessness of speaking about "marriage" where there exists only hatred and malice, etc.

In this area, virtually everything is topsy-turvy, and much filth has to be cleared away. Steps must be taken to remove sexual guilt feelings and to replace the external compulsory morality with an inner awareness of responsibility. The time is ripe for it; the necessity of a radical legal reform is accepted everywhere, except in those circles which benefit economically from obsolete sexual legislation which is ruinous to mental hygiene.]

Compulsory marriage, which is only one stage in the development of the institution of marriage in general, is the result of a compromise between economic interests and sexual needs. Of course, sexual needs are not as many sexologists present them, e.g., the "natural" need to live permanently with one partner in a sexual relationship, or in the interest of "taking care of the brood." In examining the marriage problem, we must consider these two facets separately. This will enable us to distinguish clearly between that form of sexual relationship which springs from sexual needs

and tends to endure, and the other form which corresponds to economic interests and the position of
the woman and children in society. The first will
be called an enduring sexual relationship; and the
second, a marriage.

1. THE ENDURING SEXUAL RELATIONSHIP

The social prerequisites for the enduring sexual relationship would be the financial independence of the
woman, the care and raising of her children by society,
the absence of any interference by economic interests.
Transitory, purely sensual relationships would have
to compete with enduring ones. From the sex-
economic viewpoint, the transitory relationship has
disadvantages which we can study very closely in
today's society. For there has been no other society
in which promiscuity—emotionally degrading and sex-
economically worthless because of its association with
financial interests—has been so widespread and
"normal" as it is in the age of the ideology of strict
monogamy.

The temporary sexual relationship, which is most
clearly expressed in the one-hour or the one-night
experience, is distinguished from the enduring relationship by the absence of tenderness toward the
sexual partner. A tender attitude has several possible
determinants:

1 A sexual attachment as a result of previously
shared pleasurable experiences. It has a strong admix-
ture of gratitude for past pleasure and devotion (not
to be confused with bondage) relating to anticipated
sexual pleasure. Together, they form the basic
elements of the natural love relationship.

2. An attachment to the partner resulting from
repressed hatred: reactive love. It precludes sexual

gratification. We will discuss this later in connection with marriage.

3. A relationship resulting from ungratified sensuality. Its hallmark is overestimation of the partner; its nature is precisely that of inhibited sensuality and an unconscious, unquenchable expectation of sexual gratification. It can quickly turn to hatred.

The constant absence of tenderness in a sexual relationship diminishes the sensual experience, and with it sexual gratification. But this is true only from a certain age on, when the sensual storms of puberty and post-puberty have passed and a certain equilibrium of sexual affectivity has taken their place. Unless a neurotic inhibition has suppressed the sensual striving, tender attitudes are felt only after a certain gratification of sensual needs. This tenderness is not to be confused with the childish pseudo-tenderness of the enthusiastic adolescent, who, in his fantasies, hunts for a feminine ideal corresponding to his mother, who condemns sensuality and suffers from the pressure of masturbatory guilt feelings, and who becomes a candidate for impotence unless favorable circumstances (for instance, joining a youth community or undergoing psychiatric treatment) set him free from his neurosis. The casual, short-term sexual relationships, as we find them among certain strata of our youth, seem to be natural, healthy sexual experiences in harmony with their age. They approximate the sexual life of adolescents in primitive societies both in appearance and in the forms of sexual experience. They certainly show a high degree of tenderness, which does not aim, however, at permanence in the relationship. They do not contain a lewd avidity for a renewal of sexual stimulation as we find it among neurotic forms of polygamy of adult roués and Don Juans; rather they show an exuberance of ripened sensuality, a libidinous reaching out toward any suitable sexual object. It could be compared with the agility of a young animal, which also decreases with advancing age. Unless it is neurotic, this sexual agility of the healthy adolescent is easily distinguishable to the trained eye from hysterical hyperagility.

In the more mature years, short-term love relationships need not always be neurotic. In fact, if we are honest about our sexological experience and disregard moralistic considerations, we must conclude that those who never had the courage or the strength for a casual sexual relationship (even at an older age, whether man or woman) were under the pressure of neurotic guilt feelings that cannot be rationally explained. But, according to clinical experience, anyone who is incapable of establishing a lasting relationship is dominated by an infantile fixation in his love life, i.e., he is sexually disturbed. This incapacity arises either because the sexual striving is anchored in some form of homosexual tie (which we typically find among athletes, academics, the military, and others) or because a fantasized ideal overshadows and devalues any real sexual object. We very often find that the unconscious background of continuous and ungratifying promiscuity is a fear of an attachment to a love object because such an attachment has incestuous overtones which act as an inhibtion. Most frequently, we find a disturbance of orgastic potency which prevents a tender relationship with the sexual partner because of the disappointment which reappears with every sexual act.

From the viewpoint of sex-economy, the most important disadvantage of the temporary relationship is that it precludes a complete sensuous communion of the partners and therefore the complete sexual gratification that is possible in the enduring relationship. That we do not use these sophisticated byways again to smuggle in the moralistic concept of permanent monogamy will soon be shown, to the regret of the exponents of marriage ideology. For what we describe as an enduring relationship has no set time span. It is unimportant whether it lasts weeks, months, two or even ten years. Neither do we mean that this relationship must, or should be, monogamous; we do not establish any norms.

As I have shown elsewhere,[1] the view that the first sexual intercourse with a virgin and the honeymoon are sexually the most gratifying experiences is false. Clinical data contradict it. This idea has developed only from the contrast between the lusting of virginal women and the later numbness and sexual aridity of the permanent monogamous marriage. A satisfying sexual relationship between two people presupposes that an accommodation of the sexual rhythms takes place and that the partners gradually learn to know each other's sexual needs, which are seldom conscious but always accessible. In the long run, this is the only way to insure the orderly regulation of sexual energy and the corresponding gratification. To marry without previous mutual sexual knowledge and adaptation is unhygienic and generally leads to catastrophes.

Another advantage of a gratifying enduring relationship is that it makes unnecessary the constant search for a suitable sexual partner and thereby frees interests for social accomplishments.

The capacity for an enduring sexual relationship presupposes:

Full orgastic potency of the partners, i.e., no disparity between tenderness and sensuality.

The overcoming of incestuous ties and infantile fears of sexuality.

No repression of any unsublimated sexual impulses, be they homosexual or nongenital.

The absolute affirmation of sexuality and joy in living.

Overcoming the basic elements of moralism.

The capacity for intellectual companionship with the partner.

---

1 Cf. *Die Funktion des Orgasmus* [The Function of the Orgasm] (Int. Psa-Verl., 1927). [This work will appear in English as part of Reich's early writings. It should not be confused with the book by the same title, *The Function of the Orgasm*, first published in 1942.—Editor]

If we consider these prerequisites from the standpoint of the masses and not of individual persons, we must admit that none of them can be realized in authoritarian society. Since sexual negation and repression are specific and inseparable characteristics of authoritarian society, sexual education must necessarily be conditioned by them. We also see that education within the family structure strengthens incestuous ties instead of weakening them, that the incest taboo and the inhibition of infantile sexuality destroy the connection between sensuality and tenderness, thereby producing a sex-negating ego structure which breeds pregenital and homosexual tendencies, which in turn lead to repression and the weakening of sexual life. Furthermore, the education for male dominance precludes companionship with the woman.

As with every lasting relationship, the sexual relationship also contains abundant material for conflict. But we are not interested here in the general human difficulties that arise in every relationship but only in those that pertain specifically to sexuality. The basic difficulty of an enduring sexual relationship is the conflict (temporary or final) between the dulling of sexual desires and the growing tender attachment to the partner.

Sooner or later, we will find in every sexual relationship shorter or longer periods of reduced sensual attraction, even indifference. This is an empirically established fact, in the face of which moralistic arguments are helpless. The better the sexual partners harmonize sensually and tenderly, the less frequent and definitive will be the break in the sensual relationship. But every sexual relationship is exposed to sensual dulling. This fact would be less important if three other factors did not combine to complicate matters:

1. The dulling can occur in one partner only.
2. Most sexual relationships are also tied to

economics (the dependence of the woman and the children).

3. Regardless of such external difficulties, there is an internal factor, inherent in the enduring relationship, which, even when the partners are not tied economically or by children, often complicates the only conceivable remedy, the separation and finding of other partners.

Everyone is constantly exposed to new sexual stimulation by persons other than one's partner. During the peak of a relationship these external stimuli are ineffectual. But they can never be totally eliminated, and no ecclesiastical regulation of dress or other ascetic or moralistic measures will accomplish anything except to heighten the stimulation, because sexual needs are invariably intensified by suppression. The overlooking of this fundamental fact creates the tragedy, even tragi-comedy, of all ascetically oriented sexual morality. The new sexual stimuli, against which there is only one effective protection, namely neurotic sexual inhibition, produce in every person who is sexually intact desires for other love objects. (These desires vary in intensity and degree of consciousness; the healthier the individual, the more conscious he is of his desires.) If the existing sexual relationship is gratifying, these wishes are at first inconsequential and can be successfully suppressed to the same degree that they are conscious. This suppression is clearly less harmful if it is based more on sex-economic considerations than on moralistic ones.

If these desires for other objects intensify, however, they affect the sexual relationship with the partner and, in particular, they accelerate the dulling process. The surest signs of this dulling are reduction of sexual desire before the act and of pleasure during it. Gradually, sexual intercourse becomes a matter of habit or obligation. The decrease in gratification with the partner and the desire for others mount and reenforce each other. No good intentions, no love techniques, will help here. Now the critical stage of irritation

with the partner sets in. Whether it breaks out or
is concealed depends on temperament and upbringing.
In any event, the hatred of the partner is increasingly,
though unconsciously, intensified, as proved by the
analysis of such conditions; the partner is a hindrance
in the fulfillment of those desires for other love objects.
It only seems to be a paradox that the unconscious
hatred can become all the more intense the kinder
and more tolerant the partner is. For then there is
no reason to hate him (or her) personally and yet
one still experiences him—or, rather, one's feelings
for him—as a hindrance. Thus, the hatred is rendered
inactive by extreme, reactive tenderness. This tenderness and the guilt feelings that are rampant in this
stage form the specific components of the sticky attachment in an enduring relationship and are the real
reason why even unmarried couples cannot separate
although they have nothing more to say, let alone
give, to each other and their relationship has become
a mutual torment.

This dulling need not be permanent. But it can
easily change from a transitory to a permanent state
if the sexual partners ignore their mutual hate impulses
and reject their desires for other love objects as indecent and immoral. When this occurs, it is usually
followed by a repression of the impulses, with all
its resulting unhappiness and damage to the relationship between two people. If such facts are faced
directly, however, without the prohibitions of sexual
morality, the conflict is milder and can be remedied.
It is essential that feelings of normal jealousy do
not turn into possessiveness and that the desire for
another partner be recognized as natural and self-evident. No one would think of reproaching someone
for not wanting to wear the same dress indefinitely
or to eat the same food. Only in the sexual realm
has the exclusiveness of possession acquired strong
emotional overtones because the commingling of
economic interests and sexuality has transformed
natural jealousy into a claim of possession. Many

mature and judicious persons have told me that after they had painfully mastered the idea that, at one time or another, their sexual partner had had another relationship, it lost its terror for them and not to be able to consider the possibility of an "infidelity" appeared ludicrous. Countless examples teach us that, in time, *fidelity based on conscience* damages a sexual relationship. It has been clearly shown that an occasional relationship with another partner is beneficial to a lasting relationship which is on the verge of becoming a marriage. For enduring relationships that are not bound economically, there are two possibilities. Either a relationship with another person is only transitory, which proves that it cannot compete with the one that already exists. In this case, the first relationship has, if anything, been strengthened; the woman has lost the feeling of being inhibited or incapable of being with another man. Or the relationship with the other partner will become more intense than the old one, more pleasurable and gratifying; then the first relationship will be dissolved.

What happens to the partner whose love has not yet deteriorated? He will no doubt have a severe battle on his hands, primarily with himself. Jealousy and a feeling of sexual inferiority will struggle with understanding for the partner's decision. He will perhaps strive to regain the partner's interest, which will eliminate the automatic character of their relationship and destroy the security that goes with possession; or perhaps he will prefer to wait passively and let matters run their course. In any event, the difficulty is not as great as the unhappiness produced by two people clinging to each other for moral or other considerations. The concern shown for the partner in so many cases while one's own desires are constantly suppressed without being eradicated turns all too often into its opposite. Anyone who has been too considerate feels justified in placing an obligation on the other person, regards himself as a victim, and becomes intolerant. All these attitudes are far more damaging to the relationship and turn it into something uglier than an "infidelity" could ever have done.

We do not want to conceal the fact, however, that, given human structure and sexuality as they exist today, such respect for the partner's needs is possible only for an infinitesimal number of people. For, owing to the economic dependence of the woman, sexual relationships are formed quite differently from the relationship between two independent people that has just been described. In addition, the problem of bringing up children in our society erases with one stroke all sex-economic considerations. Also, the prevailing sexual education and social atmosphere turn the solution of such difficulties into uninteresting individual events.

In this context, one difficulty should be mentioned which may have serious consequences if it is not clearly understood. If the sensual attraction of the partner is decreasing or fades altogether, there may be a disturbance of potency in the man. Usually, it takes the form of an insufficient erection or the absence of excitation in spite of stimulation. In a relationship in which tenderness persists, or in one in which previously there was no fear of impotence, such an incident may trigger a depression and even lead to a chronic impotence. In an attempt to hide his coldness, the man may try to engage in sexual intercourse time and again. This can become dangerous. At first, lack of erection is not true impotence but simply the expression of a lack of desire for the partner and, usually the unconscious desire for another. A woman can become impotent, but the disturbance does not have the same effect on her as it has on the man. For one thing, the sexual act can be carried out in spite of the woman's disturbed sensuality, and for another, the woman does not feel so offended by her disturbance as does the man. Provided that the relationship is otherwise good, an open discussion of the causes of the trouble (sensual aversion, desire for another partner) can often eliminate the difficulty. In any case, one has to wait for the aversion to disappear. In otherwise good relationships, the sexual desire recurs sooner or later. An attempt to have intercourse with another person at this time may easily fail because of guilt feelings toward the original partner. In other cases, intercourse with someone else is helpful.

Given a certain neurotic disposition, repression of the desire for another partner and the attempt to overcome the aversion toward the present partner may lead to neurotic illness. Quite frequently, such a conflict results in a disturbed capacity for work. The illness comes about when the gratification that is lacking in reality is sought in fantasy. In these situations, there is a strong urge to masturbate. The resolution of such conflicts varies greatly, depending on the partners' personalities, the character of their sexual relationship, and their moral attitudes. Our moralistic sexual prejudices often cause infinite harm by regarding even the mere idea of sexual experience with someone else as adultery, as indecency, and so on. If it were generally known that such conditions are self-evident, absolutely inherent in the nature of the sexual drive, and have nothing to do with morality, the murders and tortures among lovers and married couples would certainly decrease, as would many of the causes of emotional illness which represent nothing more than an inadequate way out of the situation.

So far, I have reviewed the difficulties inherent in an enduring relationship. Before I proceed to the ways in which these difficulties are complicated by the interference of economic interests, several facts will have to be discussed which, although economic in the wider sense of the term, are facts of social ideology which further aggravate the sexual relationship that is not yet a "marriage." I am referring to the ideology of monogamy which is accepted and represented particularly by the woman.

The dissolution of an enduring sexual relationship

is not a simple matter for the woman, even if she is economically independent. For one thing, there is so-called public opinion, which feels called upon to interfere in private matters. To be sure, it is inclined to look the other way today if a woman has an extramarital relationship, but it easily becomes venomous and brands as a whore any woman who has the audacity to have relationships with several men.

Sexual morality, pervaded with the notions of property, has made it a foregone conclusion that the man "possesses" the woman, while the woman "submits" to him. Since possession is considered honorable, whereas submission is degrading, the attitude of women toward the sexual act has developed into a shunning of the act itself. This attitude is reinforced by similarly oriented authoritarian education. And since for most men the possession of a woman is more a proof of their virility than an experience of love, since the conquest is more important than the ensuing love, this shyness of women acquires a tragic justification.

Furthermore, from infancy the girl has absorbed the demand that she may have intercourse with only *one* man. These educational influences have a deeper and stronger effect (because they are unconsciously retained by guilt feelings) than sexual enlightenment which is begun too late. Time and again, we encounter women who against their better judgment cannot bring themselves to leave an unloved man and reject any idea of it with more or less tenuous arguments. The real, unconscious motive might be expressed in these words: "My (lower-middle-class) mother has spent her whole life in a dreadful marriage, and I must be able to do the same." In most cases, this identification with the faithful, monogamous mother is the most effective inhibiting element.

Enduring sexual relationships which do not turn into marriage generally do not last forever. The earlier such relationships are entered into, the greater the likelihood—and, as can be shown easily, the psychological and biological justification—that they will dissolve more quickly than those entered into later. Until about his thirtieth year, if he is not too much held down by his economic situation, man lives in a state of continual emotional development. Generally, it is only about this time that interests are consolidated and become permanent. The ideology of asceticism and permanent monogamy is therefore in glaring contradiction to the physical and emotional process of development and cannot be achieved in practice. This brings us to the contradiction in every marriage ideology.

2, THE PROBLEM OF MARRIAGE

The difficulties just described in an enduring sexual relationship are aggravated by economic ties and are in reality insoluble. In consequence, this relationship, which has been based on biological and sexual psychological factors, becomes a compulsory marriage. Its ideological hallmarks are the ecclesiastical demands that it be lifelong and strictly monogamous. While it is true that society has relaxed the ecclesiastical form of marriage, it never penetrates the inner contradictions because, in so doing, it would come into conflict with its own liberal views. Economically, it must retain the institution of marriage, but from the viewpoint of liberal ideology, it would have to draw impractical conclusions. These contradictions can be found, without exception, in all scientific and literary treatises concerning marriage and might be summarized as follows: marriages are bad, but marriage must be cultivated and maintained. The first is a statement of fact, the second a demand corresponding to the reactionary compulsory morality of which the institution of marriage is an integral part.

On the basis of these two binding factors—established facts on the one hand, moralism on the other —the authors reach the most peculiar and absurd arguments for retaining marriage. For example, they try to prove that marriage and monogamy are "natural" arrangements, i.e., biological phenomena. They search eagerly among the millions of varieties of animals, which unquestionably live sexually irregular lives, and come up with the finding that storks and doves sometimes live monogamously; hence monogamy is "natural." In this instance, man is no longer a "spiritual" creature who cannot be compared to animals, for here the comparison supports monogamous marriage. However, the fact that promiscuity among animals is the rule is studiously avoided in discussing the problem of marriage *biologically*. But it cannot be overlooked altogether and therefore man must be different from the animals and because of his "higher calling" must retain marriage as the "highest" form of sexual relationship. Here, man is no longer an animal but a "higher being" with as inborn morality. So the slogan becomes: fight against sex-economy because it has unequivocally proved that innate morality does not exist. But if "morality" is not inborn, it must be the result of education. And who has done the educating? Society and its ideology factory, the compulsory family, which is rooted in monogamous marriage. But, with this, marriage ceases to be a natural arrangement; its social character has, in principle, been admitted.

The reactionary position, however, is stubborn and knows how to reinforce itself. Granted that marriage is neither a natural arrangement nor the requirement of a supernatural destiny of man; it is then, logically, a social institution. Consequently, some attempt to prove that man has always lived monogamously, and deny every development and change in forms of sexual living. One even falsifies ethnology, as Westermark did, and reaches the conclusion that if men have always lived in monogamous marriage, the institution of marriage must be necessary for the preservation of human society, for state, culture, and civilization. But, beware! Such reference to the past, already logically an error, does not derive from the established findings that polygamy and promiscuity have played an even greater role than monogamous forms of living. To evade this argument, the idea of eternal monogamy is given a developmental connotation. It is decided that there has been a development toward "higher" forms of sexuality; suddenly it is found that primitive people lived in a state of animalistic immorality, and that we can be proud of having conquered these "anarchic" conditions of sexual life. One does not even ponder the important fact that man differs from the animal not by lesser but by more intense sexuality (constant readiness for sexual intercourse. Thus, "superiority over the animal" is not valid in sexual matters: man is "more animalistic" than the animal. It is clear that the moralistic evaluation falsifies observation and avoids recognition of the fact that the sexual economy among primitives is far superior to our own.[2] With such a viewpoint, any possibility of examining the material and the social basis of forms of sexuality, which vary with time and place, is precluded. One becomes increasingly mired in the moralistic attitude and engages in interminable and fruitless debates. One tries to justify—morally, metaphysically, or biologistically—social phenomena which have long been doomed. And all this is done under the guise of inviolable, allegedly objective science. The fact is that the more moralistic this kind of science becomes, the more awe and respect it inspires in the philistine.

To let the facts speak for themselves, to refrain from drawing hasty conclusions from these facts and to study their development, to let that which is dying off die and to uncover new forms of existence in human society—all this requires the application of objective observation and deduction.

2 Cf. Malinowski: *The Sexual Life of Savages;* and Reich: *The Invasion of Compulsory Sex-Morality.*

If we strictly observe the facts, two questions
arise:
1. What is the social function of marriage?
2. Wherein lies the contradiction of marriage?

THE SOCIAL FUNCTION OF MARRIAGE

The social function of the institution of marriage
is three-fold: economic, political, and social. It corresponds exactly to the social function of the authoritarian family structure.

Economic. Just as historically marriage began to
develop with the private ownership of the means of
production, so it continues to draw its *raison d'être*
from this material basis. This means that as long
as there is private ownership of the means of production, marriage is socially necessary and meaningful.[3]
That classes which have no such economic interests
live with the same sexual forms is an unjustified objection, because the prevailing ideologies are the ideologies of the ruling class. Marriage is not only the
product of its material basis, it is also sustained by
the moral attitudes of the prevailing ideology and
by the human structure which is afraid of life. That
is why the average person is not conscious of the
real foundation of this form of sexual living; he merely
develops rationalizations for it. But when the material
basis requires it, the ideology is modified. After the
Thirty Years' War, when the population in Central
Europe had dwindled, the district council of Nurem-
berg abolished monogamy with an edict of February
14, 1650: "The urgent needs of the Holy Roman
Empire require that the population decimated by
sword, illness, and hunger be increased . . . therefore,
for the next ten years every male shall be permitted

---

3 With the reestablishment of compulsory marrriage in the Soviet
Union, Reich supplemented this formulation to indicate that state ownership of the means of production serves the same function as private
ownership. [Editor]

to marry two women." (This is quoted from Fuchs, *Sittengeschichte: Renaissance* [Moral History: Renaissance], p. 40ff. And this constitutes God-given monogamy.

Political. Since permanent monogamous marriage is the core of the compulsory family, which, in turn, as we have shown, is the ideological breeding ground for every member of authoritarian society, it also has a political *raison d'être.*

Social. The material dependence of wife and children is characteristic of patriarchal society. Thus, secondarily, marriage becomes a material and moral protection (moral in the sense of patriarchal interests) for wife and children and all phases of patriarchal society must adhere to it. It is not a question of whether marriage is good or bad, but whether it is socially justified and necessary. Hence there can be no desire to eradicate marriage from a society in which it is rooted economically. One can only "reform," without shaking the fundamentals. For instance, after ten years of debate, "incompatibility" is allowed to replace "guilt" as a ground for divorce.

Reforms of this kind spring from the contradictions in marriage which arise not from economic but from sex-economic factors within the marriage situation. They often have the character of tragi-comic jokes, as in the following report from the *Pester Lloyd* of January 25, 1929:

> *Card games as a school subject.* Surprising news comes from Cleveland in America. The teachers' faculty of the municipal school has decided to introduce bridge as a required subject. The reason for this strange innovation, it is stated, is that the American home is doomed because the game of bridge is tapering off. How many marriages have already foundered on the fact that, instead of playing bridge together or in congenial company, each partner went his separate way. Twelve bridge teachers are to be hired for the mu-

nicipal school. It is hoped that by being taught
bridge, the children will not only be prepared for
a sound marital life but will also exercise a good
influence on their parents who live in marriages
that have gone to pieces.

That marriages break up is not news. Nevertheless,
here are some figures. First, some statistics of marriages and divorces in Vienna from 1915 to
1925.[4]

Year	Number of Marriages	Divorces
1915	13,954	617
1916	12,855	656
1917	12,406	659
1918	17,123	1,078
1919	26,182	2,460
1920	31,164	3,145
1921	29,274	3,300
1922	26,568	3,113
1923	19,827	3,371
1924	17,410	3,437
1925	16,288	3,241

Thus, while the number of marriages remained
more or less constant and doubled only in the years
after World War I, divorces have steadily increased,
as much as fivefold in the course of ten years. Whereas
in 1915 the ratio of marriage to divorce was about
20 to 1, in 1925 it had narrowed to 5 to 1.

The *Pesti Naplo* of November 18, 1928 published
an article about marriage:

4 Walter Schiff: *Die natürliche Bewegung der Bevölkerung der Bun-
deshauptstadt Wien in der Jahren 1905–1925* [The Natural Movement of
population in the Federal Capital of Vienna in the years 1905 to 1925],
1926.

It is true that the trend toward marriage has increased, but many more people run to the divorce courts than to City Hall. It can be said that between 1878 and 1927 the number of marriages increased fourfold, but during the same period the number of divorces increased eightyfold; in 1926, one hundredfold.

The article further established that most of the marriages were dissolved during their fifth or sixth year. Of 1,645 divorces in 1927, the reason given for 1,498 was "arbitrary desertion," and only in two cases were the marriages dissolved because of adultery.

The *Budapesti Hirlap* of November 24, 1928, reported that members of the upper chamber of Parliament discussed with concern the rapid increase in divorces. Whereas there were 1,813 divorces in 1922 and 1,888 in 1923, in 1897 only 21 and in 1879 only 15 marriages ended in divorce. Since the economic and bank crises of 1898, divorces have increased rapidly (255 in 1900, 464 in 1905, 659 in 1910). It is evident that the highest divorce rate coincides with times of economic crisis.

The following table shows the number of divorces (per 1,000 marriages) in various European countries for the years 1931-1934:

	1931	1932	1933	1934
Germany	514.4	509.6	631.2	781.5
Italy	276.0	267.8	289.9	309.2
Portugal	44.9	45.4	45.8	47.5
Poland	273.3	270.3	273.9	277.3
Netherlands	59.5	55.8	59.2	60.6
Hungary	76.4	71.2	73.1	77.7
Czechoslovakia	129.9	128.0	124.3	118.3

With the exception of Czechoslovakia, however, the number of marriages in Europe during that same period of time have also increased—reflecting the increased pressure of political reaction (366,178 marriage loans in three years in Germany to further the family ideology). In addition, the statistics do not tell us anything about the intrinsic state of these marriages or about any change in the actual sexual living conditions. Nothing has altered the basic contradiction in the institution of marriage.

In Soviet Russia, where marriage was virtually eliminated, both legally and practically (the registration of a sexual relationship was voluntary, not mandatory), the statistical data are as follows:

In Moscow, the number of registrations rose from 24,899 in 1926 to 26,211 in 1929, while divorces rose from 11,879 to 19,421 during the same period. In Leningrad, the number of registrations for 1926 was 20,913, and for 1927 it was 24,369; but the separations for the same period rose from 5,536 to 16,008 (!).

In his book *The Companionate Marriage*,[5] Lindsey gives figures for the United States. In 1922, in Denver, Colorado, the combined number of divorces and desertions exceeded that of marriages. Of 2,090 marriages, 1,492 ended in divorce, and there were 1,500 cases of malicious desertion, altogether 2,992. In 1922 there were 45 more divorces than in 1921 and about 618 fewer marriages. Marriages had dropped from 4,002 in 1920 to 3,008 in 1922. In Chicago, there were 39,000 marriages and 13,000 divorces, i.e., exactly one third. "People are losing their heads," Lindsey reported with despair.

Here are further figures about conditions in America which clearly show that the deterioration of marriage is not an invention of the Bolsheviks. According to a United Press report for 1924, there were 3,350 marriages in Atlanta and 1,845 divorces (more than half); in Kansas City, 4,821 marriages and 2,400 divorces (almost half); in Ohio, 53,000 marriages

---

5 Judge Ben B. Lindsey and Wainwright Evans: *The Companionate Marriage* (New York: Boni & Liveright, 1927).

and 11,885 divorces (almost one fifth); in Cleveland, 16,123 marriages and 5,256 divorces (one third). Lindsey added to his report:

> Marriage, as we have it now, is plain Hell for most persons who get into it. That's flat. I defy anybody to watch the procession of wrecked lives, unhappy men and women and miserable, homeless neglected children who pass through my court, and come to any other conclusion. [*Revolt,* p. 174]

In Chicago it is reported that there were 39,000 marriage licenses issued in 1922 as compared with 13,000 divorce decrees actually signed. If 13,000 divorce decrees were actually signed, how many couples do you suppose there were who *wished* they could get somebody to sign a divorce decree for them, but who never acted on their wish? For divorce is a troublesome, expensive, embarrassing business, and persons who wish for it resort to the courts only when at the extreme limit of their endurance. If there were 39,000 marriages in Chicago in the year of grace 1922, it is absurdly conservative to say that fully 26,000 would have gotten divorces if they could, in addition to the 13,000 who did. I base this belief on the proportion of married couples who come under my own observation, coming as they do confidentially for advice and consolation, and who never go after the divorce they wish for. I believe their number is many, many times larger than the number of those who go to court with their problems. [p. 212]

There is no escaping the conclusion if such facts be compared with the statistics of former years, that divorces and separations are steadily increasing, and that if this continues, as it probably will for some time to come, there will be as many di-

vorce cases filed in some parts of the country as
there are marriage licenses granted . . .

There are tens of thousands of cases where the
flat failure of the individual marriage is recorded
in our courts, not as "divorce" or "legal separation" but as failure to provide, non-support, desertion, and the like. *Materially and psychologically
there is no reason why these should not be
classed as divorces—for they would be just that if
the parties to such marriages could have their
way,* and were not held together by circumstance,
children, and their legal obligations. The general
name which would cover all such cases, including divorces, separations, and all others are Marriages That Have Failed. Under that title it would
be conservative to say that there are as many "divorces" annually as there are marriage licenses
granted. [pp. 213f.]

Here is an embarrassing talk with an American
girl:

For instance, Mary, this girl of whom I have
been telling, avoided marriage because she objected
to entering on a contract so nearly irrevocable
and so hard to break away from . . . What she
demanded was a kind of marriage that would leave
her a free agent; but she couldn't have it. Therefore
she rejected the whole institution, even while admitting that, with certain amendments, she was for
it, and could see many advantages in it.

It may be contended that it was Mary's duty, as
a law abiding member of society, to conform to
the institution of marriage as we have it, and take
her chance with it; and that if she could not bring
herself to that she must remain celibate and deny
her sex life the normal expression it craved.

To that Mary gives answer, rightly or wrongly,
that she will not sacrifice herself to any such fetish
of conformity; that she will not submit to having

to make a choice between two such demands, both of which she considers monstrous and unreasonable.

Instead, she raises a flag of defiance, and says, "No, I and my generation will find a third way out. Whether you like it or not we will make among ourselves a marriage pact of our own, one that will meet our needs. We believe we have a natural right to a companionship and an intimacy which we instinctively crave; we have a knowledge of contraception which precludes the likelihood that unwanted babies will complicate the situation; we don't admit that such a course on our part imperils the safety of human society; and we believe that this effort to replace tradition with what we think is common sense will do good rather than harm." —In substance that is the way they put it.

Now what am I, a man occupying a responsible judicial position, to say to a challenge like that? On the one hand I can't commend Mary's conduct without disregarding the grave practical difficulties and social dangers which may be involved in any headlong application of her theories—the kind of application she herself is making of them, for instance. On the other hand, I cannot, with sincerity or honesty, say to Mary or anybody else that I think the institution of marriage *as we have it* capable of guaranteeing happiness to persons who enter it. I cannot escape admitting that if marriage is ever to merit the unqualified support of society it must be able to show results reasonably commensurate with its claims; and that for whatever unhappiness it produces by reason of its present rigid code it must be held answerable. Nor can I pass in silence over the fact that marriage is ordained for the welfare and happiness of mankind, and that mankind was not made for it; that marriage is not an end but a means; that when a shoe does not fit, it is the shoe rather than the foot that must be altered. As to the demand for celibacy as

an alternative to a possibly disastrous marriage,
why waste one's breath making demands which
people would never meet and which would do violence to a necessary instinct if they did meet it? [pp.
138ff.]

What conclusions does Lindsey draw from his own
findings and from the embarrassing discussion with
Mary?

And yet this is by no means to say that marriage is a failure and should go into the discard to
make way for Free Love or any other social Ism.
However imperfect the institution may be *we can't
do without it*. It must be preserved by means of
sane and cautious alterations in its code, to the
end that it may create in people's lives the kind of
happiness it should, under right conditions, be
capable of creating. I believe enormously in the
beneficent possibilities of marriage, but I can't ignore the fact that we are not permitting it to fulfill
those possibilities. I hope I make myself clear.
[p. 140]

We can see that even an exceptional man like Lindsey jumps from confirming the deterioration of marriage, and its pointlessness in terms of sex-economy,
into the realm of ethics, which after all mirrors the
economic necessities of the ruling system. That in
America marriage is deteriorating so rapidly is attrib-
utable no doubt to the fact that there capitalism
has been furthest developed and consequently produces the sharpest contradictions in the field of sex-
economy: strictest puritanism on the one hand and
the breakdown of compulsory morality on the other.
We have already seen this in connection with the
problem of adolescence.

Lindsey is convinced that marriage can be maintained because of "the kind of happiness it should"
bring. But it is not a question of whether it *should*

bring it; it must be proved that it really *does* bring it. And if it does not, it must be investigated. The economic and sex-economic causes of its disintegration must be understood.

Hoffinger, a nineteenth-century scientist, concluded in one of his investigations:

Although he probed conscientiously and arduously into the number of happy marriages, his research has been in vain insofar as he could never regard happy marriages as anything but *extremely rare exceptions to the rule.*[6]

Gross-Hoffinger also found:

1. About half of all marriages are completely unhappy.

2. Considerably more than half of these are quite obviously demoralized.

3. The morality of the remainder does not in the least include marital fidelity.

4. Fifteen percent of all married people are engaged in prostitution and procuring.

5. The number of orthodox marriages above and beyond all suspicion of infidelity (provided there is the capacity for it) is—in the eyes of any reasonable man, who knows nature's stormy demands and needs—tantamount to zero.

Bloch investigated 100 marriages and found:

Decidedly unhappy	48
Indifferent	36
Undoubtedly happy	15
Virtuous	1

Among those 100 marriages, Bloch found 14 "deliberately immoral," 51 "indiscreet and slovenly," 2 beyond suspicion. (The moral value assess-

6 Quoted from Bloch: *Das Sexualleben unserer Zeit* [The Sexual Life of our Time], 2nd and 3rd eds., p. 247.

ments should be noted.) I investigated the individual cases and found that, among those described as happily married, 3 were of long duration; in 13 one or both of the marriage partners had been unfaithful; 3 could be described as "phlegmatic," i.e., sexually undemanding (impotent or frigid); while 2 could be characterized as apparently happy. When, among 15 described as "undoubtedly happy," we find 13 in which there is infidelity, this means that in the long run a marriage can be happy only if it sacrifices the most important demand of its ideology, marital fidelity, or if it is sexually undemanding. My own statistical investigation of 93 marriages, whose conditions were well known to me, yielded the following:

Bad or decidedly unfaithful	66
Resigned or ill marriage partners	18
Highly questionable (outwardly calm)	6
Good	3

Of the three marriages I found to be good, none was older than three years. These figures date back to 1925. Since then, one of the marriages has ended in divorce, another degenerated emotionally, though as yet without separation, and the man came for analytic treatment, and the third was still stable in 1929.

In a lecture for foreign physicians in Moscow, Lebedeva reported some interesting statistics about the duration of sexual relationships. She included only those registered marriages which were, for all practical purposes, enduring sexual relationships. Nineteen percent lasted one year; 37 percent, three to four years; 26 percent, four to nine years; 12 percent, ten to nineteen years; 6 percent, more than 19 years.

These figures prove that four years is the average length of time for the sexual basis of a relationship. How will marriage reform cope with this fact?

Here are more observations about marriages that are described as "good" and "serene." "Serene"

---

7 *Das Sexualleben unserer Zeit,* p. 253.

means that no conflicts are apparent, and marriages are called "good" when quiet resignation overlays everything. If a partner in such a marriage comes for analytic treatment, one is astounded time and again by the abundance of repressed hatred that has accumulated in the course of several years of marriage and, without ever becoming conscious, has finally found expression in an emotional illness. It is wrong to reduce this hatred only to experiences in childhood. The transference of a childhood hatred to the marriage partner does not occur until ample material for conflict has accumulated in the marriage itself, reactivating the former difficulties. In my experience, marriages disintegrate in analytic treatment when the analysis is carried out without consideration for marital morality, i.e., if, consciously or unconsciously, one does not leave untouched those subjects which might imperil the existence of the marriage. Additional experience points to the fact that marriages which have to tolerate the pressures of analysis will remain intact only if the analysand becomes sexually alive and determines not to obey unquestioningly the strictures of marital morality. Such blind obedience is invariably maintained by mechanisms of neurotic repression.

Furthermore, the analysis of married couples yields the following unequivocal conclusions:

1. There is no woman who does not have so-called "prostitution fantasies," but only very few imagine themselves as prostitutes. It is almost always the desire to have intercourse with several men, not to have her sexual experiences restricted to *one* man. This desire is understandably connected with the idea of prostitution. Character-analytic clinical experience demolishes the belief in the monogamous nature of women. Many psychoanalysts regard these "prostitution fantasies" as neurotic and consider it essential to free the woman from them. Such a viewpoint, however, robs the analyst of the necessary nonmoral attitude and the analysis is conducted solely in the interest of pathogenic morality. But, as a physi-

cian, one must consider the health of the patient,
i.e., his libido economy, and not official morality.
If one finds that there is a contradiction between
the libidinal demands of the patient and social morality, it is "un-analytic" to dismiss the demands as "infantile," as "machinations of the pleasure principle,"
and to call for the necessary "adjustment to reality"
or "resignation," before investigating whether the sexual demands are really infantile and whether the
reality demands are really acceptable from the standpoint of human health! A woman who, according
to her needs, has sexual intercourse with several men
cannot be dismissed as infantile. She just does not
fit into the ideology of compulsory marriage. This
does not mean she is sick, but she will probably become sick if she submits to the current morality. More
notice should be taken of the fact that those upright,
reality-adjusted women who have accepted the onus
of marriage without apparent conflict, because they
are inhibited for economic and moral reasons, show
all the signs of a neurosis. But they have "adapted to
reality."

2. Including the patient's social existence in
analysis teaches us to recognize the motives of the
ideology of monogamy. We find: strong identification
with the parents, who at least outwardly represent
monogamy, particularly the identification of the
daughter with the monogamous mother, but also its
opposite, the reaction to the monogamous mother
in the form of neurotic polygamy. Further, we find
reactive guilt feelings toward the spouse who restricts
sexual freedom. But the most effective elements in
the series of psychic motivations of the monogamous
attitude are the prohibitions of infantile sexuality
and the anxiety created by sexual activites in
childhood. Thus, ideology of monogamy in the individual is a strong reactive protection mechanism
against his own sexual drives, which do not know
the difference between monogamy, polygamy, or
polyandry, but know only gratification. Here, the in-

cestuous tie to the parent of the opposite sex plays
a significant role, and the resolution of this fixation
overcomes a large part of the monogamous attitude.
Of course, the economic subjugation of the woman
is also operative in her monogamous tendency. We
have seen time and again that the rigorous moral
demand for monogamy is resolved without difficulty
when economic independence is achieved.

3. The husband's insistence on his wife's fidelity
also has its specific reasons. (According to experience,
the economic basis of the demand for monogamy
has no direct psychological expression.) In the first
place, we find fear of competition, particularly with
those who are more potent, and the narcissistic
aversion to social ostracism, to the stigma attached
to the "cuckold." The deceived wife is not despised
but pitied because, in her dependent position, the
husband's infidelity signifies a real danger. But, in
public opinion, the infidelity of the wife is proof that
the husband could not assert his rights, that perhaps
he was not male enough, in the sexual sense, to keep
his wife's fidelity. Therefore, the wife bears the
husband's faithlessness more easily than does the
husband his wife's. If economic interest had a direct
influence on ideology, the opposite would be the case.
However, between the economic basis of moralistic
views and these views themselves, there are many
connecting lines, e.g., the man's vanity, so that in
the final analysis the social import of marriage is
preserved: the husband may be unfaithful, the wife
may not.

THE CONTRADICTION IN THE
INSTITUTION OF MARRIAGE

The contradiction in the institution of marriage
results from the conflict between sexual and economic
interests in marriage. The economic interests make
very consistent and logical demands. Since it is

unlikely—sex-economically impossible—that someone who leads a completely gratifying sexual life will subject himself to the conditions of marital morality (only one partner, for life), the first requirement is a deep-seated repression of sexual needs, particularly in the woman. Therefore, morality demands —without, of course, being able to enforce it on a general scale—that the woman have no sexual intercourse prior to marriage, and if possible the man, too, although his transgressions are generally overlooked. Not sensual sexuality, they say, but children are the essence of marriage (this is true for the economic side of marriage but not for the lasting sexual relationship). During their marriage the spouses may not have sexual experience with another person.

It is correct to say that these requirements are necessary for the permanence of a marriage. But it is these same requirements that undermine the marriage, which doom it to failure even from the start. The demand for a permanent sexual relationship carries within it a revolt against the compulsion which, consciously or unconsciously, becomes the more violent, the more lively and active the sexual needs. Until marriage, the woman has lived in chastity; she is sexually inexperienced and has had to repress her genital needs in order to remain faithful. Now these needs are no longer or only barely at her disposal, she is anesthetized, cold; she can neither excite nor gratify her husband once the stimulus of novelty has worn off. The healthy man soon loses interest and looks for other women who can give him more; here is the first rift in the relationship. According to prevailing morality, the man also should not risk too many "escapades"; he, too, especially if he is married, must repress a large part of his genital interests. This is good for preserving the marriage, but it is bad for the sexual relationship because repression produces disturbed or damaged potency. If the woman's sexuality is aroused and she knows what it really means, she is soon disappointed. She will look for another partner, or she will become ill from sexual stasis, from the lack of gratification, in one or another neurotic form. In either case the marriage has been undermined by the same element which was meant to guarantee its stability, the sex-negating education for marriage.

To this is added the ever-increasing economic independence of the woman that helps to sweep aside sexual inhibitions. She is no longer tied to home and children but gets to know other men. Inclusion in the economic process teaches her to reflect on matters which up to now were beyond her perspective.

Marriages could be good, at least for a while, if there were sexual compatibility and gratification. This would be predicated, however, on a sex-affirmative upbringing, on sexual experience prior to marriage, and on the overcoming of the prevailing social morality. But what sometimes establishes a good marriage simultaneously destroys it, because once sexuality is affirmed and moral attitudes are overcome, there is no inherent argument against intercourse with other partners, except for a period of time (certainly not a lifetime) during which fidelity is based on mutual gratification. Marriage ideology then founders; marriage is no longer marriage but rather an enduring sexual relationship which, precisely because there is no repression of genital desires, can, all things being equal, develop into a happy relationship, far better than can strict monogamy. The advocates of the marriage license and authoritarian laws notwithstanding, the cure for an unhappy marriage is, in many instances, marital infidelity.

Gruber writes:

There are certainly times, perhaps just moments, in every marriage when there is great moodiness, when being chained to one another is felt as an oppressive burden. Those spouses will most easily overcome such unhappy disturbances if they

entered the marriage chaste and have remained
faithful to each other.[8]

He is certainly right: the more chaste before marriage, the more faithful in marriage. This fidelity owes
its existence to the atrophy of sexuality resulting from
premarital abstinence.

The futility of marriage reform is thus explained
by the contradiction between the ideology of compulsory marriage, from which marital misery and
reformist aspirations emanate, and the fact that the
type of marriage which is to be reformed belongs
specifically to the social order in which it is economically rooted. We tried to show earlier that
the basic elements of the general sexual misery spring
from the contradiction between natural sexual needs
on the one hand and the ideology of extramarital
abstinence and monogamous permanent marriage
on the other.

The sex reformer states that most marriages are
miserable because complete sexual gratification is
lacking, because the men are clumsy, the women cold.
Therefore he proposes an eroticization of marriage,
in the manner of Van de Velde, by teaching the
spouses sexual techniques, hoping that this will improve the relations among married people. His fundamental idea is correct; a marriage built on an erotically satisfactory basis is indeed better than its
erotically unsatisfactory counterpart; but he overlooks
all preconditions for eroticizing an enduring sexual relationship. One such precondition would be the sexual
experience of the woman, which would indicate a general affirmation of sexuality. But normal education is
conditioned by the goals of chastity for the girl and
compulsory fidelity for the married woman. Together,
they necessitate a very considerable if not total sexual
repression of women. The sexually undemanding,
not very independent, sex-negating woman who
merely tolerates eroticism is the most faithful wife. A

8 *Hygiene des Geschlechtslebens*, p. 148.

sex-affirmative education would make the woman more independent and would be basically antagonistic to marriage. A sex-negative education is absolutely logical from the standpoint of lifelong monogamous marriage, whereas the demand for eroticization of marriage contradicts marriage ideology. This was recognized by Professor Häberlin of Basel, who wrote in his book *Über die Ehe* [On Marriage] that the true motive for marriage was sexual love, that "although without it no marriage in the true sense is possible, it constitutes, on the other hand, the dangerous and unpredictable element in marriage whose presence makes the marriage a constantly problematical matter." He then draws this conclusion: "Marriage as a permanent relationship can be realized in spite of the sexual love which is connected with it." This means: people have an economic interest in monogamous compulsory marriage and cannot take the sexual interests into account.

From a practical standpoint, therefore, any alleviation of legal formalities of divorce is meaningless for the masses. The divorce law means only that one is willing, in principle, to allow divorce. But is one also willing to create economic prerequisites which are indispensable for the woman if she really wishes to obtain a divorce? One of these prerequisites would be a rationalization of production without creating unemployment but shortening the work period and raising wages. The woman's economic dependence on the man and the lower value placed on her participation in the production process transform marriage into a protective institution for her, even though she is doubly exploited in this "production setup." Not only is she the sexual object of her husband and the birth apparatus of the state, but her unpaid work in the household indirectly raises the profits of the employer. For the man can produce surplus value at current low wages only if a certain amount of work is taken off his shoulders at home. If the employer had to take care of the worker's household, he would either have to pay a housekeeper for the worker or put the worker into an economic position where he could afford such help. But this work is accomplished by the wife gratuitously. If the woman, too, works in a factory, either she must do additional, unpaid work to keep her house in order, or else she neglects it, the familial relationship suffers, and the marriage has ceased to be a conventional marriage.

Added to these economic difficulties is the fact that most women are adjusted to a sexual life only in marriage, with all its misery, its compulsion, its absence of genuine experience, but also with its outward peace and quiet, its circumscribed routine, which spares today's average housewife any reflections on her sexuality as well as the wearing struggle of extramarital sexual life. Such a woman is not aware that the avoidance of these problems is dearly paid for by emotional suffering and neurosis. Consciousness of her sexuality would probably spare her the neurosis but not the sexual suffering which threatens her today.

Contradictions in the institution of marriage are logically reflected in the contradictions in marital reform. The reform of marriage by eroticization (à la Van de Velde) is inherently contradictory, while Lindsey's proposal of "companionate marriage" suffers not from the fact that he has confirmed the decline of marriage as such and examined its causes but from his desire to patch up a crumbling institution with the idea that "marriage is the best sexual reform." Lindsey's writings also clearly express the leap from adherence to the development of facts to the presentation of compulsory moral judgments. For instance, he is opposed to trial marriage for moral reasons but fights for the system of companionate marriage, i.e., the "legally sanctioned" relationship between man and woman with "legalized birth control." If we seek the reason for legal sanction, we find nothing but the attitude that sexual relationships "must" be legally recognized. Therefore, companionate marriage would differ from conventional marriage only by the inclusion of birth control and by the fact that it could be dissolved at will, in contrast to a marriage with children. This proposal is undoubtedly the most far-reaching in conservative society. But we must clearly recognize that it is bound to that society and the sex-economic requirements *must* therefore be secondary to the problem of the economic care of wife and children. Thus it can contribute nothing to the solution of the problem of marriage.

The facts are as follows. Within the framework of the existing order of marriage conflicts become insoluble. On the one hand, the sexual drive can no longer be satisfied in the form imposed on it—hence the deterioration of marriage morality; on the other hand, the economic dependence of wife and children necessitates the preservation of that form. This results in the continued endorsement of the existing form of sexual life: marriage. The conflict is only the continuation of another, on a higher level. This other conflict arises from the fact that work-democratic methods of production are developing within the framework of the authoritarian social order, and marriage morality is changing as the economic independence of women and the collectivization of working youth, as well as the sexual conflict itself, precipitate sexual crises. Marriage belongs specifically to the capitalistic economic system and is necessarily maintained in spite of all crises. Its deterioration and the insoluble contradiction within this social framework, with its economic base, are only signs of the general chaotic state in this mode of existence. Marriage collapses automatically and dies of its inherent contradictions the moment its economic foundation crumbles. This occurred historically in the Soviet Union.

How fragile the institution of marriage is sex-economically could be gauged by the rapidity and completeness of its disintegration after the Revolution, particularly among the advanced strata of the population, the labor leaders and employees. The

latent marriage crisis always appears in times of social
crisis in the form of the disintegration of marriage.
"Decline of morality in stormy times," some will
say. But let us examine the facts in their social context
and finally stop looking at them moralistically. The
disintegration of compulsory morality was only a
symptom indicating that the social revolution would
also result in a sexual revolution, that it would not
be stopped by any "sanctified good."

As long as there is a normalization of sexual life
in the sense of an ideology of compulsory monogamous marriage, sexual life is apparently balanced but
internally anarchic and uneconomic. If the marriage
ideologues cannot be convinced by the actual effects
of the regulation of sexual life, which is approved
and demanded by them, including the degradation
of love life, suffering in marriage, adolescent misery,
sex murders, and other fine things, they will also
not respond to the argument that the natural necessities
of life do not need the patronage of society, if only
society does nothing to disturb their gratification.
Man's socialization is meant to facilitate the gratification of hunger and love; yet virtually all of humanity
has been restricted in the gratification of love. It is
precisely the interference of economic interests in
the gratification of basic drives that has caused
anarchy. Will the elimination of social regulation
of sexual life bring natural self-regulation, i.e., sex-
economy? Will there still be scientists, as in our own
day, who support the destructive compulsory moral
regulation of human life with their "scientific" pronouncements? We can neither hope nor fear but only
study whether the development of society aims at
improving the natural conditions of material as well
as sexual economy, improvements which take account
of human needs. One thing is certain: when a scientific
and rational view of life prevails, it will destroy the
altars of every kind of deity; it will no longer be possible to sacrifice the health and vitality of millions of

PART TWO

The Struggle for a "New Life" in the Soviet Union

If the building of the future and its completion for all time is not our concern, it is all the more certain what we have to achieve now; I mean the ruthless criticism of everything that exists, ruthless in the sense that criticism does not shrink from its own results any more than it fears the conflict with the powers that be.

—KARL MARX

Sexual Reaction in Russia

Over the past years, news of reactionary sexual and cultural-political developments in Soviet Russia has accumulated, destroying many hopes.

In June 1934, the law against homosexuality was reintroduced in the Soviet Union, and rumors about the persecution of homosexuals became more frequent. For fifteen years, Austrian and German sex reformers, in their struggle against such laws, had pointed time and again to the progressive Soviet Union, where punishment of homosexuals had been abolished.

Abortion in general and particularly for women carrying their first child and for mothers with only one child has been made increasingly difficult. Germany's birth control movement had derived its strongest support against political reaction from the original Soviet attitude toward birth control. Now we hear more and more frequently that the opponents of birth control have triumphed on the question of free abortions and that the Soviet Union has turned its back on its original views.

In Germany, the Verlag für Sexualpolitik, in collaboration with various youth organizations, published my book *Der sexuelle Kampf der Jugend,* which was intended to develop a theory and practice in this area. We pointed to the sexual freedom offered to youth in the Soviet Union. Then, in 1932, the

German Communist Party prohibited the distribution
of my book; a year later, the Nazis put it on the
index for prohibited literature. We hear that youth
in the Soviet Union are fighting hard against conservative physicians and many high state functionaries who are regressing more and more to the old
ideology of asceticism. Thus we can no longer refer
to sexual freedom in the Soviet Union and we notice confusion and conflict among Western European
youth who do not understand what is going on.

We read and hear that the compulsory family is
again being highly esteemed and "fortified" in the
Soviet Union, and that the marriage regulations issued
in 1918 are going to be revoked. In the struggle
against compulsory marriage laws, we could always
use the example of Soviet marital legislation. Marx's
dictum that the social revolution "abolishes" the compulsory family had been confirmed. And we had only
to endeavor to explain to the family-oriented person
the necessity and usefulness of this process. Now
reactionary family politics triumphs: "There you are!
Your theories have gone sour. Even the Soviet Union
has given up the heresy of destroying the authoritarian
family. The compulsory family is and remains the
basis of society and state."

We read and hear that, due to the problem of delinquency, parents are again responsible for rearing their
children. In our pedagogic and cultural work we
pointed to the fact that in the Soviet Union the power
of parents over their children had been removed and
the educational task had been transferred to the whole
community. We regarded the collectivization of child
education as a basic process of socialist society. Every
progressive worker, every clear-thinking mother,
recognized and affirmed this orientation in Soviet
Russia. We struggled against the possessive instinct
and the abuse of power by women vis-à-vis their
children. We did all we could to show mothers that
their children were not being "taken away" from
them but that collective education would merely spare

them burdens and cares. We were successful. However, political reaction in pedagogy can now say: "You see, even the Soviet Union has given up this nonsense while the natural right and the eternal power of parents over their children have been restored."[1]

In Soviet schools, the Dalton plan has long been dropped; we hear that the methods of teaching are becoming more and more authoritarian. For some time now, we have not been able to rely on the Soviet Union in our pedagogic struggles for the self-regulation of children and for the elimination of authoritarian forms of education.

In our battles for the rational sexual enlightenment of children and adolescents we have always drawn upon the success of the Soviet Union. But for years we have heard nothing further about it, except that the ideology of asceticism has assumed increasingly rigid forms.

Hence we are compelled to conclude that there is an inhibition in the Soviet sexual revolution, even a regression to authoritarian moral forms in the regulation of human love life.

We learn from various sources that sexual reaction in the Soviet Union is gaining the upper hand and that progressive circles cannot explain this; that people are looking for clarification and cannot find it and are therefore helpless in the face of reactionary encroachment. The confusion inside as well as outside the Soviet Union raises questions about Soviet sex politics. What has happened? Why does sexual reaction win out everywhere? Why did the sexual revolution fail? What can be done about it? These are the questions that preoccupy every educator and social worker and should interest every political economist.

---

[1] I would recommend that the reader obtain a copy of the Russian book *I Want to Be Like Stalin*, by Jessipov and Goncharov (1947). This volume was published by the Russian Commissariat for Education and is thus official. It reflects the most infamous abuse of the child's character, for reasons of power politics, which I have come across in thirty years of psychiatric practice.

The argument that political reaction might disrupt an open discussion of these questions is not valid.

First, political reaction can never take a scientific, sex-political position *against* today's measures in the Soviet Union. On the contrary, it triumphs because of these measures.

Second, the clarification of these questions within the European and American working-class movement is more important than any consideration of prestige. Confusion is harmful. In France, the Communist newspaper *L'Humanité* has already proclaimed the salvation of the "race" and the "French family." Reactionary Soviet measures are known to everyone and can no longer be denied.

In the Soviet Union, regression in the sexual realm is connected with general questions of revolutionary cultural development. We know that the trend toward self-regulation of social life has yielded to authoritarian regulation of society. This regression is expressed best in the sexual realm and can also be most clearly comprehended here. Not without reason. The sexual process of society has always been the core of its cultural process. This is as clearly evident in the family politics of Fascism as in primitive society during its transition from matriarchy to patriarchy. In Russian Communism, the economic revolution during the first years paralleled the revolution in sexual life. This sexual revolution was the objective expression of the revolutionary restructuring of culture. Without an appreciation of the sexual process in the Soviet Union, its cultural process cannot be understood.

It is catastrophic when leaders of a revolutionary movement try to defend reactionary, philistine views by calling the sexual revolutionary "petty bourgeois." The return to trash in various forms merely expresses the fact that the revolutionary breakthrough did not succeed. The connection between the inhibition of the sexual revolution and cultural political regression can be merely sketched here. Perhaps it will be possible in the near future to obtain material which will clarify the general cultural problem. But first it would be more helpful to deal with the heart of the matter; to deal with the general problem of culture without knowledge of its basis in human character structure would be confusing.

VIII

The "Abolition of the Family"

The sexual revolution in the Soviet Union began with the dissolution of the family. It disintegrated in all segments of the population, sometimes sooner, sometimes later. This process was painful and chaotic, causing fright and confusion. It provided objective proof for the accuracy of the sex-economic theory about the nature and function of the compulsory family: the patriarchal family is the structural and ideological breeding ground of all social orders based on the authoritarian principle. With the elimination of this principle, the institution of the family is automatically weakened.

The disintegration of the compulsory family was an expression of the fact that human sexual needs broke the chains imposed on them by economic and authoritarian family ties; it effected the separation of economy and sexuality. In patriarchy, the sexual needs served and were thus subordinated to the economic interests of a minority; in primitive communist (work-democratic) matriarchy, the economy served the gratification of all needs, including the sexual. The genuine social revolution aims at restoring an economy that will satisfy the needs of all productive workers. This reversal of the relation between need and economy is at the heart of social revolution. The

disintegration of the compulsory family can be understood only in terms of this general process. It would
develop rapidly and thoroughly, and without friction,
if nothing else were involved but the burden which the
familial economic tie imposes on the family members
and the strength of the sexual needs bound up in
it. The problem is not so much why the family
disintegrates; the reasons for this are clear. The more
difficult question is why this disintegration is so much
more painful psychically than any other upheaval.
The expropriation of the means of production hurts
only their former owners but not the masses, the
carriers of the revolution. But the disintegration of
the family strikes precisely those who are to carry
out the economic revolution: workers, employees,
farmers. It is here that the conservative function of
family ties becomes most obvious. Intense family
feelings effect an inhibition in the carrier of the revolution. His ties to wife and children, his love for the
home if he has one—never mind how shabby it is—his
tendency to follow a circumscribed routine, etc.,
hinder him to varying degrees when he is supposed
to carry out the main function of the revolution, the
restructuring of man. Just as the developing Fascist
dictatorship in Germany used family ties to restrain
the revolutionary élan (enabling Hitler to build an
imperialistic, nationalistic ideology on the firm foundation of these ties), so the family ties in the revolution
acted as a brake on the intended transformation of
life. There is a grave contradiction between the disintegration of the social foundations of the family, and
the old familial human structure, which is not easily
changed and which, emotionally, the family wants
to maintain, though usually this occurs unconsciously.
There is no doubt that the replacement of the patriarchal family form by the workers' collective is the
core of the revolutionary cultural problem. One should
not be deceived, however, by the often loud, rebellious
cry "Away from the family!" Frequently those who
most loudly demand the destruction of the family

are unconsciously most strongly bound up in their
own familial childhood. Such people are unsuited
for resolving the most difficult of all problems, the
dissolution of family ties and their replacement by
collective social ties, both in theory and in practice.
If it is not possible to establish a self-regulating work
democracy simultaneously with its anchoring in the
psychic structure of man, if the family feeling is maintained over a long period of time, an ever-widening
gulf must arise between the economic and the mass-
structural, i.e., the cultural, development of work
democracy. The cultural revolution fails to occur
because the carrier and cultivator of this revolution,
the psychic structure of man, was not qualitatively
changed by the social revolution.

In Trotsky's *Problems of Everyday Life* we find
rich material on the process of family disintegration
from 1919 to 1920:

The family, including the proletarian family, was
"disintegrating." During a discussion of Moscow
propagandists, this fact was plainly established and
disputed by no one. It was regarded in various ways.
"Some were disquieted, others were aloof, and still
others could not make up their minds about it." It
was clear to one and all that they were facing "some
significant, very chaotic process that soon would
assume tragic dimensions," that "could not yet manifest a new, higher family order which lay concealed
in its possibilities." Indications of family disintegration were also reported in the press, "although extremely rarely and in generalized form." Many believed that the disintegration of the workingman's family should be regarded as "a bourgeois influence on
the proletariat." Many others felt that this explanation
was wrong; they thought the matter went deeper and
was more complicated. Of course there was some
bourgeois influence, past and present. But the main
process was said to be in the pathological and crisis-rid-
den "evolution of the proletarian family"; the first
chaotic phases of this process were being observed.

In the area of family life, the first period of disintegration was by no means ended; disintegration and deterioration were still in full swing. Everyday life was described as far more conservative than the economy, because, among other things, it was much less conscious than the latter.

It was further ascertained that the disintegration of the old family form was not limited to the upper stratum of society, which was most forcefully exposed to the influence of newly created conditions, but penetrated far beyond the vanguard. In the final analysis, the consensus was that the Communist vanguard was merely passing through an earlier and harsher form of what would become more or less inevitable for society as a whole.

Both husband and wife were caught up more and more in public functions; this destroyed the claims that the family could impose on its members. Children grew up in the collective. This produced a competition between familial and social ties. But the social ties were new, young, scarcely born, while the familial ones were deeply anchored in everyday life, in every expression of the psychic structure. The emotional barrenness of sexual relationships in most marriages could not compete with the new, joyous sexual relationships in the collective. And all this occurred against the background of an ever-increasing uprooting of the family's main tie—the economic power of the father over wife and children. The economic bond was broken and the sexual inhibition with it. But this did not yet mean "sexual freedom." The external freedom necessary for sexual happiness is not yet that happiness itself, which primarily requires the psychic capacity for shaping and enjoying it. In the family, genital needs were largely replaced by infantile dependencies or pathological sexual habits which were endowed with all the power of sexual energy but destroyed the capacity for every biologically normal orgastic experience. Family members hated each other, consciously or unconsciously, and superimposed on their hatred a spasmodic love and a sticky attachment which poorly camouflaged their origin in concealed hatred. In the foreground of these difficulties were the women, genitally crippled and unprepared for economic independence, unable to renounce the slavish protection of the family and the substitute gratification of ruling over their children. Economically dependent, their lives a sexual desert, these women had regarded the rearing of their children as the central meaning of their life. Every limitation, even if it was beneficial to the children, was experienced as a severe restriction, and they knew very well how to defend themselves against it. This resistance is quite understandable and must be taken into account. Gladkov's novel *Cement* shows clearly that the struggle for the collective encountered no difficulties that were even remotely comparable to the struggle of the women for home, family, and children. At first, the collectivization of life was imposed from above, by edicts, and was supported by revolutionary youth who broke the chains of parental authority. But the average person felt the inhibitions of familial ties in every step he wanted to take toward collectivization, particularly in the form of his unconscious familial dependence and longing.

These difficulties and conflicts in everyday life did not correspond to an "accidental chaotic" condition produced by the "unreasonableness" or "immorality" of the people; rather, they harmonized with a law that governs the relationships between sexual forms and forms of social organization.

In primitive society, which is structured collectively and in terms of "original communism," the unit is the clan, the sum of all blood relationships derived from the first mother. Within this clan, which also represents the economic unit, there exist only the loose ties of a mating relationship. To the extent that, as a result of economic changes, the clan becomes subordinated to the patriarchal family of the chieftain, the destruction of the clan by the family sets in. Family and clan are now antithetical. The family increasingly replaces the clan, becomes an economic unit and, with it, the social crystallization point of partriarchy. The chieftain of the matriarchal clan organization, who originally was not in opposition to the clan society, gradually becomes the patriarch of the family, achieves an economic predominance, and develops progressively into the patriarch of the whole clan. This produces for the first time a class contrast between the family of the chieftain and the lower strata of the clan. Thus the first classes were the family of the chieftain on the one hand and the *gens* (clan) on the other.

In the development from matriarchy to patriarchy, the family acquires, along with its economic function, another function which is more important: to modify the structure of each individual from that of a free clan member to that of a subjugated member of the family. In today's large East Indian family, this function is expressed most clearly. By developing as an independent unit in opposition to the clan, the family becomes the original organization not only of class relationships but also of social suppression inside and outside its boundaries. The emerging "family man" begins to reproduce the increasingly patriarchal class organization of society by changing his own structure. The basic mechanism of this reproduction is the shift from sex affirmation to sex suppression; its basis is the dominating economic position of the chieftain.

Let us briefly summarize the nature of this psychic change: in place of the free, voluntary relationship of clan and tribe members, based only on common interests, there is now a conflict between economic and sexual interests. In place of voluntary work accomplishment, there is now a requirement to work, and the rebellion against it; in place of natural sexual sociality, there is moralistic demand; in place of camaraderie among warriors, there are authoritarian-minded followers; in place of clan solidarity, there

is the family bond, with the rebellion against it; in
place of a sex-economically regulated life, there is
the restriction of genitality and with it the first neuroses
and sexual perversions. The naturally strong, self-con-
fident biological organism becomes helpless, dependent, and God-fearing. The experiencing of nature
in the orgasm is displaced by mystical ecstasy, the
later "religious experience," and an unquenchably
vegetative longing. The weakened ego of the individual
looks for strength in associating and identifying with
the tribe which gradually develops into a "nation,"
with the tribal chieftain gradually becoming tribal
patriarch and finally king. With that, the birth of
a submissive structure is achieved and the structural
anchoring of human subjugation is guaranteed.

The initial phases of the social revolution in the
Soviet Union reveal the latest reversal of this process:
the restoring of conditions as they existed in primitive
communism, but on a higher, civilized plane, and
the shift from sex negation to sex affirmation.

According to the findings, of Marx, which are
developed in the *Communist Manifesto,* one of the
main tasks of the social revolution is the abolition
of the family.[1] What Marx inferred theoretically
from the social process was later confirmed by the
development of social organization in the Soviet
Union. In place of the family, there begins to appear
an organization which shows certain similarities with
the clan in primitive communism—the socialist collective in the factory, in the schools, on the farm, etc.
The difference between the primitive clan and the
modern communist collective is that the former was
founded on blood relationships and, as such, also
became an economic unit. The latter does not consist
of people related by blood and is based on common
economic functions; it develops as an economic unit
and leads of necessity to the formation of personal
relationships which may also be characterized as a

---

1 "That the elimination of a separate economy cannot be separated
from the abolition of the family is self-explanatory" (Part I).

sexual collective. Just as the family destroyed the
clan in primitive society, the communist economic
collective destroys the family, which had already
begun to crumble during the crisis of capitalism. The
process reverses itself. If the family is retained
ideologically or structurally, the development of the
collective is inhibited. If it does not succeed in overcoming this inhibition, it destroys itself in the restrictions of man's family structure, as occurred, for instance, in the youth communes (cf. Chapter XII). At
the beginning of communist development, *the process
may be characterized as a conflict between the
economic collective, with its inherent sex-affirmative
tendency toward sexual independence, and the dependent, familial, sex-fearing, structure of individuals.*

IX

The Sexual Revolution

1. PROGRESSIVE LEGISLATION

Soviet sexual legislation was the clearest expression of the first surge of the sexual revolution against a life-negating sexual order. Most traditional legislation was literally turned upside down in the new laws. It will be shown that where this change did not succeed completely, sexual reaction regained a foothold, as, for instance, in the gaps in marital legislation, abortion laws, etc. In order to appreciate the antithesis between moralistic and sex-economic regulation, it is necessary to compare the legislation of the revolution with earlier Tsarist legislation. It is superfluous to prove in detail that the liberalized and "democratic" sexual laws do not differ in principle from Tsarist laws and show only minor differences in the degree of sexual subjugation. Sexual, moral, and authoritarian measures for regulation remain basically the same. It is important to emphasize this because we must deal with the argument which maintains that Soviet measures merely put another authoritarian order in the place of the capitalistic one, that, for instance, Soviet marriage law merely provides for a removal of suppression and not a *basically different* regulation. Sex-economy is concerned precisely with the nature of this other kind of "order."

194

Let us first examine a passage from Tsarist legislation:

> From Article 106 of the Penal Code: The husband is obligated to love his wife as he does himself, to live with her in peace and harmony, to respect her and to assist her during illness. He is obligated to provide for his wife in accordance with his position and capacity.
>
> Article 107: The wife is obliged to obey her husband as the head of the family, to stay at his side with love, respect, and unlimited obedience, and to show him every favor and devotion as a housewife.
>
> Article 164: The rights of the parents: the power of the parents extends to children of both sexes, regardless of age. . . .
>
> Article 165: The parents are empowered to use corrective measures at home in dealing with recalcitrant and disobedient children. If these measures fail, the parents can exercise the following powers:
>
> 1. To put children of either sex, who are not in the civil service, in jail for stubborn disobedience of parental authority, for immoral conduct, and for other obvious vices. . . .
>
> 2. To file complaints against them with the proper legal institutions. Without special legal preliminaries, stubbornly disobedient children who defy parental authority, behave immorally, or engage in other obvious vices are subject to jail sentences of two to four months if the parents so desire. In such cases, the parents are entitled to shorten or suspend jail sentences in accordance with their judgment.

Let us look carefully at how moralistic authoritarian regulation is expressed. The parents are under the compulsion of a moral, legally sanctioned obligation. The husband *must* love his wife, whether he can or not, whether, later, he wants to or not; the woman

must be a submissive wife; to change situations which
have become untenable is not possible. The law in-
structs parents to exercise their power over children
and to use it for purposes which coincide with the
interests of the authoritarian state: punishing "stubborn disobedience of parental authority" (representative of state power); safeguarding the submissive
structure of the state's subjects; preventing "immoral
conduct and other obvious vices" in order to establish
the most essential means for such safeguarding. In
the face of such obvious, ingenuous avowal by the
patriarchal-state order, it is almost impossible to
believe how little significance the revolutionary movement attached and still attaches to sexual suppression
as the principal means of achieving human subjugation.

Sex-economy did not have to reveal the content
and mechanisms of every kind of suppression; they
were, and still are, plainly visible in all legislation
as well as in the cultural phenomenon of patriarchy.
The problem is why they were *not* seen, why the
powerful weapons which such revelations furnish us
were *not* used. Tsarist as well as any other reactionary
sexual legislation clearly reveals the sex-economic
viewpoint: *the purpose of authoritarian moral order
is sexual subjugation.* Wherever we find moral regulation and its principal tool, sexual suppression, there
can be no possibility of real freedom.

The importance which the social revolution attributed to the sexual revolution is expressed in Lenin's
two edicts, proclaimed on December 19 and 20,
1917, which essentially abolished all previous regulations. One of these edicts was called "On the Dissolution of Marriage"; its content was not as unequivocal as its title. The second edict was entitled
"On Civil Marriage, Children, and Civil Registration." Both laws took away the man's right to a
dominating position in the family, gave the woman
full economic and sexual self-determination, and
clared it to be self-evident that the woman could

freely determine her name, domicile, and citizenship. As everyone with any insight knew, such legislation alone merely safeguarded the seemingly free development of a process to come and gave it a specific ideological form. That the revolutionary law unmistakably expressed the abrogation of patriarchal power was self-evident. As the former ruling class lost its power and its suppressive state apparatus, the paternal power over family members was also removed, and with it the man's position as representative of the state within the compulsory family. If this logical and inherently necessary connection between authoritarian state and patriarchal family as its structural breeding ground had been recognized clearly and handled practically, the revolution might have been spared many fruitless discussions and failures, and even very crucial regressions. Most of all, the right words and measures would have been found with which to combat the representatives of the old ideology and morality who gradually began to take over. They held the highest offices and the revolutionary movement had no presentiment of the harm they were causing.

In accordance with the Soviet tendency to simplify life, the dissolution of a compulsory marriage was made considerably easier. A sexual relationship which was still known as a "marriage" could be dissolved just as simply as it had been established. All that mattered was the "free will and determination" of the partners. No one was allowed to force another into a relationship against his or her "free will." It was no longer the state which determined the relationship of the partners, but only the partners themselves. It became meaningless to require grounds for a divorce. If one partner decided to terminate the sexual relationship, he or she was not obliged to furnish reasons. Marriage and divorce became purely private matters, and the principle of "guilt" or "incompatibility" was "absolutely alien" to Soviet law (Batkis).

Registration of a relationship was voluntary and other sexual relationships of one of the partners were "not prosecuted" in spite of a registration. But not telling one's partner of a second relationship was regarded as "deceit." Originally, registration was intended to be a "temporary measure," as was the obligation to pay alimony. Mandatory alimony after separation lasted six months and was valid only if the woman was unemployed or unemployable. It is self-evident that mandatory alimony could have only a temporary character, since the Soviet Union intended to establish full economic independence for all members of society. In the first years of the revolution, alimony was meant to help the parties concerned through the initial difficulties which hindered the social order from creating full personal and economic freedom.

One of these difficulties was the institution of the family, which had been abolished in law but not in reality. For as long as society cannot guarantee the care of all adults and adolescents, the family, as the representative of society, is left to assume this function for its members. Thus if someone lived over a period of time in a registered marriage and took care of his family, the family would be harmed if he undertook new obligations. If he did not notify his wife of a new relationship, he unquestionably deceived her. This familial situation itself produced an inhibition or, rather, a contradiction in the meaning of Soviet law which explicitly guaranteed personal freedom, even in relationships with several partners.

Here we recognize for the first time a real contradiction between a part of the Soviet ideology of freedom, which had anticipated sexual freedom in marital legislation, and the actual conditions of family life. Mandatory alimony payments and the interests of the woman who was not yet fully independent contradicted the aspirations of freedom. We will later find such contradictions in abundance. However, it is not important that they existed, but, rather, *in what form* they were resolved, whether the solution was in the direction of the original goal of freedom or in the direction of inhibition.

Soviet law clearly shows elements which ideologically anticipate the final goal as well as elements which take a transitional period into account. Only if we follow the dynamic course of these contradictions between final goal and momentary conditions will we comprehend the mystery of the inhibition of the sexual revolution in the Soviet Union which later stood out so sharply.

Lenin is often invoked by cultural and sexual hypocrites as having authorized reactionary attitudes. It is all the more useful to learn how clearly Lenin realized that legislation alone was merely a beginning of the sexual and, with it, the cultural revolution.

Discussions of the "new order of personal and cultural life," of the so-called *"Novy Byt,"* continued for years. They were characterized by an enthusiasm and an active participation that can be produced only by people who have thrown off their heaviest chains and realize clearly that they have to rebuild their lives completely. These discussions about the "sexual question" began at the start of the revolution and continued with mounting intensity but then faded away. Why they disappeared and made way for regressive activity is precisely what this book tries to comprehend. It is significant that in 1925, when, according to Fanina Halle, discussions about the sexual revolution had reached their peak, People's Commissar Kursky had to introduce new marital legislation with the words of Lenin:

> Of course laws alone are not enough, and we will certainly not content ourselves with decrees. However, in the area of legislation we have already accomplished everything that was demanded of us in terms of the woman's equality with the man and we are entitled to be proud of it: the present position of the woman is such that, from the standpoint of even the most progressive nations,

it can be described as virtually ideal. And yet we continue to say that this marks only a beginning.

"Beginning" of what? If one follows the discussions, which at that time aroused all segments of the population, one can see that the conservatives had at their disposal the entire stock of old arguments and "proofs," while progressives and revolutionaries felt that the "old" should be replaced by something "new" but could not articulate this "new" element and consequently could not express it properly. They fought bravely and indefatigably, but they finally became paralyzed and failed in the discussions because they had first laboriously to forge their weapons and pick their arguments from the tumultuous life of the revolution itself, because finally they were caught in the old concepts which clung to them like underwater creepers to a swimmer.

Every effort to expose the contradictions in the Soviet cultural revolution would be in vain unless we understood this most tragic of all revolutionary struggles in such new terms as to be better equipped to confront sexual reaction when this society ultimately becomes aware of its true nature and proceeds to reorder its life.

In the Soviet Union, the people were neither theoretically nor practically prepared for the difficulties which such restructuring of life would produce. These difficulties resulted partly from factual ignorance about the deep psychic structure of humanity as taken over from Tsarist patriarchy, and partly from the transitional problems of the revolution itself. Let us establish what was clearly required and formulated in terms of revolutionary intentions, confronting it with what was expressed in uncertainties and later forced a retreat.

2. WARNINGS FROM THE WORKERS

It is generally believed that the essential aspect of
the Soviet sexual revolution was to be found in the
changes set down in legislation. But a legal or otherwise formal change achieves social significance only
when it really reaches "the masses," i.e., when the
mass psyche is restructured. This is the only way for
an ideology or a program to become a historically revolutionizing force—solely by a deep-seated change in
the feelings and instinctual life of the massses. For
the often quoted and yet so little understood "subjective factor of history" is to be found exclusively in
the psychic structure of the masses. It is crucial for
the development of society; be it that despotism and
suppression are passively tolerated; be it that society
has become adapted to the process of technical
development initiated by the ruling powers; be it finally that it has actively interfered in the course of social development, as in a revolution. Therefore, no investigation of historical developments may call itself
revolutionary if it regards the psychic condition of
the masses merely as a product of economic processes
and not also as their motor force.

From this point of view, the *effect* of the Soviet
sexual revolution should be judged not by the legislation it instituted (these laws are proof only of the
revolutionary spirit of Bolshevik *leadership*) but by
the revolutionary upheavals experienced by the
masses of the Russian people after this legislation
was initiated and by the outcome of this struggle
for a "new life." How did the masses react to the
legal changes in terms of sex politics? How did the
low-ranking functionaries of the party, who were intimately connected with the masses, react? Later,
what was the response of the leadership?

Let us first consider a report by Alexandra Kollontay, who very early became concerned with the
problem of the raging sexual crisis:

> The more protracted the [sexual] crisis, the
> more it assumes a chronic character, the more in-
> extricable becomes the condition of the people who
> live through it, and the greater the bitterness with
> which humanity pounces on the solution to this ac-
> cursed [!] problem. But with every new attempt to
> disentangle the tortuous knot of the sexual prob-
> lem, the interrelationships become even more com-
> plicated, and it is as though no way could be found
> to unravel this stubborn tangle. Frightened humanity
> goes from one extreme to the other, but the magic
> circle of the sexual question remains as closed as
> ever . Not even the peasants have been spared
> the sexual crisis. Like an infectious disease which
> knows neither rank nor station, it pours down
> from castles and villas into the drab dwellings of
> the workers, glances into peaceful homesteads,
> rushes into the numb Russian village. . . . There
> is no defense against the sexual crisis. It would
> be an enormous error to assume that only the rep-
> resentatives of the economically secure classes of
> people are struggling in this net. More and more
> often the muddy waves of the sexual crisis roll
> across the thresholds of workers' homes, creating
> tragedies which, in their acuteness and bitterness,
> equal the psychological conflicts of a sophisticated
> bourgeois world.[1]

The crisis of sexual life, of the private life, of family
life, had erupted. The new marriage law, the "abolition
of the family," had only eliminated external obstacles.
The actual sexual revolution took place in daily life.
For that matter, the fact that the leading functionaries
of a state became concerned with the sexual problem
was a minor revolution in itself. Then the low-ranking

---

1 *The New Morality and the Working Class.*

functionaries picked it up. At first, when the old order collapsed, there was only chaos. But the simple, untrained bearers of the revolution approached the monstrous problem bravely. The "cultured" and distinguished academicians, however, indulged in "speculation," insofar as they had any idea at all of what historical processes were taking place.

In his booklet *Problems of Everyday Life,* Trotsky, with the support of Moscow's functionaries, called the attention of Soviet public opinion to daily life. Of course he did not raise the sexual question! He merely let the functionaries discuss topical questions of everyday life. And it was as if the functionaries were already familiar with sex-economy because they talked almost exclusively about the "family question." They were not concerned with legal or sociological family questions but with the uncertainties and insecurities of sexual life which until then had been tied up with the economic unit of the family but which now, with its disintegration, raised questions that had never arisen before.

In the first years of the revolution the low-ranking functionaries behaved in an exemplary manner, a model for any future revolution. The *beginning* of the sexual revolution (as the nucleus of every cultural revolution) was correct not only in its legislation but also in the manner in which difficulties were recognized and the right questions asked. Here are some examples. Functionary Kosakov said:

> Outwardly, there has been a change in family life, i.e., one has a simpler attitude toward family life. But the basic evil has not changed, i.e., there has been no alleviation of the family in its day-to-day cares, and the domination of one family member over others has remained. People aspire to public life, and if these aspirations cannot be fulfilled because of family needs there will be restlessness and neurasthenic illness, and the individual who cannot come to terms with this will either

leave the family in the lurch or torment himself
until he himself becomes neurasthenic.

Kosakov's understanding of the problems can be
summarized in a few sentences:
1. Ostensibly, the familial situation has changed
basically; actually, it has remained the same.
2. The family acts as a brake on the revolutionary
trend toward establishing the collective.
3. The familial inhibition acts unfavorably on the
psychic health of its members; this is tantamount
to diminished capacity for work and joy in work
as well as to producing psychic illnesses.
The following statements reveal the effects of
economic upheaval on the progressive deterioration
of the family:

Kobosev: No doubt the revolution has brought
about great changes in the workers' family life;
particularly if husband and wife are active in the
production process, the wife considers herself
economically independent and acts as an equal.

On the other hand, prejudices have been overcome, e.g., that the man is the head of the family,
etc. The patriarchal family is falling apart. Under
the influence of the revolution, both workers' and
peasants' families show a strong trend toward
separateness, toward independent living, as soon
as they begin to feel economically secure.

Kuljkov: No doubt the revolution has wrought a
change in family life, in ideas about the family and
even about the emancipation of the woman. The
man is accustomed to being the head of the family. . . . Added to this is the religious question, the
denial of petty bourgeois needs of the woman—but
since not much can be accomplished with the available means, there have been scandals. The woman
on her part demands greater freedom; she wants
to leave the children somewhere, she wants to be

with her husband more often wherever he is. This is how all manner of scandals and scenes begin. Hence, divorce. *Ordinarily, the Communists' answer to such questions is that family quarrels and particularly those between husband and wife are a private matter.* [Emphasis added.]

We may well describe the difficulties of the "religious question" and the "denial of petty bourgeois needs of the woman" as expressions of the contradiction between family ties and the aspirations for sexual freedom. The lack of facilities, such as rooms for privacy, was bound to lead to scandals. The attitude that sexuality is a "private affair" was detrimental. Members of the Communist Party were faced with the task of coping with this revolution in personal living, but frequently resorted to legal formulas because they had no answers. Functionary Markov understood this:

I call attention to the fact that we are approaching a terrible calamity inasmuch as we have misinterpreted the concept of "free love." The result is that with this free love the Communists have produced innumerable children. . . . If the war has brought us innumerable invalids, the wrong interpretation of free love will reward us with even more cripples, and *we have to declare honestly that we have done nothing in the area of educating the working masses to a proper understanding of this question. And I am of the opinion that if someone asks these questions we will be unable to answer them.* [Emphasis added.]

Unquestionably the Communists had the *courage* to cope with the problem. But it will be shown that this courage was useless because they could not resolve the difficulties with the knowledge available to them.

Anyone who looks at these statements from the viewpoint of later developments must conclude that it

was like a magnificent symphony in which the chords
and themes of the finale were already imperceptibly
hinted at in the opening sounds. They were themes
announcing a tragedy.

The Communist functionary Koltsov warned:

> *These questions are never discussed; it is as
> if they are avoided for some reason* [emphasis
> added]. Up to now I have never thought them
> through. . . . For the moment, these questions are
> new to me. I regard them as extremely important.
> One ought to ponder them. I think that for the
> same reasons, although undefined, they don't get
> into the press.

And functionary Finkovsky recognized one of the
reasons for avoiding these questions:

> . . . Discussions on this subject are seldom
> started because *they strike too close to the
> core.* . . . *I think they haven't started yet because
> they might cause embarrassment* [emphasis
> added]. . . . Everyone understands that a way out
> of this fraud might be for the state to take com-
> plete responsibility for the education and care of
> all workers' children, freeing the woman from the
> kitchen, etc. The Communists usually invoke the
> beautiful future and thereby evade any discussion
> of the question. . . . The workers know that in this
> matter the Communists' families are even worse
> off than they are.

Zeltlin showed his revolutionary instinct when he
said:

> The literature does not even mention the ques-
> tion of marriage and the family, the question of the
> relationship between husband and wife. *But these
> are precisely the questions that interest the workers
> of both sexes. If we make these questions the sub-*

*ject of our gatherings, the workers hear about it
and fill our meetings.* Furthermore, the masses feel
that we gloss over these matters in silence, and that
is just what we are doing. I know that some of
them say that the Communist Party holds no specific opinion on this question, and *cannot* hold an
opinion. *Workers of both sexes raise these questions often and find no answer to them.* [Empha-
sis added.]

These views of workers, totally untrained in sexology and drawing solely on their feeling for life,
are worth more than lengthy treatises on the
"sociology of the family." They prove that the abolition of the authoritarian power of the state laid bare
a critique and conviction which were formerly invisible. Zeitlin knew nothing about sex-economy and
yet described exactly what it contends: the interest
of the average person is not oriented toward state
politics but toward sex politics. He expressed the
mute criticism of the masses with regard to the
avoidance of sexual questions on the part of revolutionary leadership. He determined correctly that
proletarian leadership, in acting this way, obviously
had not formed an opinion and hence had to be eva-
sive. Yet it was precisely these questions for which
the average person awaited an answer.

There was also criticism of what were regarded
as merely historical reflections on topical questions,
on the inability to put a living theory to the test.

Gordon reports that a lecturer who was supposed
to speak about the sexual question talked only about
Engels' *Origin of the Family,* adding nothing of his
own:

Of course I don't want to say that this is bad,
but one should have drawn conclusions from
Engels' work with reference to the present; and
this is precisely what we cannot do. Therefore it
has now become an extremely burning question.

Thus the functionaries emphasized the interest of the masses in clarification and a new order of sexual relationships. They were asking for good, inexpensive literature on the subject. They talked about "family" and meant sexuality. It was known that the old order was decayed and untenable, but they looked for the new order with old concepts or, even worse, with economic information alone. Let us visualize how this looked in reality. A functionary in Moscow, Lyssenko, tried to understand the "phenomena of the street," which were generally disquieting. It was observed that children "were up to mischief." For instance, they played "Red Army." The "bitter taste of militarism" as recognized but regarded as "good." At times, "other" games were seen which were "worse," i.e., sexual, and there was general astonishment that no one interfered. Yet people were racking their brains as to how the children could be steered "onto the right path." The revolutionary element was revealed in the feeling that no one should "interfere"; but conservative sexual anxiety brought on troubled thoughts. If the old mode of thinking, in the form of sexual anxiety, had not confronted the new one, there would have been no concern about "steering" children onto the "right," meaning the asexual, path. One would have carefully observed the sexual expressions of children and faced the question of how to handle a child's sexuality. But since childhood and sexuality could not be viewed as related people became frightened, and natural expressions, which probably appeared in a turbulent form because they were socially unorganized, were regarded as degeneracy. "We must find out," it was said, "what children should read; maybe something about athletics or some other useful subject."

Revolutionaries warned: "We are often told that we speak only of earth-shaking matters, that we should instead talk about things that are closer to life. We must turn our attention to the small matters in life."

Concretely applied to children's games, this clearly means:

1. Should we favor these games or not?
2. Is the child's sexuality natural or not?
3. How should we understand and regulate the relationship between childhood sexuality and work?

The control commissions were worried but the functionaries comforted them. "The control commission need not shake its head in confusion. The Communist will go and live with the workers; he will do his job among them, i.e., he will keep them in check. For, if we do not live with them, we will lose touch with the masses." However, the task of the Communist was not only to keep in close contact with the masses but also to use this contact for specific purposes. To want to keep the masses in check meant that one did not know how to cope with the new life expressions of those who had just thrown off the chains of authoritarian power; it meant erecting a new compulsory authority in place of the old one, with its same meaning. However, the task was to organize a *new* type of authority in order to lead the awakening life of the masses toward independence, enabling them finally to do without constant authoritarian supervision.

Unable to formulate it in so many words, responsible workers faced the decision whether to go ahead toward new forms of life or to go back to the old ones. Since the Communist Party had not formed any opinion on the sexual revolution, and since they could not master the revolutionizing upheaval of life with the historical analysis of Engels alone (which furnished merely the social background but not the essence of the problem), a struggle broke out which will show all future generations the birth pangs of a cultural revolution.

At first, one took comfort in alluding to the need for purely economic prerequisites. But the attitude of "first the economic questions, then the problems of everyday life" was wrong and merely exposed the unpreparedness for the seemingly chaotic forms of the cultural revolution. Often, it was just an evasion. A society which, in the depth of poverty, bleeds from the wounds of a civil war and cannot immediately and adequately organize public kitchens, laundries, and kindergartens, first has to think of the simplest economic essentials. These prerequisites of a cultural revolution, and particularly of sexual life, were understood correctly. In a backward, authoritarian country like Tsarist Russia, the first steps had to be taken to educate the masses of workers and peasants to cleanliness, to brushing their teeth, to stop cursing and spitting. But it was not merely a question of raising the masses to the cultural level of capitalist countries; that was only the most immediate task. From a wider vantage point one had to become clear in one's mind about the *quality* of the "new culture," the socialist Communist culture.

In the beginning, no one was at fault. The revolution had collided with unexpected problems, and the practical experience for overcoming such gigantic difficulties could be acquired only when the difficulties themselves had fully developed and required a solution. Retrogression is inevitable unless such a envelopment is seen and understood in time. We must not forget that this was the first successful social revolution. There was a serious struggle to recognize its purely economic and political prerequisites. But today it is evident that the cultural revolution raised infinitely more difficult problems than the political revolution did. This cannot be otherwise, for political revolution requires "only" a steeled, trained leadership which has the confidence of the masses. Cultural revolution, however, requires the *restructuring of the masses*. It cannot be achieved with figures and statistics, and the concepts needed for its scientific elucidation barely existed. Here is a brief look at the results.

On August 29, 1935, the journal *Weltbühne* published an alarming article by Louis Fischer on the growing reactionary sexual ideology in the Soviet

Union. That a leftist journal would publish this article shows the seriousness of the situation. The article emphasizes the following facts:

Young people find no privacy for their love life in the crowded homes of the city. The girls are warned that abortion is harmful, dangerous, and undesirable; it would be much better to have children. A film, *The Private Life of Peter Vinogradov,* promotes conventional marriage—"a film," as Fischer writes, "that would be approved in the most conservative quarters of certain conservative countries." *Pravda* writes: "In the land of the Soviets the family is an important and serious matter." Louis Fischer feels that the Bolsheviks never really attacked the family. They knew of course that at certain times in man's history there was no family, but they did nothing to undermine it; on the contrary, they had strengthened it. The regime which no longer needs to fear [!] the parents' bad influence now welcomes their "necessary moral and cultural influence," i.e., the sex-suppressive function of the older generation toward the new.

In 1935, a *Pravda* editorial announced that a bad paterfamilias could not be a good Soviet citizen. "This was unthinkable in 1923," Fischer writes. At the same time, the following also appeared: "In the Soviet Union, only great, pure, and proud love should be cause for a marriage." And: "Anyone contending today that it is petty bourgeois to show interest in the family belongs himself to the lowest category of the petty bourgeois." An injunction against aborting the first child would probably put an end to many love affairs and to promiscuity and would further "serious marriage." In recent months the newspapers have been crammed with articles by academicians and clinical experts describing the great damage caused to the body by abortion.

"If the press thunders every day against abortion; if this propaganda is accompanied by praise of festive marriage ceremonies; if the sanctity of marital obligations is stressed and if it is proclaimed that mothers giving birth to triplets or quadruplets receive special prizes; if articles are written about women who never resorted to abortion; and if an underpaid village teacher, the mother of four, is openly praised because she did not reject a fifth 'even though it is hard to feed them all,' then one thinks of Mussolini," Fischer writes. "One has gained inner and outer security and therefore believes that birth control can be reduced. . . . One will also fight against cheap 'summer affairs.' Girls who resist the urgings of men are no longer regarded as conservative or even 'counter-revolutionary.' Not the gratification of physical needs, but love should be the basis of the family."

This brief résumé shows that the sexual *ideology* of leading circles in the Soviet Union does not differ from that of the leading circles in any other country. The return to life-negating sexual morality cannot be disputed. The only question is how the more relaxed young people who have tasted freedom, e.g., the industrial workers, will react.

The social ideology of the Soviet Union also affected Western Europe. We read in *L'Humanité* of October 31, 1935:

> *Save the family!* Help us on November 17 to organize our great investigation in the interest of the right to love.
>
> It is known that births in France have decreased with alarming rapidity. . . . Therefore the Communists are confronted with a very serious fact. The country which, according to their historic mission, they are supposed to transform, the French world which they plan to put on the right track, threatens to become crippled, stunted, depopulated.
>
> The malice of dying capitalism, its immorality, the egotism it develops, the misery it creates, the social diseases it propagates, the secret abortions it provokes, are destroying the family.

The Communists want to fight in defense of the French family.

They have broken once and for all with the bourgeois, individualistic, and anarchic tradition which makes sterilization an ideal.

They want to take over a strong country and a populous race. The U.S.S.R. will point the way. But we will have to take immediate measures to save the race.

In my book *The Misfortune of Being Young* I have spoken of how difficult it is for today's youth to have a home and I have defended their right to love.

The right to love, the love of man and woman, of the one for the other, children's love, parents' love, shall be the subject of this new investigation. . . . It is supported by the letters of our readers who report on their difficulties, fears, and hopes.

This is an investigation which will examine the means of saving the French family by giving motherhood and childhood and the family with many children the rank and advantages they should have in this country. Write to us, young people, write to us, fathers and mothers. . . .

[signed] P. VAILLANT-COUTURIER

These are the thoughts of a Communist who competes with the National Socialists in the race theory and the concept of the large family. Such an article in a Communist organ is nothing short of catastrophic. The competition is hopeless; the Fascists understand this business much better.

Arrogant criticism and a know-it-all attitude would only be the sure signs of a complete misunderstanding of the situation. There has to be respect for the greatness, complexity, and diversity of the tasks. It is the most important prerequisite for the necessary seriousness and courage which such historical processes demand.

In the Russian cultural revolution a "new life"

broke through, unrecognized, misunderstood, but the old forms of life impeded it. The old thinking and feeling sneaked into the new. At first the new element freed itself from the old and battled for clear expression, but it did not find it and sank back again.

Let us try to understand in what manner the old suffocated the new, so that we will be better prepared the next time.

From the course of the Russian revolution, we must learn that economic revolution, expropriation of private ownership of the means of production, and the political establishment of a social democracy (dictatorship of the proletariat) automatically go hand in hand with a revolution in attitudes toward man's sexual relationships. Just as the economic and political revolution, so the sexual revolution must be consciously understood and guided forward.

What does this "forward," which has been preceded by the disintegration of the old order, really look like? Only very few know how fiercely the struggle for the "new life," for a gratifying sexual life, raged in the Soviet Union.

X

The Retarding of the Sexual Revolution

1. THE PREREQUISITES FOR THE RETARDATION

About 1923 the first steps of a development were noted which was directed against the upheavals in personal and cultural life; it was not until 1933 to 1935 that they were expressed in reactionary legislation. This process is best described as the retarding of the sexual and cultural revolution in the Soviet Union. Before we investigate its important symptoms, we will have to familiarize ourselves with some of its prerequisites.

From an economic and political viewpoint, the Russian revolution was consciously guided by the Marxist doctrine of the economy and the state. Everything that occurred in the economic sector was measured, and essentially confirmed, by the theory of historical materialism. But for the cultural revolution—let alone its core, the sexual revolution—neither Marx's nor Engels' investigations contained anything that would have been suitable to guide the leaders of the revolution in a similar manner. In his critique of a pamphlet by Ruth Fischer, Lenin himself emphasized that the sexual revolution as well as the process

of social sexuality in general had not been understood
at all from the viewpoint of dialectical materialism,
and that it would take enormous experience to master
it. If someone, he said, would comprehend this question in its totality and real importance, he would
render the revolution a great service.[1] We have
learned from the functionaries that here was entirely
new territory to be explored. In his writings on culture, Trotsky also showed that the field of cultural and
sexual revolution was new and little understood.

Therefore, first of all, the Soviet sexual revolution
had no theoretical basis.

A second prerequisite for the later successful
retardation was that all those who might have been
called upon to understand and guide the spontaneously developing process of the sexual revolution were
caught in the old concepts and formalisms. To a large
extent the concepts of conservative sexology were
taken over, without anyone stopping to consider that
a clear distinction between the useful and the worthless
elements would have been necessary for the revolution.

Some of the false concepts which contributed heavily to the retardation were: the idea, which still exists,
that sexuality is antithetical to sociality; and the prejudice, which also still exists, that sexual life is a
"diversion from the class struggle." Sexpol in Germany found out about the ineradicability of these
erroneous concepts in a very unpleasant manner. People did not ask: What kind of sexuality is a diversion
from the class struggle? Under what conditions and
suppositions does sexual life divert energies from the
class struggle? Under what conditions and suppositions can the sexual crisis be totally absorbed into
the class struggle? Rather it was said: Sexuality itself,
as a fact, is at variance with the class struggle.

The alleged incompatibility of sexuality and culture was taken over from the old moralistic concept in
which sexuality and culture are made to appear as

---

1 From a conversation with Clara Zetkin.

absolute opposites. Furthermore, the whole question of the sexual process, i.e., the forms of the gratification of sexual need, was obscured by speaking of the "family" instead of "sexuality." However, a superficial glance into the history of sexual reforms would have shown that the patriarchal family is not intended to protect sexual gratification but is a sharp opposite to it. It is an economic institution and as such restricts sexual drives.

Another precondition for the inhibiting process was the widespread dissemination of incorrect, economistic views about the sexual revolutionary. According to these views, with the fall of the bourgeoisie and the enactment of Soviet sexual legislation, the sexual revolution had "already been accomplished"; or the sexual question would be resolved "spontaneously" once the proletariat had taken power. It was overlooked that sexual legislation and the seizure of power were only the external prerequisites for the restructuring of sexual life. They were not life *itself*. The plot of ground that one buys for building a house is not the house itself; it is only a prerequisite before the actual task of building the house can begin. For instance, G. G. L. Alexander, of Moscow, wrote in the journal *Die Internationale* (1927, No. 13):

> With the solution of the large social question, with the abolition of private property, the question of marriage, which is basically a question of property, was also resolved in principle. . . . The Communist view consistently proceeds from the fact that, with the step-by-step realization of Communism, i.e., with the development of basically different organizations of social life, the marriage problem will disappear as a social problem. . . . Unrequited love, with its loneliness and pain, will scarcely play a role in a society which sets collective tasks and offers collective pleasures, in which individual pain can no longer weigh so heavily.

On the question of the future form of sexuality, he continues:

> If Communism means the dissolution of the family within the community—and the development in Soviet Russia points in that direction—it is clear that with this kind of dissolution of the family the marriage problem will also disappear.

This manner of comprehending difficult problems of mass psychology is misleading and dangerous; e.g., if the economic basis of society and its institutions is changed, then human relationships automatically change themselves. That these relationships become independent and, in the form of the psychic, sexual structure of men in a certain era, become an independent force which influences economy and society, can no longer be doubted after the success of the Fascist movement. To disregard this means to eliminate living man from history.

Briefly, matters have been oversimplified; the ideological upheavals had been derived all too quickly from the economic basis. This has nothing to do with Marxism.

What are the forms which express the often quoted and little understood "repercussion of the ideology on the [economic] basis"?

The woman with a strict marital and familial orientation becomes jealous when the man begins to participate in public life. She fears that he will become involved with other women. The patriarchal jealous man behaves in the same manner when his wife awakens politically. He fears she will become unfaithful. Parents, even proletarian ones, do not want their growing daughters to join organizations. They are afraid they might become "depraved," i.e., begin to have a sexual life. Children should join the Pioneers or the collective, but the parents make their old claims on them. They are horrified if the child begins to look at his parents with a critical eye. These examples can be multiplied ad infinitum.

Many an attempt to deal with such problems ended with the meaningless slogan of "raising culture and the human personality."

The revolutionary view that the distinction between nature and culture should be eliminated and that nature should be brought into harmony with culture was correct. But when it came to devising a practical solution to these problems, the old habits, in the form of antisexual, moralizing attitudes, sneaked in.

Batkis, the director of the Institute of Social Hygiene in Moscow, wrote in his pamphlet *The Sexual Revolution in the Soviet Union*:

> During the revolution, the element of eroticism, of sexualism, played only a subordinate role because youth was completely carried away by the revolutionary élan and lived only for great ideas. But with the quiet times of reconstruction it was feared that youth had now cooled off and would follow the path of unlimited eroticism, as in 1905. . . .
>
> On the basis of experiences in the Soviet Union, I contend that the woman who had experienced liberation and became familiar with public social work, also experienced a certain sexual frigidity during the transition from mere female to human being. Her sexuality was repressed, even if only temporarily. . . . It is the task of sexual pedagogy in the Soviet Union to bring up healthy men and women, citizens of a future generation in full harmony with their natural drives and the great social mission which awaits them. The guidelines for this would be: to further everything creative and constructive that is latent in the natural drives, but to eliminate everything which could become harmful for the development of the personality of the member of the collective. . . .
>
> . . . Free love in the Soviet Union is not an un-

reined, wild living out but the ideal relationship
between two free, independent people in love.

Thus, while starting out correctly, even the otherwise clear Batkis remains stuck in slogans.

The sexuality of youth is characterized as "sex-
ualism," the sexual problem as an "element of eroticism." It was calmly stated that women experienced
a certain frigidity, that they turned from a "mere
female" into a "human being"; everything that was
harmful to the development of the personality had
to be eliminated (of course, what was meant was
sexuality), and "unreined, wild" sensuality was confronted with the "ideal relationship" of "two free,
independent people in love." The masses were caught
in these concepts as in a net. If one takes a closer
look, one can see their complete emptiness or, rather,
their antisexual, i.e., reactionary, tendency. What
does "wild living out" mean? Does it mean that man
and woman in an embrace are not allowed to live
out their feelings? And what is this "ideal relationship"? Is the relationship ideal if the couple is
capable of full "animal" surrender? Yes—but then
again they are "wild." Briefly, these are mere words
which, instead of grasping the reality of sexual life
and eliminating the contradictions that govern it,
obscure truths in order to avoid any contact with
such embarrassing matters.

Where did the thinking go wrong? In not dis-
tinguishing between the pathological sexuality of
youth, which runs counter to its cultural tasks, and
healthy sexuality, which is the most important
physiological basis of social accomplishment; in the
contrast between "mere female" (sensual woman)
and "human being" (actively sublimating woman),
instead of seeing the psychic basis of her revolutionary
emancipation and activity in the woman's sexual self-
awareness; in making the distinction between "living
out" and "ideal relationship," instead of regarding
the capacity for full sexual surrender to the beloved

partner as the most secure basis of a companionable relationship.

2. MORALIZING, INSTEAD OF UNDERSTANDING AND MASTERING

It was one of the most important characteristics of the retarding process that the upheavals and chaotic conditions produced by the sexual revolution were judged morally, instead of being understood as the sign of a revolutionary transition. People shouted that chaos had broken out and that discipline would have to be reintroduced, that "an inner discipline must replace outer coercion." "The value of the ties between husband and wife" was emphasized; people spoke of "individual culture." As an "inner discipline" was being spoken about, the old element had sneaked in in new guise. Inner discipline cannot be exacted; it either exists or it does not. In asking for an "inner discipline" instead of external compulsion, one still exercised coercion. One should have asked: How do we achieve voluntary discipline in people without having to force them? The "equality of the woman" had a revolutionary ring. Economically, the principle of equal wages for equal work had been achieved. With regard to sex, the woman's claim of equality with the man was originally uncontested, but this was not the main point. The point was whether the women were emotionally capable of making use of this guaranteed equality. Were the men ready for it? Were they not all characterized by a structure which was antisexual, moralistic, timid, depraved, lecherous, jealous, possessive, neurotic, and ill? First of all, it was necessary to understand the events, to comprehend the chaos, to distinguish the revolutionary from the reactionary, inhibitory forces, to know that a higher form of living can be born only amid pain.

The retarding of the spontaneous sexual upheaval soon crystallized around various centers. At first, the high-ranking Soviet authorities remained passive. The complaints of the functionaries show that the leaders were blind to what was happening, or else underestimated it. The formula "We will solve the sexual question later; the economy comes first" was often heard. The press was exclusively or predominantly at the beck and call of economic interests. Whether there were publications devoted exclusively to the problems of the sexual revolution, I do not know.

The influence of intellectuals was crucial. By their very structure, background, and thinking they had to be *against* the sexual revolution. They idolized the old revolutionaries who, owing to their difficult tasks, could not have a gratifying sexual life, and without qualms they transferred this ascetic form of living to the masses as an ideal. This was harmful. One can never expect from the masses what great tasks require of the leadership. Why should there be such a demand anyway? Fanina Halle praises this ideology in her book *Die Frau in Sowjetrussland* [The Woman in Soviet Russia], instead of explaining that this ideology was catastrophic for the influencing and restructuring of the masses. She writes (on pages 101, 110, 112) about the old revolutionaries:

. . . They were all young, these women revolutionaries, some of them radiantly beautiful and artistically gifted (Vera Figner, Ludmilla Wolkenstein), feminine through and through and thus made for happiness in their personal lives. In spite of their capacity for intense relationships with their male comrades, however, the personal and erotic element, the woman herself, was relegated to the background in favor of a general love for mankind which overshadowed everything else. And the strong trait of chastity, purity in the relationships between the sexes, which left its imprint on the entire generation of intellectuals and those who came after them, as well as the comradely atmosphere in Russia student circles, often misunderstood in Western Europe, still rules between man and woman in the Soviet Union and astounds time and again those foreigners whose attitude toward this problem is quite different. . . . This complete detachment from all philistinism, this absolute rejection of all social barriers which encircle those who struggle to be free, have furthered the growth of pure, intimate, comradely relationships based on common intellectual interests and a warm, serious friendship in a way that can seldom flourish freely. . . .

. . . With an even greater enthusiasm, some of these women who had been imprisoned devoted themselves to mathematics, and they were called fanatics because they had reached such a level of tension that even their dream life at night was preoccupied with mathematical problems. . . .

Again, it is not explained specifically and in a manner understandable to the ordinary mortal whether a so-called "pure" relationship between man and woman permits or prohibits the genital act; whether a "pure" relationship includes or precludes a vegetatively uninhibited surrender and release, which temporarily suspends all culture and intellectuality. It is completely pointless to set up an ideal for the masses whereby mathematics becomes such an intense sensation as to replace the most natural need of all living beings. We cannot admit that such an ideology is honest and true to reality. This is not what life is like! The revolution does not have to defend and safeguard fraudulent ideals, rather it should uphold the real life of sexuality and work!

In 1929, I heard in Moscow that youth was being sexually enlightened. I could see at a glance that this enlightenment was *anti*sexual, e.g., lectures on venereal disease to discourage sexual intercourse;

no trace of an open discussion about adolescent sexual conflicts, only instructions on procreation.

When I asked at the Narkomsdrav, the People's Commissariat for Health, how masturbation among adolescents was treated, the answer was that "of course" one tried to "divert" youth. The medical point of view, which in Austrian and some German sexual-counseling centers had become a matter of course, that a guilt-ridden adolescent should be counseled so as to enable him to experience gratification in masturbation, was rejected as horrendous.

The answer of Madame Lebedeva, director of the Office for the Protection of Mothers, to the question of whether adolescents should be instructed in the necessity and use of contraceptives was that such measures could not be brought into harmony with Communist discipline. On the same evening that a Narkomsdrav representative had revealed his timidity in sexual matters, I visited a youth group in a glass factory on the outskirts of Moscow and conversed with adolescents about various questions. Finally we got to the topic of girls, and I reported the opinion of the Narkomsdrav representative. There was hearty laughter, and the adolescents reassured me that they did not bother about such things and knew how to handle themselves. That was their opinion. It turned out that they had no place to go with their girl friends, that they had grave reservations about resorting to masturbation, that, in brief, they found themselves in the typical conflicts of puberty.

Some poorly understood pronouncements of Lenin's were invoked in a particularly harmful fashion to inhibit the sexual revolution. Lenin was extremely reserved in making specific statements about sexual questions. His true understanding of the tasks of the revolution in this field was evident when he said: "Communism is not supposed to bring asceticism but joy in life and vitality by means of a gratified love life." But thanks to the reactionary sexual convictions of responsible circles, what became most widely known was that passage of Lenin's, in his conversation with Clara Zetkin, which dealt with the "chaotic" sexual life of adolescents.

The changed attitude of adolescents toward the questions of sexual life is of course "basic" and refers to a theory. Some describe their attitude as "revolutionary" and "Communist." They honestly believe that this is the case. But I, as an older man, am not impressed. Although I am anything but a gloomy ascetic, it sometimes seems to me that the so-called "new sexual life" of youth—and even of the older generation—is often purely bourgeois, an expansion of the good old bourgeois bordello. But all this has nothing to do with the freedom of love as we Communists understand it. You no doubt know the famous theory that in Communist society the gratification of instinctual life, the needs of love, is as simple and inconsequential as drinking a glass of water. This "glass of water" theory has driven part of our young mad, quite mad. It has become fatal to many young boys and girls. Their adherents claim that the theory is Marxist. I want none of such Marxism which directly deduces all phenomena and transformations in the ideological superstructure of society from its economic basis. Things are just not that simple. . . .

It would be rationalism, not Marxism, to reduce the transformation of these relationships to the economic basis of society by taking them apart and severing their connection with the total ideology. Of course, thirst wants to be quenched. But will the normal person under normal circumstances lie down in the gutter and drink from a dirty puddle? Or drink from a glass greasy from many lips? More important than anything else is the social aspect. Drinking water is really an individual matter. For love, you need two, and a third

being may be conceived. This fact involves an obligation toward society.

Let us try to clarify what Lenin meant here. First
of all, he rejected the economism which directly infers
all culture from the economic basis. He recognized
that youth's rejection of tender relationships in sexual
life was merely the old conservative view in another
guise. Furthermore, he realized that a life based on
the glass-of-water theory was nothing but the absolute
opposite of ecclesiastical ascetic ideology. Lenin also
knew that this was not the desired, sex-economically
regulated life; it was antisocial and ungratifying. What
then was missing in Lenin's formulation? First of
all, a *positive* view of what would replace the former
life among adolescents. Since there were only three
possibilities—abstinence, masturbation, or a gratifying heterosexual love life—Communism should have
established one of the three as a guideline. Lenin
assumed no programmatic attitude, but he did reject
the sexual act devoid of love and pointed in the direction of a "happy love life," which precludes both abstinence and masturbation. Lenin never endorsed abstinence! But, as we said before, this passage of his
about the glass-of-water theory was quoted time and
again by the fearful and the moralizers to support
their pernicious views in the struggle against adolescent sexuality.

The well-known Communist Smidovitch wrote in
Pravda:

> Youth seem to believe that the most primitive
> view of sexual life is Communistic, that every-
> thing that goes beyond the borders of a primitive
> view, which might apply to a Hottentot or an even
> more primitive version of an aborigine, is phils-
> tinism and a bourgeois attitude toward the sexual
> problem.

She had nothing positive to say, except to express
her deep disdain of aborigines and to sneer at the

violent battle waged by adolescents for a new form of sexual life. Instead of understanding and helping, instead of developing something new from the old forms, la Smidovitch summarized the sexual ideology of young Communists in order to ridicule it:

1. Every member of the Komsomol (the Communist youth organization), every Rabfakov (a student of the workers' faculty), and every other greenhorn can, and may, live out his sexual drive. For reasons unknown, this is valid as irrefutable law. Sexual abstinence is condemned as "petty bourgeois."

2. Every little Komsomolka (female member of the Communist youth organization), every Rabfakovka, and any other female student who has been selected by this or the other boy—why among us, in the North, such African passions have developed is beyond my knowledge—must be beholden to him, or else she becomes a "petty bourgeois" unworthy of the name of a proletarian student.

3. And now comes the third part of this extraordinary trilogy: the pale, harassed face of a girl who thinks she will become a mother—with the touching expression of a pregnant woman. In the waiting rooms of the Commission for the Approval of Abortion you can see and read many such tortured stories about a Komsomol love affair. . . .

From this attitude radiates the pride of the "Nordic," i.e., the sexually "pure" human being, the Smidovitch, in contradistinction to the typical sub human, e.g., the Hottentot. But the simple means of preventing pregnancies among youth—instructing them in the use of contraceptives and providing hygienic conditions for a sexual life—did not occur to the Nordic. The words of Smidovitch were even displayed on German billboards as "Communist sexual ideology!"

And, as always when people dare not face the reality of adolescent sexuality, the Soviet Union, after a period of grave conflicts with adolescents, resorted to the slogan: Abstinence! A slogan which was as convenient as it was catastrophic and impossible to realize. Fanina Halle reports:

> The older generation, which was drawn into the discussion—scholars, sexual hygiene experts, party functionaries—at that time endorsed a view similar to Lenin's which Semachko, the People's Commissar for Health, summarized in a letter to students:
>
> "Comrades: You have come to the universities and technical institutes in order to study. This is now the main goal of your lives. And even as all your impulses and views are subordinated to this goal, as you must deny yourselves not infrequently many extraneous pleasures because they would be detrimental to your main goal—that of studying and becoming educated collaborators in the reconstruction of the state—by the same token you will have to subordinate all other activities of your life to this same goal. For at this time the state is too poor to support you, to undertake the rearing of your children, and to care for parents. Therefore we advise you: Abstain!"

And what invariably follows abstinence appeared also in the Soviet Union: sexual delinquency.

We must register an energetic protest against the misleading invocation of Lenin. Lenin never advocated asceticism for youth. Who believes that Lenin was so benighted as to see in "joy in life and vitality by means of a gratified love life" the asceticism of impotent scholars and warped sexual hygienists?

We should not reproach the leaders of the Soviet Union, who carried the responsibility in those crucial years, for not solving the existing difficulties. But they ought to be blamed for evading these difficulties, for resorting to the line of least resistance and greatest failure. As revolutionaries, they did not stop to consider what all this meant; they talked about the revolution of life but did not seek this revolution in life itself or try to master it in those terms. They regarded the real chaos as a "moral chaos" in the sense of political reaction and not as a chaos of a transitional nature leading to other forms of sexual living. And last but not least, they should be blamed for rejecting the incipient understanding of the problems of sexual life, which German revolutionary sex politics had disclosed to them.

What exactly were those difficulties which, once they had become so great, led to the retarding process?

First of all, a sexual revolution runs a different course from an economic one; not in forms which could be grasped in legislation and planning but in the tortuous, subterranean, emotionally charged, myriad details of daily life. To master the sexual chaos by coping with these details is impossible if only because they are too numerous and complicated. Consequently the theory arises that "private life impedes the class struggle; hence there is no private life!" Of course one cannot try to escape the chaos by mastering each single case individually. This would not correspond to our basic view that problems should be solved on a mass basis and not individually. Still, there are some individual difficulties that concern millions. For instance, there is the question which preoccupies and burdens every halfway healthy adolescent: how can he be alone with his girl? There can be no doubt that the solution of this question alone, i.e., to make it possible for youth to be together sexually without being disturbed, would win over all adolescents because they would feel understood. It would also, at one stroke, eliminate an essential part of the chaos. For if four thousand adolescents in one neighborhood do not know where they can embrace their girls, they do it in dark corners and behind walls; they disturb each other, provoke jealousy and quar-

rels, feel unsatisfied, become angry, and are driven
to excesses. In brief, they create "chaos." But in none
of the existing political organizations and associations
can one find an unequivocal demonstration of support
for providing facilities for adolescents with the explicit
purpose of enabling them to have an undisturbed
sexual relationship. This is only *one* detail of what
Sexpol tried to realize with the slogan "politicization
of private life."

3. OBJECTIVE CAUSES OF THE RETARDING PROCESS

The retarding processes as described up to now
stemmed from the lack of training and the prejudices
of responsible functionaries. But the élan of the revolution was so great that these obstacles would have
been overcome in spite of individual functionaries
and old reactionary academicans if there had not
been difficulties in the *objective* process itself which
supported the insecurity of the officials. Hence it would
be wrong to say that the sexual and cultural revolution
in the Soviet Union had foundered on the ignorance,
sexual timidity, and anxiety of its leaders. This would
be a subjectivistic view, contrary to historical materialism. The retarding of a revolutionary movement of
the dimensions of the Soviet sexual revolution can
come about only if there are weighty, objective obstacles. They can be grouped as follows:

1. The laborious rebuilding of society from the
old to the new, especially in the face of the cultural
backwardness of old Russia, the civil war, and
famine.

2. The lack of a scientific theory of sexual revolution
which would have mastered the tumultuous course
of events. Let us not forget that the Soviet sexual
revolution was the first revolution of its kind.

3. The sex-negating structure of people in general,

i.e., the specific form in which a sexually repressive patriarchy had preserved itself for thousands of years.

4. The genuine entanglements and complexities of such an explosive and comprehensive area of life as sexuality.

These four groups are not all-encompassing, but they offer us a perspective on those objective premises which supported the inhibiting action of individual functionaries.

There can be no doubt that the civil war between 1918 and 1922, which had been preceded by a devastating three-year war, provoked an almost grotesque and dangerous trend in the deterioration of the old forms of living brought about by the social revolution. The dreadful years of starvation, 1921 and 1922, reduced the psychic and material level of the suffering people and produced large-scale migrations. According to the reports of Kollontay, Trotsky, and many others, thousands of families inhabiting whole townships were forced to leave their homes to try to make a living elsewhere. It was not unusual that mothers deserted their children and husbands deserted their wives on the road. Many women had to sell their bodies for their own and their children's mere subsistence. The number of neglected children rose to tremendous proportions. Under these circumstances, youth's craving for sexual freedom assumed different forms than it would have under quiet conditions. The painful and restless struggle for clarity and a new order was replaced by the brutalization of sexual life. No one knew exactly what should replace the old order. Basically, this brutalization revealed a structure which from time immemorial has characterized patriarchal man and which has remained more or less concealed, though on occasion it has exploded into excesses. The so-called sexual chaos was no more the fault of the revolution than was civil war or famine. The revolution had not wanted civil war. It had only overthrown

Tsarism and driven away the capitalists and it had to
defend itself when those who were expelled wanted to
regain the lost ground and their former power. The
sexual chaos which now followed was, among other
things, a consequence of the fact that the aging functionaries did not know how to deal with the old character structure which was incapable of enjoying freedom.

If we examine the opinions and judgments of responsible Soviet leaders on the chaos which developed, we can state unequivocally that a fear of sexual freedom, well known to us, clouded their view
of the real difficulties and their causes. The victims
and supporters of the sexual revolution were accused
of losing all sense of responsibility; but for thousands
of years a corrupt sexual morality had prevented
the growth of the capacity for sexual responsibility,
which is firmly tied to a fully developed genital structure. Youth in particular was accused of letting relations between the sexes become looser and looser.
It was forgotten that really healthy and responsible,
genitally gratifying relationships had never existed;
and what had never existed could not be loosened.
What had actually relaxed was the compulsion of
economic dependence in family relationships and
the pressures of an antisexual conscience in youth.
What went to pieces were not healthy sexual relationships but an authoritarian morality which had
kept the people in a state of inner rebellion; a morality
which achieved precisely the opposite of what it intended. There was no need to mourn its passing.

Whenever explanations for prevailing conditions
were needed, there was nothing but helplessness. For
instance, the casual sexual relationships among youth
(as later among youth in Germany, where they were
taken for granted) were interpreted as the result of
an economic emergency. This was incorrect. Economic deprivation alone never leads to casual relationships, except in the form of prostitution. No
distinctions were made between those abuses that

sprang from the civil war and the difficult economic situation and the manifestations of a new life which, in itself healthy and optimistic, must have looked like "sexual chaos" to those burdened with the old concepts. Sexual intercourse between a boy of seventeen and a girl of sixteen can be chaotic or healthy. It is chaotic, sexually uneconomic, harmful to the young, and socially dangerous if it takes place under poor external circumstances, with sick structures, with anxiety, under the pressure of a moralistic conscience which makes gratification impossible; in brief; if it is pervaded by the chaos of our time. It is part of the life-affirmative sexuality of the future if it occurs under favorable circumstances with young structures capable of experiencing happiness in love, fully aware of the value and importance of this love life, without feelings of guilt and fear of authorities and unwanted children whom no one can raise. There is a great difference between two sex-starved men who rape a woman or wheedle her into sexual intercourse by getting her drunk, merely to empty themselves into her, and two independent people of the opposite sex, conscious of their sexuality and capable of enjoying it, who during a vacation spend only one happy night together. There is a difference between a man irresponsibly deserting his wife and children because of a superficial realtionship and the man who, because he is sexually healthy, makes an unbearably oppressive marriage which he cannot dissolve more bearable by maintaining a secret happy relationship with another woman. These examples may suffice to show what we mean:

1. What looks like chaos to persons twisted by an authoritarian sexual order need not necessarily be chaos; on the contrary, it may be the expression of an organism rebelling against impossible conditions of life.

2. Much of what is really chaos is not the moral failure of youth but the manifestation of an insoluble contradiction between natural sexual needs and a

society which opposes their gratification in every manner and form.

3. The transition from a life that is actually chaotic but gives the appearance of order to one that is genuinely ordered but, to the philistine, appears disordered cannot be achieved except by passing through a phase of grave upheavals.

Moreover, consideration for social stability alone is not the deciding factor. We must understand that people of our era develop a boundless fear of precisely the kind of life they yearn for but which they cannot cope with emotionally. While the sexual resignation into which the majority of people have fallen means dullness, desolation, paralysis of every activity and initiative, or is the basis for brutal, sadistic excesses, it also offers a relative peace and quiet. It is as if death has been anticipated in this particular kind of life; one lives toward death! And this living death is preferred if the psychic structure cannot deal with the uncertainties and violent emotions of life. Think only of the jealousy with which power politics does not concern itself but which nevertheless plays a far greater role in the background of major political events than anyone suspects. Think of a person's fear of not finding a suitable partner after having lost a previous one, even if he was a torment. Think further of the thousands of murders that are committed because the idea of the partner embracing someone else is simply unbearable. This fact plays a much larger and more significant role in real life than do the travels of a politician like Laval. Parliaments can trample on the people and dictators can do as they please supported by the masses as long as people wrestle unceasingly, unconsciously, and hopelessly with the most personal difficulties and needs that touch the core of their lives. In a city of a hundred thousand people one ought to seek out all the women who grieve and torture themselves because of their troubles with raising children, the infidelities of their husbands, their own sexual inadequacy or their lack of gratification, and ask them what they think of Laval's diplomatic trips. Their answers will prove that millions of women, men, and adolescents are too preoccupied with their personal problems to realize that they are being treated abominably.

XI

Abolition and Subsequent Reinstatement of Laws Against Birth Control and Homosexuality

1. BIRTH CONTROL

From the beginning, there was complete clarity with regard to birth control. The basic features of the revolution in legislative policy and social hygienic attitudes were the following:

Only when the responsibility for the rearing of children is assumed by the whole community can one contemplate explicit birth control and population policies. As long as a society is neither willing nor able to undertake this responsibility, it is not entitled to require that mothers bear children against their will or in spite of the prevailing economic distress. All women therefore were entitled to interrupt a pregnancy during the first three months. The abortions were to be performed in public obstetric clinics. Only those who carried out secret abortions without permission were severely punished. These measures, it was hoped, would uncover illegal abortions and do away with the activities of charlatans. They succeeded in the cities, but in the country it was much harder to persuade women to give up their old views. This reinforces our opinion that the abortion problem is not only a legal matter; it is also conditioned by the sexual anxiety of women. The secrecy and shame which have surrounded all sexual life for thousands of years prompt a simple worker or peasant woman to go to a quack midwife rather than to a clinic, even if the latter is available.

No one ever thought of making abortion a permanent social feature. The Soviets clearly intended that the legalization of abortion would be only one means of opposing quackery. The principal goal was *to prevent abortion* by thorough instruction in the use of contraceptives. The Soviets, composed of workers and peasants who exerted strong pressure on intellectuals and physicians, knew very well that the legislative and sanitary measures would have to be supplemented by other steps before the conception of a child would become a happy event for the woman.

The taboo against the unwed mother soon disappeared. Progressive inclusion of women into the production process gave them an economic independence and security which not only made motherhood less difficult but also made it seem much more desirable. Fully paid pregnancy vacations, which began two months prior to childbirth and ended two months after it, were introduced. Increasingly, factories and peasant collectives arranged for nurseries and clothing and for the training of competent nurses who could take care of the infants while their mothers worked. Women were not required to do hard work at the beginning of pregnancy or in its advanced stages; they were also assured that once they resumed work they did not have to worry about their children. Anyone who saw the Soviet Russian infant and child cribs (*yasli*) could no longer doubt that the Soviet system was extremely effective in making improvements in social hygiene. Women received bonuses during the entire period they nursed their children. The budget for mother and infant care rose from year to year in almost geometric progression. Hence it is not surprising that the decline in birth rate, so feared by timid philistines and moralists, did not take place; on the contrary, over a period of ten years births in the Soviet Union increased on the average of three to four million per year.

The Soviet government made every effort to penetrate to the most remote regions of their vast country. For instance, mobile birth-control units were organized. Trains equipped with all that was needed for birth control covered the provinces. That it took ten to twelve years of hard work to reduce illegal abortions to a minimum shows the power that sexual timidity exerted on the masses, preventing immediate acceptance of useful measures.

As always, the self-evident sex-hygienic principles clashed with the reactionary convictions of hygienists of the old school. As always, the masses had a sure instinct for these vital questions. The "trained" expert in social hygiene, however, has so many arguments, pro and con, that he acts like the centipede that could no longer walk when it learned it had a hundred legs. Let us find out at which point in time and by what means the reactionary forces were able to gain influence in questions concerning abortion and ultimately to inhibit its use.

A historical statistical presentation of the abortion problem is not needed; there are innumerable good books on this subject. We only want to try to understand the dynamics of the conflict between the progressive and the reactionary forces. The ethical, disguised religious argument not only preserved but became more successful in the course of time. Here, as always, reactionary morality can be recognized by its empty phrases. From the beginning, the reactionary forces fought against the complete revolutionizing of the use of abortion, partly with old arguments taken over from Tsarist times and partly with new ones adapted to Sovietism but no less reactionary. One heard that "humanity would die out," that "morality would disintegrate," that "the family must be protected" and that "the desire to have children" must be strengthened. People prattled about the emotional and physical turmoil that women would experience. As always, however, the greatest worry of political reaction was whether the birth rate would decline.

We must distinguish between reactionary arguments which are meant sincerely and those which, subjectively and objectively, are nothing but empty pretexts intended to avoid the vital questions of sexual life. These cultivated people are genuinely concerned with preserving "morality," meaning the non-fulfillment of love needs, so that the family does not founder. In the discussion about abortion it becomes increasingly clear that the unconscious dread of genital activity clouds the assessment of real needs in an irrational manner.

One pretext turns on the worry that humanity might die out; another on the idea of protecting germinating life. The gentlemen who endorse these ideas do not realize that in nature everything multiplies a million-fold, perhaps because there are no educated population politicians to hinder it. It is neither arrogant nor false but absolutely accurate to contend that population politics, as it is practiced today, is in its vagueness and dishonesty an apparatus of sex negation, a means of diverting people from the problems involved in transforming conditions so as to make sexual gratification possible.

Unmistakably Fascist-National Socialist tendencies were expressed in the views of those persons whose first duty should have been to the mothers rather than to the "state." If one has concern for the mothers, the revolutionary state is automatically protected.

In 1932, at the Congress of Kiev, Dr. Kirilov expressed the following opinion:

> . . . We regard the interruption of the first pregnancy as particularly dangerous in terms of the woman's possible subsequent sterility. We therefore consider it our duty to prevent the mother

from aborting and, at the same time, to ascertain why she wants an abortion. But we find in the answers scarcely anything motherly, scarcely anything about an inner struggle and search; in 70 percent of the cases the reason given is a "love that failed." A brief comment such as "He left me," "I left him," and toward the end some scornful remark about "him" or herself: "What kind of a man is he anyway?" In the women's answers *we almost never find an indication of a germinating family as the initial unit of society*.

Not free love as a protest against old bourgeois family marriage, not free love as an unconscious selection of eugenics, but a frivolous feeling culminating in the decision: to the hospital! *Unbridled haste to surrender the grown young body*, as a result of the transition to new, not yet crystallized forms that have arisen out of the sexual chaos! *. . . I have to compare work in the field of abortion with the extermination of the first-born in ancient Egypt who had to die because of the sins of their fathers* who devastated man and society. This kind of abortion must be suppressed as a socially negative, misshapen phenomenon of life. It must be replaced by a persistent effort to enlighten. A change in psychological mood, in the sense of recognizing motherhood as a social function, is absolutely mandatory. . . . Conclusions:

Criminal abortion is an evil practice based on the awareness that abortion is legal. . . .

Social abortion often wrongly protects *the distorted caricature of sexual problems* and new forms of life which have not yet crystallized. It blocks the road to motherhood and often diminishes the woman's success in public life. Therefore it is alien to true communal living.

Abortion seems to be a mass means of destroying a new generation. It does not have the inherent intention of serving mother and community and is therefore alien to the clear goals of protecting maternal health. . . . [Emphasis added.]

In contrast to these phrase makers whose structure and thinking would enable them at any time to adapt themselves to Fascism, there were sexologists and physicians who, with little theoretical knowledge and acting solely on the true instinct they had acquired in their practice, endorsed the correct revolutionary viewpoint. Among them was Klara Bender, of Breslau. In 1932, September 11–14, there was a conference in Frankfurt of German groups affiliated with the International Criminological Association. Bender courageously argued against the bigots when they attempted to play off the statements of reactionary population politicians in the Soviet Union against revolutionary abortion policies.

The talk about physical and emotional damage was nonsense, she rightly said, as long as the interruption of pregnancy was carried out under proper hygienic conditions. The concern about a decreased population was refuted by the actual results in the Soviet Union. The prattling about the "female primitive instinct for a child" was revealed as nonsensical when confronted with the brutality which made it impossible for women to raise their children properly. Abortion under capitalism was simply a matter of finances and the abortion law was therefore a transparent class law, driving women without means to the quack. In Moscow's clinic for birth control, however, in one year there was not one fatality among 50,000 abortions.

The inefficacy of such clear arguments is always astounding. Anyone who attended the discussions on birth control and abortion in Germany about 1930 could not avoid the impression that reactionary population politicians and hygienists of the caliber of a Grotjahn were in no way concerned with rational arguments. It was reminiscent of the discussions on the Nazi's reactionary race theory in which it had

been clearly shown that benighted prattlers and impotent, but all the more vain, academicians could not
be convinced, even after the most laborious proofs,
that the Germanic Nordic race was *not* the most
superior race in the world; that, for instance, the
baby of a Negro need not be less intelligent and charm-
ing than that of a German. If these were reasonable
debates, revolutionary argumentation would have
long ago defeated the ideologies of reactionary population politicians and race theorists. But both were
supported by irrational forces anchored in the thinking of the masses, which could not be reached by reason alone. Reactionary population politicians succeed
because hundreds of thousands, even millions of
women have an unconscious fear of genital injury
and therefore vote against their better interests to
preserve the murderous abortion law. The same unconscious fear was revealed in the collection of signa-
tures by Christians against the repeal of the abortion
law in Denmark in 1934. Race theorists exist only
because the German citizen can compensate for his
feelings of inferiority when he hears that he belongs
to the "leading," "most intelligent," "most creative"
race, namely, the Nordic. We must emphasize that
irrational ideas like the race theory and today's
eugenics cannot be eliminated by rational arguments
alone; the rational arguments must rest on the firm
foundation of powerful natural feelings. It is not a
question of "putting across" an igeniously reasoned
theory of sex-economy; social life itself, if the revolution allows the source of human life to flow anew,
reveals the facts which are described by the sex-
economic concept. For the moment we are not concerned with procreation, but only with the protection
of sexual happiness. The fact that the problem of
birth control in the Soviet Union was not confined
to private associations and groups but was officially
and nationally debated in a positive manner was
already a tremendous step forward. This alone made
it possible for a courageous and intelligent revolu-

tionary like Selinsky to throw the following excellent arguments into the faces of the conservative authorities:

> Considering all the lectures on the harmfulness of free abortion that have been given at this Congress, my comments will seem heretical. But a good doubt is better than a bad conscience. It is hard to believe in the social honesty of those speakers who, with their coats properly buttoned and their backs turned to human problems, have stubbornly presented us with abstract truths about abortion. It is as if we dealt with blindness, a social nearsightedness, or a social hypocrisy. These people do not see, or do not want to see, those real conditions, those socioeconomic and psychological conditions of the masses in which the abortion epidemic runs its course. The verdicts on abortion contain more moralizing prejudice than objectivity. Many horror stories have been told on the subject. We have been scared off with just about everything: infection, perforation of the uterus, deterioration of the nervous system, with a decline in the birth rate, the burial of the instinct for motherhood, and the degeneration of the nation. But one is tempted to say with Tolstoy, "They frighten me, but I am not afraid." Operations in the dark, operations in dim corners, working with a crowbar. But is not probing down into the stomach and further into the duodenum also a work in the dark? And are not the manipulations with the esophagoscope like work with the crowbar? And if you inject into the veins everything including sublimate, thereby irritating the tender tissues of the intima, do you know in advance the consequences of such actions? And if, for diagnostic reasons, without any medical symptoms, you blow out ovarian tubes and inject acid solutions for an X-ray examination—does all this do no damage to the organism? In any event, we

cannot dispense with all this, and never will. Is the connection between hormonal disturbances and abortion an irrefutable fact? Why do the city women, who regularly turn to abortion when they have reached thirty, Balzac's favorite age, continue to compete successfully with friends in their twenties in terms of the suppleness and beauty of their bodies, while their conscientiously childbearing sisters in the country look like death in their thirties after six or eight births, dried out like squeezed lemons? Apparently hormones are not the simple answer. And who says that giving birth to fewer children harmfully affects a person's looks? I insist that under certain circumstances it can even be helpful. Gardeners know that when a chrysanthemum shrub has too many blossoms it has to be trimmed to save the shrub from dying off and to produce large, full flowers. . . . Of course, the chrysanthemum shrub can also be forced to yield more magnificent flowers, but then the condition of the soil must be changed and the cultivation of the shrub must be improved. Change the culture, and these statistics will show different figures, of different dimensions . . . and they will speak a different language about abortion. Look openly into the eyes of life and you will see under what socioeconomic and psychological conditions women must live and give life to another human being. The family, with its instability and transitory character, does not guarantee women the necessary conditions for rearing their children. Alimony payments do not always fulfill their purpose. The man who is obligated to pay alimony but does not have the money is of greater theoretical interest to lawyers than of practical interest to women. Contraceptives are unreliable. The right to motherhood is not always realizable because only those earning 40 to 50 rubles per month are in a position to make use of this right, while many women are unemployed. Remember in

a Zola novel how an illegal abortionist scorns
an accredited physician: "You push the women
into prison and into the Seine; we, however, pull
them out of it." Do you want the "dragging out of
the Seine" to be turned over again to illegal abortionists? One of the speakers called out in fright:
"A physician's prescription and a woman's wish—
that's all that is needed for the abortion." Yes,
and this is how it should be: the will of the woman
is sufficient because the right to determine her social needs belongs to her alone, and to no one
else. We men would never tolerate it if some commission were to decide, according to its social
viewpoint, whether or not we could marry. Therefore, do not prevent women from taking care of
themselves and deciding the cardinal question of
their lives. Women have the right to a sexual life
and should be able to realize it just as men do.
This is essential to guarantee their social and biological equality. There should be no mass production of old spinsters who would only be harmful to
the collective.

Selinsky, with his true instinct, came forward at
the very time when sexual reaction in the Soviet Union
was about to eliminate free birth control and abortions
by means of commissions, decrees, and so-called
humanitarian pretexts.

Thus, at the aforementioned congress there was
a grave struggle between sex-affirmative and sex-
negating views of population control. For example,
the possibility of reintroducing the abortion law as
a means to stem the rising number of abortions was
seriously discussed. Yefimov, a People's Commissar,
felt that abortion was such an "obvious biological
and psychic sexual trauma for the female organism
that further proof was irrelevant." In spite of this,
he considered abortion a lesser evil than its prohibition.
Of course criminal abortion, which still existed, had
to be fought by all available means. Yefimov shared

Selinsky's opinion that prohibiting abortions would not decrease their numbers and would "drive women back to the abortion mills." Furthermore, the socioeconomic conditions of life and the raising of the cultural level absolutely require birth control. "What is better," it was asked, "a humanitarian attitude toward those not yet born, and with it a burden on today's family, or birth control?" Yefimov's answer was correct: "The demands of life are stronger than humanitarian considerations. Present conditions are such that there can be no question of forbidding abortion."

Ten years after the legalizing of abortion, not only was sexual reaction not destroyed but, on the contrary, it was obstructing the revolutionary movement. Yefimov demanded a thorough investigation of contraceptives. He complained that contraceptives were openly sold in the streets of Moscow without any medical control; the doors were wide open to speculation and fraud. Benderskaya wanted contraceptives to be placed at anyone's disposal free of charge. Belinsky and Selinsky insisted on a medical prescription; uncontrolled dissemination of contraceptives might cause the population incalculable damage. The question of how to disseminate contraceptives remained undecided. No consensus could be achieved.

The concern about "population policies" was in reality apprehension about the "moral" behavior of the population. The enjoyment of sexual pleasure seemed incompatible with the desire for children. Dr. Benderskaya, for instance, endorsed the following principles:

1. To make abortion again punishable by law would bring about a great increase in the number of quack abortionists.

2. Quack abortions must be fought with the help of legal abortion.

3. The battle against legal abortion must be

fought by means of propaganda for contraception.

4. In a socialist society, the woman will exercise the function of motherhood according to the demands of the collective to which she belongs.

Point 4 instantly obscures the clarity of the first three points. By means of sex-hygienic measures it was intended to guarantee sexual freedom and pleasure; but giving birth would be subordinated to a moral demand, the "demand of the collective." It was overlooked that enjoying a child is a function of pleasure, the joy one takes in a new human being. No one ever has or will succeed in forcing women to bear children to oblige an external power. Either having children will be part of the general joy of life, in which case it will rest on firm foundations, or it will become a moral demand and, as such, an insoluble problem.

Why does population politics time and again run contrary to the sexual interest of the masses? Is this conflict insoluble, eternal? As long as there is hostility between nations, as long as there are national borders and customs barriers, as long as there is an interest in maintaining sufficient human cannon fodder for wars, population politics cannot be brought into harmony with the requirements of sexual hygiene. Since one dare not admit that a population increase is needed for such purposes, one talks about the "morality of procreation" and "the preservation of the race." In reality, women's refusal to bear children merely expresses the crisis in human sexual life. It is no pleasure to have children under poor living conditions with an unloved partner; moreover, sexual life itself has become a torment. Demographic politicians do not see this contradiction; they cannot see it because they represent nationalistic interests. Only if the social causes of war itself disappear, and society can turn to the building and securing of a happy life for all the people, will the contradiction between sexual happiness and population interests also disappear; for then the joy in sexual pleasure is translated immediately into the joy in having a child. With this, the motive for the demand to procreate is also eliminated.

The legalization of abortion contained an implicit affirmation of sexual pleasure which required a *conscious* transforming of the whole sexual ideology from sex negation to sex affirmation. According to statistics compiled by obstetricians at the congress, the majority of women—60 to 70 percent—were unable to enjoy their sexuality. There was talk of a "lack" of sexual drive, of its "attenuation," and it was claimed that the decrease in sexual potency could be traced to planned abortion. Medical experience with sexual disturbances refutes this contention. It is an attempt to conceal the abortion problem by all available means and to justify the prohibition of abortion. The majority of women are sexually disturbed, with or without abortion. Women have been known to have as many as fifteen abortions; many had had seven and some women had it performed two or three times a year. This is proof that women are afraid of using contraceptives; otherwise they themselves would demand an adequate supply of such devices. We know from our work in German Sexpol clinics that almost all women are dominated by this fear while at the same time they wish for nothing more fervently than the regulation of contraception. Women must be freed from this fear and we must express their burning, unspoken wish and see to its fulfillment. The elimination of the abortion law alone does not create the desire for children. There must also be an inner capacity and all the external prerequisites for a happy love life. Instead of eternally struggling with the question whether contraceptives should be dispensed by medical prescription or otherwise, it would be more important and useful to find out, from properly trained physicians and social workers, which contraceptives are most suitable for sexual gratification. What use is a pessary if the woman walks about with the sensation of carrying a foreign object inside her, thereby interfering with gratification? What use is a condom if it blunts sensations of pleasure and causes neurasthenic complaints? What use is the best propaganda for contraception unless there are enough factories to supply everyone with the best devices? What finally would be the use of those factories unless women overcame their fear of using contraceptives?

Although the congress fully endorsed legalized abortion, it did so in a general atmosphere of fear, fear of actually guaranteeing the opportunity for sexual gratification.

It was an atmosphere about which Fanina Halle reported in 1932:

> People aboard learned little about the protests of the older Bolsheviks, some of whom went far beyond Lenin and preached ideals that were virtually ascetic. The fable about the "socialization of women in the Soviet Union" was all the more energetically disseminated and even today is frequently recited particularly in anti-Soviet propaganda. Meanwhile, however, the flood of sexual interest has finally receded, and maturing Soviet youth, the vanguard of the revolution, momentarily faces such serious, responsible tasks that their preoccupation with sexual problems appears unimportant. In this way, relationships between men and women have again reached a stage of de-erotization which is perhaps developing on a more comprehensive scale than ever before. The platonic quality in the relationships between men and women which characterized a small group who paved the way for the revolution has now become a characteristic of the Russian masses. This time, the power which has accomplished this is called the "Five-Year Plan."

Soviet ideology is proud of the "de-erotization" of life and people. But this "de-erotization" is a figment

of the imagination. Sexuality continues to exist and,
lacking conceptual understanding, it exists in a
pathological, distorted, and harmful way. There is
no alternative of sexuality or sociality. The one alternative is socially affirmed, gratifying, happy sexual
life *or* pathological, secretive, socially ostracized sexual life. To the degree to which a seeming de-erotization—in reality, the degeneration of natural sexuality—makes the people of the Soviet Union sick and
antisocial, the responsible functionaries of the state
will feel they should strengthen the moralistic regulations and reintroduce the law against abortion. In
a vicious circle, suppressed sexuality will require further moral pressures, and the moral pressures will
increase the degeneration of sexual life. Professor
Stroganov has already complained that formerly
women were ashamed of abortion, "but now they
boast of it as their right; they acquired this right,
however, through the legalization of abortion."
Madame Lebedeva, director of the Organization for
the Protection of Mothers, remarked that legalizing
abortion had "unchained the woman's psychology."
Abortion had become a "life style," a fashion; it
was a kind of "psychosis" which, like an epidemic,
overran everything. Krivky thought that this "psychosis" was progressive; no one could predict when
it would begin to recede. The result of this "degeneration" of "morality" was that the woman's maternal
feeling had become dulled and deeply affected. Some
Soviet physicians were correct in concluding that
economic need did *not* play the dominant role in
the frequency of abortions. A foregone conclusion,
for otherwise a woman who does *not* suffer from
economic deprivation would not interrupt her pregnancy. In reality, abortion is a clear indication that,
above all, people want to enjoy sexuality without
having to bear children.

On the basis of all this confusion, sexual freedom
was considerably curtailed during the second Five-
Year Plan. Mothers carrying their first child were

not allowed to interrupt the pregnancy. Even if an interruption was indicated, the commissions quietly exerted heavy moral pressure. It is impossible to foresee the outcome of this development. It will not be decided on its own merits but by the outcome of the struggle in the Soviet Union between sex-affirmative, revolutionary currents and those of sex negation and reaction. It is to be feared that the tendency toward sexual revolution will not be able to gather sufficient force quickly enough to prevail over the old miserable rut of thinking. The result will then be a brilliant technological economy guided by neurasthenics and living robots; but it will not be socialism.

Let us summarize what has been learned from this struggle so we can be better equipped when society is again faced with the problem of reconstructing its life on a rational basis. The following will be essential:

1. The elimination of all pretexts and dishonest interpretations; e.g., the concern about preserving the race; the idea that economic need is the only motive for abortion. Removal of the separation between population politics and sex politics in general.

2. Recognition of the sexual function, independent of procreation.

3. Recognition of the will to procreation as a partial function of sexuality, the wish for a child as an expression of the pleasure in life. Recognition of the fact that when there is material and sexual gratification in life, joy in having a child is self-evident; that is, the child results from the enjoyment of life.

4. Open endorsement of the viewpoint that contraception serves not only the elimination of abortion but, primarily, the security of sexual pleasure and health.

5. Courage for the bold venture of supporting sex affirmation and self-regulation of sexual life.

6. Assurance that all saints, moralists, and other-

wise disguised sexual neurotics are without practical
influence.

7. The most rigorous control of the practice and
ideology of reactionary obstetricians by sex-political
organizations of women and adolescents. Ridding
the masses of their stupid respect for today's science;
only rarely does the latter deserve the name.

The goal of revolutionary population politics
should be to awaken the interest of the people themselves, without imposing "from on high" the obligation
of "preserving the race." Today, population politics
has no interest whatever in the average person. In
order to realize this goal, it will first be necessary
to affirm sexual pleasure and to safeguard it for all
those who participate productively in the social process. People must feel that they are fully understood
on this particular point and that everything is being
done to protect sexual happiness and to enable them
to enjoy it.

The solution of these problems will turn out to
be relatively simple when compared to the main question: how can the fear of orgastic pleasure (orgasm
anxiety) which is so prevalent today be eliminated
on a mass scale? This problem is unprecedented in
its magnitude and difficulty. Once it is solved, the question of population politics will no longer be resolved
by sexually timid academicians but by adolescents,
workers, peasants, scientific specialists—and children.
Until that time, population politics and eugenics will
remain the reactionary systems they are today.

2. THE REINTRODUCTION OF THE LAW ON HOMOSEXUALITY

Soviet sexual legislation, by a stroke of the pen, had
abolished the old Tsarist law on homosexuality which
punished homosexual activity with long prison terms.
This action was based on the idea that homosexuality

should be treated scientifically and that homosexuals should not be punished.[1] The walls separating homosexuals from society were to be torn down. This act of the Soviet government gave a tremendous stimulus to the sex-political movement in Western Europe and America. It was not only an act of propaganda; it could establish a precedent for the fact that homosexuality, whether inborn or the result of inhibited development, was an activity which harmed no one. This agreed with the thinking of most of the urban and rural population. The latter was extremely tolerant in all sexual matters, even if homosexual men or lesbian women on occasion became the butt of "good-natured jokes," as one reporter expressed it. In contrast, as in all countries, petty bourgeois groups were still under the spell of sexually ascetic views and medieval prejudices. These groups were represented in the middle and higher party hierarchy and their influence gradually spread to parts of the working class. As a result, two views on homosexuality emerged with increasing clarity:

1. That it was a "sign of barbaric unculture," an "obscenity derived from half-savage Eastern people."

2. That it was a phenomenon of "overbred culture of a perverse bourgeoisie."

These views, together with the general confusion about sex-political conditions and developmental possibilities, led to grotesque cases of persecution which gradually became more frequent. Legislation alone could not solve the problem.[2] According to sex-economy, homosexuality in the overwhelming majority of cases is the result of an early developmental disturbance of the heterosexual love function. With the general retarding of the sexual revolution,

---

1 In its presentation of sexuality, the official Soviet encyclopedia drew mainly from Magnus Hirschfeld and partly from Freud.

2 In spite of the elimination of punishment, homosexual persecutions continued among the Eastern people of the Soviet Union. About 1925, in Turkestan, an additional paragraph was added to the legislative code, calling for rigorous punishment of homosexuals.

homosexuality among adolescents, in the Army, Navy, etc., necessarily became more widespread. There was snooping and informing, ostracizing by Party committees and even "Party purges." Old Bolsheviks such as Clara Zetkin and others intervened in individual cases. But in the course of time, as a result of the unsolved sexual problem, homosexuality increased until, in January 1934, there were mass arrests of homosexuals in Moscow, Leningrad, Kharkov, and Odessa. These arrests were politically motivated. Among those arrested were many actors, artists, and musicians, who, because of their alleged "homosexual orgies," were sentenced to several years in jail or were exiled.

In March 1934, Kalinin[3] signed a law prohibiting and punishing sexual intercourse between males.[4] It branded such intercourse as a "social crime" punishable by three to five years in jail in less serious cases and five to eight years in cases of more fully established relationships. Thus homosexuality was reinstated with other social crimes: banditry, counterrevolution, espionage, etc. The homosexual persecutions to some degree paralleled similar measures in Germany taken in connection with the Röhm[5] affair in 1932–1933. The Soviet press opened a campaign against homosexuality as a "manifestation of Fascist bourgeois degeneracy." According to my information, the well-known Soviet journalist Koltsov wrote a series of articles in which he mentioned the "homosexuals of Göbbels' Ministry of Propaganda" and spoke of the "sexual orgies in Fascist countries." Maxim Gorki contributed an influential article, "Proletarian Humanism," in which he wrote: "The mind boggles when one thinks of the abominations

---

3 Then President of the U.S.S.R. [Editor]

4 According to a private source, this law was a kind of emergency legislation, since any legal changes could be made only by the Soviet Congress.

5 Ernst Röhm, Hitler's Storm Trooper lieutenant, a known homosexual, was killed for political reasons. [Editor]

that Fascism so abundantly spawns." What was meant was anti-Semitism and homosexuality. Then the article said literally: "While in the Fascist countries homosexuality is rampant, degrading the young with impunity, it has been declared a punishable social crime in the country where the proletariat boldly has taken over the power of the state. In Germany, there is already a slogan: exterminate homosexuality and Fascism will disappear."

We see with what vagueness and damage this concept of homosexuality evolved. Organized homosexuality, which actually formed the basis of Röhm's organization and that of others, was confused with the incidental homosexuality among sailors, soldiers, and prisoners which must be attributed to the lack of satisfactory heterosexual relationships. Completely overlooked was the Fascist ideological attitude toward homosexuality, which was also negative. On June 30, 1934, we may recall, Hitler exterminated the whole Storm Trooper leadership for the same reasons that motivated the persecutions of homosexuals in the Soviet Union. It is clear that nothing can be accomplished with such chaotic ideas about the relationship between sexuality and Fascism and about the general questions of sexual life per se. As a result of mass arrests, there was panic among homosexuals in the Soviet Union. Numerous suicides were reported among Red Army men and their commanders. Until 1934, there was no denouncing of homosexuals in the Soviet Union, but after these events it resumed. In contrast, the population sympathized with the homosexuals.

I shall restrict myself to this brief description. The relation of homosexual persecutions to the general sex-political situation, especially among the Eastern peoples, would require a more extensive statement than is necessary here. The sex-economic view on the question of homosexuality is presented in *Die Funktion des Orgasmus, Charakteranalyse,* and *Der sexuelle Kampf der Jugend.* To summarize, I may say:

1. Homosexuality is not a social crime; it harms no one.

2. It can be restricted only by restoring all the prerequisites for a natural love life among the masses.

3. Until this goal is realized, it must be considered on equal terms with heterosexual forms of gratification and should not be punished (except for the seduction of minors).

XII

The Impeding of the Sexual Revolution in Youth Communes

During the civil war years, Russian youth immediately assumed the dominant role to which it was entitled. Lenin fully appreciated the significance of its vitality for the revolution, and he turned his particular attention to the organization of youth, to raising their economic position and securing their future power.

Official recognition of the independence of youth in the economic process and in its relationship to the older generation was fully expressed in the decision of the Second Congress concerning youth associations: "The Komsomol is an autonomous organization with its own bylaws." As early as 1916, Lenin had emphasized: "Without complete independence, youth cannot produce useful Socialists from its own ranks."

Only independent, sexually healthy young people, acting without authoritarian discipline, could, in the long run, accomplish the enormously difficult tasks of the revolution.

The following will illustrate the sex-political character of revolutionary independent youth organizations:

257

1. REVOLUTIONARY YOUTH

Until about ten years ago, Baku was among the most reactionary, sinister places in the Russian empire. In the Russo-Turkish republic of Azerbaidzhan the revolution had claimed an enormous number of victims. It is true that the laws were changed by the revolution, that the economic foundation was restructured, that religion had been declared a private matter of the individual, but "under the newly built roofs, the old cruel discipline of the harem was still raging" (Balder Olden).[1] Girls were sent to religious institutions; they were forbidden to learn how to read and write, for a literate girl might establish contact with the outside world by writing a letter, she might escape from the institution, and bring disgrace down on her family. Girls were their fathers' serfs. When they were sexually mature, they became serfs of their husbands, whom they were not allowed to select themselves, whom they had never even seen prior to marriage. Women and girls were not allowed to show their faces to a man; fully veiled, they looked through the window onto the street. They were carefully guarded on the rare occasions when they were allowed to go outside. They were not allowed to work any more than they were permitted to read a book or a newspaper. It is true that they were legally entitled to divorce, but they did not know it. Although the knout had disappeared from Russian jails, women in the harem were still being beaten. These women had to give birth unaided because there were no midwives or woman physicians, and to show oneself to a male doctor was forbidden by their religion, which they practiced in secrecy.

In the middle of the 1920's, Russian women

1 An anti-Nazi German journalist. [Editor]

founded a central women's club which organized education. Gradually, education spread. The schoolrooms became crowded and girls listened to white-haired teachers (young men were not permitted to teach). Thus, many years after the outbreak of the social revolution, the "revolution of mores" began. These girls learned that there were countries with a coeducational system where women engaged in sports, went to the theater unveiled, attended meetings and took an active role in them, and generally participated in the life of their time.

This sex-political movement became widespread. Fathers, brothers, and husbands felt their interests were threatened when they learned what was being discussed at the women's club. They circulated the rumor that the club was a whorehouse. As a result, it became dangerous to visit it. According to a report by Balder Olden, girls who attended had been scalded with hot water and had dogs set on them. Even in 1923, girls who wore sports suits that exposed arms and legs risked death. Hence it is understandable that even the idea of a love relationship outside of marriage was far from the thoughts of even the most courageous women. In spite of all, there were many girls who, within themselves, had broken with tradition and were determined to take up the fight for the sexual liberation of young women. They were exposed to incredible martyrdom. They were of course immediately recognized; public opinion considered them lower than prostitutes, and none of them could ever expect that a man would marry her.

In 1928, the twenty-year-old Sarial Haliliva ran away from home, called meetings, and proclaimed the sexual emancipation of women. She went unveiled to the theater; she addressed the women in the clubs; she walked around in a bathing suit at the beach and in sports arenas. Her father and brothers held court over her, condemned her to death, and cut her up alive. This happened in 1928, eleven years after the outbreak of the social revolution. Her murder

provoked a tremendous upsurge of the sex-political
movement among women. Her body was taken away
from her parents and was placed in the club, where
an honor guard of boys and girls guarded it day
and night. Girls and women streamed in droves to
the club. Sarial's murderers were executed, and since
then neither fathers nor brothers have dared to take
similar measures against women's and youth movements.

Balder Olden describes these events as a general
cultural movement. More concretely, it was unquestionably a sex-political upheaval which, for the first
time, stimulated the cultural consciousness of women
and girls. By 1933, 1,044 girls were studying at
the university; there were 300 midwives as well as
150 women's and girls' clubs, which produced many
writers and journalists. The chairman of the Supreme
Court was a woman; another woman presided over
a Soviet commission. Women were trained as
engineers, doctors, and airplane pilots. Revolutionary
youth had won its right to live.

2. YOUTH COMMUNES

Youth communes are particularly suited to demonstrate the role of the adolescent sexual revolution. They were the first natural expression of collective life among youth which was then developing. A
commune formed by older people immediately runs
into the difficulties of rigid psychic reactions and habits.
However, at a younger age, and particularly during
puberty, everything is in flux; inhibitions have not
yet become structured. It was precisely the youth
communes that had an excellent chance to succeed,
proving thereby the usefulness of collective life and
the great progress it was capable of achieving. Let
us see what was accomplished in the communes in

terms of progressive revolutionary life and what inhibitions impeded this progress.

The Soviet Union realized very early that the
political organization of youth and the raising of its
living standards would have to be a primary task.
It was also realized that this alone would not suffice.
Bukharin tried to summarize the principal task by
saying: "Youth needs romance." This attitude
became necessary with the decline of the proletarian
youth movement which began when the civil war
ended and the New Economic Policy period formed
a transition from the stimulating events of those first
years to the less romantic period of laborious
reconstruction. "We must not address ourselves to
the brain alone, since before a man can understand
anything he must first feel it," was said at the Fifth
Congress of the Komsomol. "All romantic revolutionary material must be utilized to educate the young:
the underground work before the revolution, the civil
war, the Cheka,[2] the battles and revolutionary ex-
ploits of workers and the Red Army, technical inven-
tions and expeditions." Above all, it was said, a
literature would have to be created in which the
socialist ideal was presented "in inspiring form," in
which the struggle of the people with nature, the
heroism of the workers, and unquestioning loyalty
toward Communism was to be glorified. Thus the
enthusiasm of youth was to be kindled or maintained
with the help of ethical ideals. Revolutionary ideals
would take the place of bourgeois concepts and
ideals.

Specifically: the youth of bourgeois society likes
to read sensational crime stories. It is perfectly possible
to replace the content of the average crime story with
a revolutionary content. Instead of the pursuit of
a criminal by a detective, we have the pursuit of
a Tsarist guard by a member of the Soviet secret
police. But the young people's experience remains

---

2 The Soviet secret police, which fought counterrevolutionary elements.
[Editor]

the same: horror, thrills, being hounded and tensed; the result is sad.stic fantasies which are bound up with unrelieved sexual excitation. The formation of the psychic structure does not depend on the content of the experience but on the kind of vegetative excitation which accompanies it. A fairy tale of horrors has the same effect whether it deals with Ali Baba and the Forty Thieves or with the execution of a Tsarist guard. It is the creepy feeling which grips the reader, and not whether forty thieves or forty counterrevolutionaries are executed. If the revolutionary movement wanted simply to achieve preeminence for its ideas, then the replacement of one ethical ideal by another would suffice. But if the movement intends to change human structure, to enable people to think and act independently, then it must realize that the conservative Sherlock Homes cannot simply be replaced by a Red Sherlock Holmes, that conservative romanticism cannot be outdone by revolutionary romanticism.

The resolution of the Fifth Congress reads: "To influence the young, demonstrations, torchlight parades, banners, mass concerts must be used to the maximum extent." That was necessary, but it was only a continuation of old forms of enthusiasm and ideological influence. In Hitler's Germany, the same demonstrations, torchlight parades, flag consecrations, and mass concerts were conducted to effectively influence youth. The German adolescent was no less enthusiastic and devoted than the Komsomol. The difference is that Germany's Hitler youth promised unquestioning and uncritical devotion to the eternal leader without even daring to think of creating "a personal life according to one's own laws." The Komsomol, however, had the task of creating a new life for all working youth out of their own needs, to prepare young people to be independent, antiauthoritarian, happy in their work, capable of sexual gratification, able to make decisions and to think critically from convictions and not from obedience.

The young had to know that they were not fighting for some "Communist ideal" somewhere in the beyond, but that the Communist goal was the realization of their own independent lives. It is characteristic of authoritarian society that youth have no consciousness of their real lives and therefore they either numbly vegetate or blindly obey. Revolutionary youth, however, develops from the consciousness of its needs the most powerful and durable form of enthusiasm: a zest for living. To be "young" and "independent" also means to be sex-affirmative. The Soviet state had to choose between ascetic self-sacrifice and a sex-affirmative zest for life. In the long run, youth could be won over and restructured only with the help of an affirmative view of life.

In 1925, Lenin's Komsomol comprised one million, in 1927 two million, in 1931 five million; in 1932, the number reached almost six million. Thus the working youth had been successfully organized. But had this youth also been "made independent" and "restructured" in the meaning of the resolution of the Second Congress? At about the same time, scarcely 15 percent of peasant youth were organized in the Komsomol. Of the 500,000 young peasants who lived in farm communes where they could easily be organized, only 25 percent were in the Komsomol. Why were the remaining 75 percent not organized? The degree to which youth can be influenced is in direct ratio to the ability of youth organizations to understand their sexual and material needs, to articulate them, and to do everything possible to fulfill them. New forms of life are created only by new contents of life, and new contents must have new forms. The structural transformation of peasant youth must be different from that of proletarian youth, because the sex-political conditions of their life are basically different.

THE SOROKIN COMMUNE

During the revolutionary upheaval there were social organizations which, while characteristic for a period of transition, must not be regarded as the germinating cells of a future Communist order. Let us try to examine these organizations by looking at the now famous Sorokin Commune.

It is the prototype of a disciplined, authoritarian, antifeminist commune, based on homosexual ties, and not specifically communist-structured.

A young worker named Sorokin was working at a steam mill in the northern Caucasus. He read in the papers about the construction of "Autostroi," the largest automobile factory in the Soviet Union and decided he wanted to work there. He took technical courses in the next town and organized a special brigade among the students. When the courses ended, all forty-two graduates, infected with Sorokin's enthusiasm, applied for jobs at Autostroi. They arrived on May 18, 1930. Twenty-two young workers formed a workers' commune under Sorokin's leadership. Each one put his wages into a common fund from which all expenditures were paid. It was truly a youth commune; no one was older than twenty-two. Eighteen of them belonged to the Komsomol, one to the party, and three had no political affiliations.

The youthful enthusiasm with which they tackled their work, their ambition and indefatigability, soon annoyed the other workers. Even the director harassed and hounded them, instead of letting them work as a closed unit, which was their wish. But Sorokin succeeded in having the director removed. His successor was more sympathetic to the commune. It immediately reported for a very difficult project in which only 30 percent of the scheduled Five-Year Plan had been completed. A marshy stretch of land had to be dried out. Four commune workers, among them the only woman of the commune, left the project because it was too difficult. The eighteen who remained formed a solid, battle-happy bunch and worked like madmen. They were ruled by an iron discipline. They even decided that anyone missing more than two hours of work would be expelled. One of the commune members who was actually guilty of this delinquency was ruthlessly expelled although they all liked him.

Soon they had accomplished twice as much as the Plan required. The fame of the Sorokin Commune spread throughout the factory. Now the commune was used systematically wherever there were difficulties. It always inspired other workers. Sometimes the commune members worked twenty hours out of twenty-four. The intense activity bound them closely together; they succeeded in obtaining two tents where they could live and eat together. Thus they developed into a people's commune. The example they set was followed by others. When Sorokin and his comrades arrived, the whole plant had 68 brigades with 1,691 members (udarniki), with the Sorokin Commune being the only one of its kind. Half a year later, in the fall of 1930, there were 253 brigades, among them seven communes. In the spring of 1931, the number of brigades rose to 339, that of the udarniki to 7,023, that of the communes to thirteen. In honor of his achievements, Brigadier Sorokin was awarded the Order of the Red Banner.

These commune members remind us of collectivist groups of Red Front battle divisions in Germany. The exclusion of women alone characterizes them as atypical of the future Communist collective. Their structure is alien to the ordinary person. The tasks which the communes set themselves were heroic and no doubt necessary in the hard struggles of the transitional period. But they do not reveal the germ of a future development. We must learn to distinguish whether a commune develops from extreme need and merely getting used to one another, as happened with the brigade members, or from the natural demands of life. The development of many communes in the Soviet Union was marked precisely by its transitory character; common work and misery in the factory, in the Army, in the farm collective formed the cornerstone. People became accustomed to one another in the brigades, the way soldiers in the trenches become accustomed to one another. It was the primitiveness of living conditions that wiped out individual differences. The work collective developed into a full collective once the workers began to live together. But it was not an actual commune because only part of the individual's wages was put into the common money fund. In some collectives everyone contributes the same amount, regardless of his wages. According to another regulation, the members pay a minimum amount and beyond that a percentage of their income. It is different in the full communes, where the communards pledge their whole salary to the common fund. The full commune was regarded as the "highest form of communal living." Its development, however, showed that disregard for structural and personal problems led to a compulsive, authoritarian, and constricted form of living. For example, at the Moscow State Library there was a commune in which coats, shoes, and even underwear were at the disposal of all communards alike. If one of the communards wanted to wear his own coat and his own underwear, he was condemned as being "petty bourgeois." There was no personal life, e.g., it was forbidden to be more friendly with one communard than with another. Love was scorned. When someone observed that a girl liked a particular communard, both were attacked in a meeting as "destroyers of Communist ethics." After a brief time, the commune disintegrated (Mehnert).[3]

It is particularly important to study the failure of such communes if one affirms the commune as

---

[3] Klaus Mehnert: *Die Jugend in Sowjetrussland* (Berlin, S. Fischer Verlag, 1932).

the "future family form," as the future unit of human society, and if one wishes to preserve and promote it. Every distortion that contradicts man's nature and his needs, every kind of authoritarian, moralistic, or ethical regulation of life, must destroy the commune. The basic problem is how the commune can develop on the basis of *natural* and not moral conditions. As an example of how the contradiction between human structure and a form of living can lead to grotesque phenomena, let us look at the commune of the Berg Academy in Moscow. This commune decided not only to plan the finances but also the time of its members. According to Mehnert, the time-table was as follows:

7:30	Get up
7:30 to 8:45	Dress, breakfast, clean up
8:45 to 14:00	School
14:00 to 15:30	Lunch and rest
15:30 to 21:00	School and study at home
21:00 to 21:30	Dinner
21:30 to 23:00	Rest, reading
23:00 to 24:00	Newspaper reading
Total:	
Studying	10 hrs. 45 min.
Eating, resting, news-paper reading	4 hrs. 45 min.
Housework	1 hr.

The commune of the AMO plant, on the basis of thorough observation, provided the following statistics on the communard's average use of the twenty-four hours in the day:

1.	Factory work	6 hrs. 31 min.
2.	Sleeping	7 hrs. 35 min.
3.	Learning	3 hrs. 1 min.
4.	Eating	1 hr. 24 min.

5.	Political social activity	53 min.
6.	Reading	51 min.
7.	Diversions (movie, club, theater, walking)	57 min.
8.	Household	27 min.
9.	Guests	25 min.
10.	Hygiene	24 min.
11.	Undetermined	1 hr. 32 min.

24 hrs. 00 min.

This is compulsive statistics mania. Such phenomena are of a distinct pathological nature, the compulsion neurotic symptoms of a life guided by duty against which the communards had to rebel inwardly. The conclusion to be drawn is not that of Mehnert, who questions the possibility of collective living altogether. Rather, while collectivist forms of life are adhered to, a way must be found in which the structure of people can adapt to these forms. As long as the thinking and feeling of the communards contradict the collective, the social necessity will prevail in the form of conscience and compulsion. It is a question of closing the gap between human structure and the form of living, not by coercion but in an organic manner.

THE "BOLSHEVO" WORK COMMUNE OF THE GPU FOR DELINQUENTS

This was the first work commune organized for neglected, delinquent children, established at the instigation of Dzerzhinsky, director of the GPU, in 1924. The basic principle was that criminals were to be educated in complete freedom. The fundamental problem was how to organize them. This was resolved as follows. Two of the founders of the Bolshevo Commune discussed the undertaking with prisoners at the Butirki jail in Moscow. The prisoners were adolescents convicted of robbery, theft, loitering, etc.

The GPU proposal was: We will give you freedom, the opportunity for cultural development, lessons, participation in the building of the Soviet Union. Do you want to come along and found a commune? At first, the delinquents were suspicious; they would not, and could not, believe that the GPU which had arrested them now wanted to set them free. They thought it was a trap and rejected it. It was later revealed that they decided to look into the matter and then run off to continue stealing and robbing. Fifteen boys were given a leader, and some carfare and money for food. They also were given complete freedom to come and go as they pleased. Arriving at the site of the future commune, they searched the shrubs and hedges for hidden soldiers. When they saw an old iron gate they became suspicious and wanted to run off; they thought this was the walls of another prison. They were calmed down and convinced that nothing of the kind was intended, so they stayed. The increase of commune members to 350 and then to a thousand was due exclusively to the fifteen original boys. They first made a list of another seventy-five boys and guaranteed their behavior. They themselves sent a delegation to the jail to recruit the seventy-five new members.

Now there was the problem of how the work could best be organized. It was decided to establish a shoe factory for the neighboring population. The boys organized everything themselves. They arranged communes for household, work, and cultural evenings. At first their wages were 12 rubles monthly with free bed and board.

The neighboring population violently protested against the establishment of the commune of delinquents. They sent petitions to the Soviet government to try to stop the plan; they isolated themselves and were frightened.

Gradually, the cultural work began. A club was organized, a theater set up. The peasants in the neighborhood were invited to come. The relationship between the delinquents and their neighbors grew so harmonious that in the course of a year boys began to "marry" girls from the neighboring villages and towns.

Gradually, the small plants were turned into factories for sports equipment. In 1929, there was a shoe factory that turned out four hundred shoes and one thousand skates per day, as well as clothes, sweaters, etc. The wages were 18 rubles for newcomers and 100 to 130 rubles for older residents. Workers paid 34 to 50 rubles for their recreation, food, housing, clothing, and 2 percent of their wages went for cultural events. The newcomers faced the problem of subsisting on 18 rubles. The answer was: we will give you credit until you make enough money.

The plant had the same system of self-administration as did all the factories in the Soviet Union. A trio of directors was elected from the ranks and a delegation was elected to supervise the functions of the directorate.

Several commissions were set up to recruit new members, and the commune was steadily expanding. If, in 1924 and 1925, the delinquents had been afraid of joining the free commune, now the rush of delinquents into the commune was so great that the rank and file decided to hold entrance examinations for newcomers, in which they had to prove that they were really neglected delinquents and not noncriminal workers. It was ascertained exactly where the applicant was captured and imprisoned, what crime he had committed, which prisons he knew, how they were arranged inside, etc. If the newcomer could not answer these questions satisfactorily—and the commissioners knew their job well—he was not accepted. Non-prisoners were also not accepted. The list of candidates was submitted to a general meeting of the commune at which the newcomer had to tell about himself. If he was unknown, two members of the commune were appointed to take care of him.

The candidacy lasted six months. If the newcomer proved himself during that period, he was accepted into the commune on a permanent basis; if he did not prove himself, he could leave without embarrassment.

Gradually, a library, a chess club, a small art collection, and a movie house were established, operated not by high officials but by elected communards. There were also so-called conflict commissions. If someone did not show up for work or was late, he was officially reprimanded; if he lapsed again, money was subtracted from his wages. In the most serious cases, the commune sentenced the communard to one or two days of arrest. The "criminal" was given the address of a jail in Moscow. Entirely without escort or supervision, he went there, served his term, and returned happily to the commune.

In the course of the first three years, thirty girls joined the 320 boys. Apparently there were no sexual difficulties, because the boys had contact with girls in the neighborhood. In reply to my specific question, the director of the commune explained to me that the commune members counseled themselves when there were sexual difficulties but that coarser excesses rarely occurred. Sexual life regulated itself because love could be experienced without restrictions.

The Bolshevo Commune may serve as a model for educating young delinquents on the principle of self-government and unauthoritarian restructuring. Unfortunately, such communes were isolated institutions, and, for reasons unknown to me, the same principle was not followed in subsequent years. This is proved by reports after 1935. Let us not forget that by 1935 the general regression toward authoritarian social measures had already made serious inroads.

YOUTH IN SEARCH OF NEW FORMS OF LIVING

At the same time that the economy was being reconstructed with the help of the NEP, the organization of private communes played a dominant role. In collective homes the young were supposed to put into practice the Communist form of community life. Mehnert reports that later these aspirations were relegated to the background and, to my knowledge, no one has contradicted him. "One has become more sober," he wrote in 1932. "It is openly admitted that there is little sense in creating small islands in which the final stage of socialism, i.e., Communism, is anticipated while, all around, the country is still in the phase of liquidating the NEP, i.e., the very first beginnings of socialism. In spite of the sweeping élan with which they were developed, the creation of communes has been largely an exercise in confusion. Today they are no longer needed." This statement of Mehnert's is unsatisfactory. It is possible that the attempt to form communes was premature in the 1920's. Why did they fail? To this day the Soviet development is marked by serious struggles between new and old forms of living. The outcome of these struggles will decide the destiny of the Soviet Union. The question of youth communes is only a part of the whole problem. We cannot accept the idea that their formation was merely an "exercise in confusion." It is much more likely that this extremely serious and important step of youth foundered on difficulties created by lack of insight. Plainly, the new form of living could not maintain itself in the face of the rampant old one. Nevertheless, people in the Soviet Union already speak of "fully realized Socialism."[4]

4 "Under the leadership of the Communist Party of the Soviet Union, its Leninist Central Committee, and its great leader, Comrade Stalin, socialism has become definitely and irrevocably victorious." (Manuilsky in his speech to the Moscow and Leningrad parties on the results of the Seventh Congress of the Komintern.)

Let us look at a commune diary which Mehnert mentions:

It was the winter of 1924. Bitter need ruled the Soviet Union, particualrly the large cities like Moscow. People were drawn closer to each other through sharing common experiences—hunger, deprivations, lack of housing. The feeling of belonging together had become so strong that some friends graduating from school felt unable to separate. They still had not agreed on their plans, but after years of collective camaraderie it seemed impossible to return to their individual families. From this there emerged the idea of staying together in the future as one large family, the idea of founding a commune. Many wanted to participate, but the selection (they were bright enough to consider it necessary) was rigorous; the rejected applicants wept. After a long and fruitless search for an apartment, several rooms became vacant in a former saloon on the second floor of a house in Moscow's old city. On the first floor there was a Chinese laundry; the steam drifted up through the cracks. Only at night, between two and six, when work stopped, could one breathe more easily. But this did not matter. The members of the commune were happy to have a roof over their heads.

In April 1925, they moved in. The apartment: two bedrooms, a living room also known as the "club," and a kitchen. The furniture: some cots, two tables, and two benches. Ten people, five girls and five young men, were to build a new life here.

At first they intended to do the housework themselves. But soon the communards became so loaded down with outside tasks that, after their first enthusiasm was spent, they began to neglect the household. It was not long before the place was a mess. A few months later we read in the diary:

"October 28. The clean-up detail overslept. There was no breakfast. The commune was not cleaned. The after-dinner dishes were not washed (incidentally, there was no water).

"October 29. Again, no breakfast. Nor dinner
either. The dishes still not washed. The larder is a
mess and so is the toilet (the toilet is almost never
cleaned). Thick dust covers everything. The door
was left unlocked when we went to bed and in two
rooms the lights were left on (a common occurrence).
About two in the morning, our amateur photographer
started developing his films, all regulations to the
contrary.

"October 30. We have started cleaning up.
Everything is on the floor, on the window sills, on
chairs, thrown around on and spilled under the beds.
In the club, newspapers, inkstands, letters, fountain
pens are scattered across the whole room. On the
table there is chaos. The kitchen is still full of dirty
dishes, there are no clean dishes any more. The kitchen
table is stacked to its very limits. The sink is clogged
up with a dirty coating of fat. The larder is a hellhole.
The communards are apathetic, quiet, and some of
them even satisfied. Is this how we build a new life?"

A few days later it is decided to hire a housekeeper
(a wage worker). But is this not open exploitation?
After some reflection it is stated that "everyone is
forced, day in day out, to pay for outside services
in household matters: clothing is taken to the laundry,
a cleaning woman is hired to scrub the floor, shirts
are ordered from a seamstress. In principle, the em-
ploying of a housekeeper is the same, except for the
fact that all individual services are united in one person." Thus, housekeeper Akulina comes into the commune, and with her a certain order and cleanliness.

Nevertheless, after the first year of the commune,
the diary paints a drab picture. The relationships
among the communards are not pleasant: "The pressure of dark times has provoked nervousness and
irritability." Four of them are already gone. One girl
left because she was ruining her health in the commune,
so she said; the second explained she had to leave
because of the quarrelsome character of one of the
boys; the third married and moved in with her husband;

a fourth boy was expelled from the commune because he had secretly kept a part of his income of 160 rubles from the communal fund, and so had to be punished. Two girls and four boys remained. This was its nadir and a decisive crisis. With the summer, things were looking better. Soon there were eleven communards, five girls, six boys, all the same age, twenty-two or twenty-three, almost all students. Of the ten original founders of the commune, only four remained.

Every question, even the smallest, was discussed in full meetings. Several "commissions" were appointed to take care of the various facets of life: the finance commission had the difficult job of balancing the budget; the economic commission was responsible for purchasing food and keeping the home in order; the student-political commission devoted itself to questions of schooling inside the commune, took care of the library and newspapers, and maintained the connection between the commune and the youth organizations, expecially the Komsomol. The clothing commission took care of clothes, underwear, and shoes, and the hygiene commission paid attention to the health of the communards and purchased soap and tooth paste.

Organizationally, the commune adopted the forms of the state government—government by "commissions." But moral considerations were revived when the commune members had overcome the first difficulties of their material existence and when so-called private life reared its head.

The difficulties burdening the commune could be divided into those which resulted directly from material need and those that expressed structured sexual anxiety. It seemed as if "egotism," "individualism," and "petty bourgeois habits" were harming the collectivist spirit of the commune. An attempt was made to eradicate these "bad qualities" by moral discipline; an ideal was set, a moral principle of "collective life" against the "egoistic trend." Thus they tried to build an organization, whose principle was self-government and voluntary inner discipline, by using moralistic, even authoritarian means. Where did this lack of inner discipline originate? In the long run, could a commune tolerate the contradiction between the principle of self-government and authoritarian discipline?

The self-government of a commune is predicated on psychic health; this in turn requires all inner and outer conditions for a gratifying love life. The contradiction between self-government and authoritarian discipline was rooted in the contradiction between the collectivist life to which the communards aspired and their psychic structure, which was incapable of living it. The collective was supposed to offer a new home to those youth who were tired of the parental home and family life. But this youth which was antipathetic to the family also simultaneously longed for it. Therefore, they failed to establish the necessary conditions for a gratifying sexual life in the commune. The problem of chopping wood and other small everyday chores became insoluble only because of the entangled sexual relationships. At first, the communards set very fair requirements. The relationships would have to be "comradely." But it never became clear what "comradely" meant. It was rightly stressed that the commune was not a monastery and the communards were not ascetics. The bylaws of the commune said:

"We are of the opinion that sexual relationships [love] should not be restricted. They must be open. We must conduct ourselves toward them consciously and seriously. Uncomradely relationships bring about the wish for secrecy and dark corners, flirtation and other undesirable phenomena." In these few sentences the communards understood intuitively a basic principle of sex-economy: restriction of sexual relationships leads to "backstairs" sexuality. Were the communards brought up without these restrictions? Were they conscious of their sexuality and healthy enough to be able to follow this sex-economically sound collectivist principle? They were not.

It was soon proved that requirements and words could not solve the difficult problem of human structure. It was discovered that the desire of a couple to be alone, to surrender to love undisturbed, was by no means the result of an uncomradely attitude. Immediately the foremost problem of adolescent life in all social strata and in all countries was raised: *the lack of a room of one's own.* Every room was full of people. Where could one embrace without being disturbed? When the commune was founded no one had considered the number of problems that would result from the need to be alone together sexually. These realities of life could not be obviated by commissions and discipline. The constitution of the commune was later amended with a clause that was supposed to solve all difficulties with one stroke: "Sexual relationships among communards are not desirable during the first few years of the commune!"

The diary claims that this decision was maintained for two years. Considering all that we know about adolescent sexuality, we think this absolutely impossible. There is no doubt that sexual relationships took place in secrecy, invisible to the eye of the "commission"; and in this way a part of the reactionary world had to break into the new one. The first correct principle of the commune, to be open and honest in sexual matters, was broken.

THE INSOLUBLE CONTRADICTION BETWEEN FAMILY AND COMMUNE

The difficulties of life in the commune did not turn on whether girls or boys should iron and darn. At the core was the question of sexual intimacy. This is proved by the partly new and revolutionary and the partly constricted, anxious manner in which the communards tried to cope with the sexual problem.

The severe conflict resulted in the conclusion that family and commune are incompatible organizations.

At the start of 1928, this difficulty appeared in an acute way. On January 12, the following debate took place in a commune conference called by Vladimir:

Vladimir: I'm getting married. Katya and I have decided to marry. We definitely want to live together, and in the commune, because we cannot imagine life outside the commune.

Katya: I wish to apply for membership in the commune.

Semyon: How does Katya want to be accepted, as Mrs. Vladimir or simply as Katya? Our decision will depend on that.

Katya: I have intended to apply for a long time. I know the commune and want to become a member.

Sergei: I'm in favor of acceptance. If Katya had applied regardless of her marriage to Vladimir, I would have thought matters over. But this concerns not only Katya but also one of our communards. We must not forget this.

Lelya: I'm against being forced to accept a marriage partner into the commune. *First we have to weigh how the newly created family fits into the commune* [!]. I do think that Katya is highly suited for this experiment because by nature she is qualified for commune living.

Misha: At the moment, the commune is in a crisis. A marriage would mean forming a group within the commune and would further undermine its unity; that is why I'm against acceptance.

Lelya: If we don't accept Katya, we'll lose Vladimir. We've already lost him, almost. I'm in favor of acceptance.

Katya: Please consider my case without "extenuating circumstances"; I want to be a proper member of the commune, and not just the wife of a communard.

DECISION: Katya is accepted into the commune.

A new cot was placed in the girls' bedroom. Neither in the commune diary nor in Mehnert's description is there any concrete information about how sexual intercourse between the young communards took place. In principle, the problem of a communard's marriage had been resolved in a positive way, but the difficulties did not occur until later. After long debates it was determined that, because of lack of space and the financial limitations of the commune, children were not desirable. Their presence would prevent the students from studying and working quietly at home. The diary contains the following:

"Marriage in the commune is possible and permitted. However, it has to remain without issue because of the serious housing situation. Abortion is not permitted."

These three sentences contain more about the problems of the historic revolution in the Soviet Union than do thousands of pages of formal reports.

First sentence: *Marriage in the commune is possible and permitted.* There had been doubts that marriage was possible, and then it was permitted after all; one could not simply prohibit a love relationship. It occurred to no one that a formal marriage was not necessary for a love relationship because the concept of marriage in official Soviet ideology covered *every* sexual relationship. No distinction was made between a relationship tied to the wish for offspring and a relationship that stemmed purely from the need for love. Neither was there a distinction between short, transitory relationships and permanent ones; no one thought of the end of a short relationship or the gradual development of a lasting one.

Second sentence: *Marriage has to remain without issue because of the serious housing situation.* On the one hand, the communards recognized the pos-

sibility of marriage without children since there was
no place to raise them. But the real problem was
where sexual intercourse without issue could be engaged in. In German youth movement this problem was occasionally solved if an adolescent who had
a room was willing to place it at the disposal of his
comrades so that couples could be together undisturbed. Despite the overriding necessity for such a
measure, no party would have dared to establish it
officially as an emergency measure.

Third sentence: *Abortion is not permitted.* This
sentence expresses the conservative tendency to permit a love relationship but to prohibit abortion; in
practice this meant abstinence. The correct decision
should have been: "Since temporarily we cannot allow
children because of insufficient living space, you may
not have any children. If you want to be together,
use contraceptives and let us know when you wish
to be undisturbed."

The debates that followed this decision showed
how hopelessly the communards were entangled in
the idea that procreation and sexual gratification are
inseparable. Not all communards agreed with the
decision; some thought it was too sharp an interference
with the laws of nature, too coarse, muddled, and
harmful to health. A year later, when the possibility
for new and larger housing facilities arose, the resolution was replaced by another: "The commune permits
the birth of children." Again, the question of undisturbed sexual intercourse was not raised, although it
was truly revolutionary to regard the children of communards as the children of the commune, to be raised
at the commune's expense.

Here the contradiction was clearly revealed. The
commune was undoubtedly the new form of "family":
a collective of persons not related by blood which
was to replace the old family. But while the longing
for the collective stemmed from the protest against
familial restrictions, it was itself the expression of
a desire to live in a community similar to the family.

Thus a new family form was established, retaining the old form within its framework. The confusion was enormous. After conditions inside the commune had become consolidated, the idea of marrying arose and led to the following conclusion in a debate:

> If any of the communards wants to marry, this is quite in order, and the commune must not stand in the way. On the contrary, the commune must do everything possible to prepare the necessary conditions for family life.

The contradiction between family and collective was expressed specifically in the following questions: What happens when a communard wants to marry a girl outside the commune, a girl who does not fit into the framework of the commune? Must she be accepted by the commune or not? What happens when this girl from the outside has no wish to join the commune? Should husband and wife live separately? In this manner, one question spawned another. The communards did not realize:

1. That there was a contradiction between the new form of the commune and the old structure of the communards.

2. That the communes were incompatible with the old concepts of marriage and family.

3. That the structures of people living in a commune had to be changed. Nor would they have known how to accomplish this change.

The conservative concept of "marriage" was connected with the idea of the insolubility of the relationship; the communards were trapped by it and found no way out.

They scarcely had time to enjoy their resolutions on family rights when something sad happened. The diary reports:

> Vladimir stopped loving Katya. He himself could not quite clarify the situation. When he mar-

ried, he was in love with Katya, but now he has only a comradely feeling for her, and it is difficult and unnecessary to live as man and wife without love.

The result was divorce, but the comrades were very upset about it, and the girls in particular made some very wild assertions:

Vladimir is a swine. He should have thought about this before he married. He cannot first get married and then run off after a while. This is damned similar to philistine romanticism: If I want to, I love, and if I want to, I stop loving. Today I can't live without you, let's get married. Then a month later: I'm terribly sorry, but I don't love you any more. Let's just be comrades.

How small was the influence of Soviet marriage legislation on the psychic structure of the communards! They took for bourgeois philistinism what the bourgeois himself fears so greatly: the dissolution of a marital relationship. Dialectics!

The boys showed greater understanding: no doubt Vladimir had loved Katya, and it was not his fault that this feeling had disappeared. The whole matter was debated in a full session of the commune. Some girls thought it peculiar that Katya had never told anyone about it and now brought it up in a full session. There was a long quarrel. Some said: "Vladimir is right in wanting a divorce, and we cannot condemn him. After all, he cannot be forced to love by a resolution of the commune." The majority, however, condemned Vladimir because he had married carelessly and had conducted himself in a manner unworthy of a Komsomol and communard. There was no unanimity. The matter resolved itself when Katya left Moscow for a few months. When she returned, Vladimir was again close to her, but this did not solve the divorce problem. In the course of time, five of the eleven communards married. Nothing had changed in the living arrangements, i.e., boys and girls had to sleep in separate bedrooms—an impossible situation in terms of sexual hygiene.

Communard Tanya wrote a desperate letter to her husband:

> I want to have a little, simple, and quite legal personal happiness. I'm longing for a quiet corner where you and I can be alone, where I can be together with you when we want to, so that we don't have to hide from the others, so that our relationship can become fuller, freer, and more enjoyable. Can't the commune understand that this is a human necessity?

We contend that Tanya had the healthier genital structure. It is now quite clear why the commune foundered. The communards understood Tanya very well and suffered themselves from housing conditions and ideological confusion, but they could not change anything. The diary notes ceased, the problem submerged and continued to rumble under the surface. The problem of the relationship between the sexes in the collective would not have been solved even if the housing question had been. The guarantee of privacy would have accomplished only one important *external* prerequisite. For instance, it did not occur to our communard couple that people should not enter into a permanent reationship unless they are convinced they are sexually and psychically compatible; that, in order to establish this, they would have to live with each other for a while without further obligations; that the adjustment often takes a long time; that one must be capable of separation if there is sexual incompatibility; that love cannot be commanded; that sexual happiness will either develop spontaneously or not at all. These bright young boys and girls would have found this out themselves after serious struggles if the concept of marriage and the equation of sexuality and procreation had not been in their bones. These concepts were not inborn; it was only that they had not been eradicated from social ideology.

3. NECESSARY STRUCTURAL PREREQUISITES

Let us summarize:

1. About 1900, the family situation was relatively simple. People lived encapsulated in their families; there was no collective which made demands that conflicted with the family situation and the familial human structure. In addition, there was no conflict between the family and the patriarchal social order. Repressed sexuality only broke out in the form of hysteria, characterological rigidity and eccentricity, prostitution, perversions, suicides, torturing of children, and bourgeois war fanaticism.

In 1930, the situation was more complicated. The compulsory family disintegrated in the contradiction between collectivist production and the economic basis of the family. The institution of the family was only very seldom maintained by economic factors, but all the more strongly by factors of human structure. It could not live and it could not die. People could no longer live *in* the family, but neither could they live *without* it. They could not live permanently with one partner, but neither could they live alone.

2. A new family form emerged in the Soviet Union, the collective, which consisted of people unrelated by blood. Since it excluded the old form of marriage, the next question is how sexual relationships in such a community are molded. We cannot predict anything, nor should we. We can only follow the process of upheaval which the current sexual revolution represents, and support that tendency which does not contradict the economic and social forms

of work democracy—in general terms, *unlimited, concrete affirmation of man's sexual happiness*. Neither customary, permanent monogamy nor casual, loveless, unsatisfying relationships ("promiscuity") correspond to this. Soviet Communism excludes both asceticism and lifelong monogamy as norms. Sexual relationships take place under totally new conditions; the collective creates opportunities for more varied human relationships among individuals, so that a guarantee against changing a partner or having a relationship with a third party becomes impossible. One must completely understand the pain and the full significance of the idea that a beloved partner is being embraced by another; it must be experienced personally, both passively and actively, in order for one to comprehend that this problem is neither mechanical nor economic, but structural. With the same number of boys and girls, men and women, in the collective, it is easier to select a partner, and there are greater possibilities for changing one's partner.

It would be a dangerous oversight if we do not learn to understand and master the painful birth process of a new sexual order. I do not mean to understand and master in the moralistic sense but rather in the sense of affirming life and securing happiness. Soviet youth has paid bitterly for its experience. They should not have suffered in vain.

Human structure must be adapted to collective living. This adaptation will undoubtedly require a diminution of jealousy and of the fear of losing a partner. Sexually, most people are extraordinarily dependent, burdened with sticky, loveless ties and hence incapable of dissolving them. They are afraid that if they lose a partner it will be difficult to find a new one. Since this anxiety is always sustained by infantile ties to mother, father, or older siblings, the replacing of the family by the collective would prevent the formation of such ties in the child. With this, the core of sexual helplessness would disappear and the possiblitity of finding suitable partners would be greatly enhanced. This alone would not solve the problem of jealousy but it would certainly simplify it, since the capacity to change permanent relationships of long duration without damage to either partner is one of the basic issues. However, the essential task to be achieved by the restructuring of man is to enable him to experience the fusion of tender and sensual genital love. It will therefore be necessary to reestablish the capacity for full surrender, for uninhibited sexual life (orgastic potency) from childhood on. The prevention of sexual disturbances of neurotic, unsatisfying polygamy, of sticky sexual demands, of unconscious sexuality, etc., will require enormous efforts. It is not a question of telling people how to live; they must be brought up in a way that will enable them to regulate their own sexual lives in the constant flux of collective life, without any socially dangerous complications. This is predicated on the unrestricted, socially supported development of natural genitality. It is only then that the ability to be candid and open with one's partner and the capactiy for tolerating jealousy without resorting to violence will develop. The conflicts of sexual life will not be totally eliminated but their solution can, and should be, eased.

A purposeful, social prevention of neuroses would have to see to it that people do not neurotically complicate the everyday conflicts to which they are exposed. The sexual self-awareness of the masses, supported by the material wealth of society, will brand any moral hypocrisy as a social crime. Struggle, pain, the enjoyment of sexuality, etc., are part of life. But what matters is that human structure should be able to experience pleasure and suffering. People who are capable of that would be incapable of becoming submissive subjects. Only genitally healthy people are capable of voluntary work and of an unauthoritarian self-regula'ion of life. The task of restructuring will fail, it will not even be understood, unless this has been clarified. The non-adaptation of human sexual structure to collective living must produce reactionary consequences. Every attempt to achieve this adaptation by way of moral authoritarian demands must end in a fiasco. One cannot demand "voluntary" sexual discipline. This discipline either exists or it does not. All one can do is to help man fully to develop his natural potentialities.

XIII

Some Problems of Sexuality in Childhood

The Soviet kindergartens I visited in 1929 had an excellent collective organization. One kindergarten had six teachers who spent five hours with the children and one hour in preparation for their work. The director and the housekeeper were factory workers. The six teachers shared one secretary. Among the approximately thirty children, fifteen were from factory workers' families; the parents of the others were attending technical high schools. The factory paid 28 rubles for each child. The council of the kindergarten consisted of the director, one teacher, two parent representatives, one Komsomol, one district representative, and one physician. The children were raised in an anti-religious atmosphere; religious holidays were not observed. The curriculum contained several unusual subjects such as "What meaning does the forest have for people?" and "What is the significance of the forest for health?" The children did a great deal of work with wood. In general, the organization reflected the orientation of a Communist collective.

The situation was less positive in respect to sexual matters. Teachers complained about the nervousness of the children. In many cases, children followed sleeping rituals as a protection against masturbation. Children who masturbated were often removed by their parents. A teacher commented: "Even doctors' children masturbate." Toward the end of my visit, I made an interesting observation: I was standing at the window of a kindergarten room which led into the garden. We were speaking with the head teacher. Outside, the children were playing, and I saw a little boy pull out his penis and let a little girl look at it. The children were near a tree. This happened just as the teacher was assuring us that in her kindergarten "such things" as masturbation and sexuality did not occur.

1. CREATING A COLLECTIVE STRUCTURE

The history of the formation of ideology teaches us that every social system, consciously or unconsciously, uses the influencing of children to anchor itself in man's structure. It we follow the way in which the social order was transformed from matriarchy to patriarchy, we can establish the sexual education of the child as its central mechanism. In matriarchal society, which rests on the social order of primitive communism, children have unrestricted sexual freedom. The ideology of asceticism for the child develops along with the development of patriarchy in the economy and social structure. This turnabout in the attitude toward the child's sexual life facilitates the producing of authority-oriented character structures in place of the previous unauthoritarian ones. In matriarchal society, the general collective life corresponds to the unrestricted sexuality of children, i.e., there are no norms for the child that would coerce him into specific forms of sexual life. The free sexuality of the child creates a firm structural basis for voluntary integration into the collective and for voluntary work discipline.

Sexual suppression of the child comes about with
the development of the patriarchal family, which is
in opposition to the clan. Sexual games with compan-
ions are forbidden. Masturbation gradually becomes
a punishable activity. From a report by Roheim about
the children of Pitchentara, it is clear that the nature
of the child changes in a frightening way once he
can no longer experience his natural sexuality. He
becomes shy, aloof, fearful, subdued, afraid of authority, and he develops unnatural sexual impulses,
such as sadistic tendencies. A free, "fearless" nature
is replaced by obedience and a personality that is
easily influenced. Suppressing sexual impulses requires a great deal of energy, attention, and self-control. To the degree that the biological forces of the
child can no longer turn to the outer world and to
instinctual gratification, he also loses vigor, mobility,
courage, and a sense of reality. He becomes "inhibited." In the center of this inhibition we regularly
find the inhibition of motor activity, of walking, running about, of muscular activity in general. It can be
generally observed that children of patriarchal cultures become rigid, cold, and "quiet," and begin to
armor against the outside world during their fourth,
fifth, and sixth year. They lose their natural charm
and frequently become clumsy, unintelligent, recal-
citrant, and "difficult to raise"; this in turn provokes
more rigorous patriarchal methods of education. From
these structural foundations religious tendencies usually arise, as well as strong ties to and dependence on parents. What the child loses in terms of
natural motor activity he now begins to replace
by fantasized ideals. He becomes introverted and
neurotic, a "dreamer." The weaker his ego is in reality,
the stronger are the ideal demands he makes upon
himself in order to remain capable of any accomplishments. We have to distinguish between the
ideals which develop from the natural biological
motility of the child and those which are developed
from the necessity for self-control and suppression

of drives. The former correspond to free-flowing productive work, the latter to a sense of duty. The principle of self-regulation in social adaptation and in joyous work accomplishment that exists with the former is replaced in the latter by the structural principle of authoritarian submissiveness, together with rebellion against the burden of work. Let us be content with this general description. In reality, conditions are very complicated and can be described only within the context of character-analytic investigations.

The question that is of primary interest to us here is how a self-regulating society is reproduced in children. There are two possibilities:

1. To inculcate the child with the ideal of self-regulation instead of with compulsory moral ideals;

2. To abandon such inculcation of ideals and, instead, develop the character structure of the child in such a manner that he regulates himself and accepts the general work-democratic atmosphere without resistance.

We may say without reservation that the second possibility corresponds to the principle of the desired self-regulation, but the first does not.

If the restructuring of children in all historical periods is accomplished by way of modifying their sexual structure, then the restructuring in terms of work democracy cannot be an exception. There were a number of attempts at this kind of restructuring in the Soviet Union, where many pedagogues, especially those who were analytically oriented, such as Vera Schmidt, Spielrein, etc., tried to bring about the sex-positive education of children. But these were isolated efforts, and by and large the sexual education of children in the Soviet Union was sex-negative. This fact is extremely important. Of necessity, the structure of the children had to be adapted to collective life. This adaptation was impossible without affirming infantile sexuality; one cannot raise children in a collective and simultaneously suppress their most vital impulses, the sexual ones. If they are suppressed,

the child will be forced to muster far more energy
to keep down his sexuality than he would in the family,
and he will therefore become lonely and develop more
conflicts. The educator has only one solution for this
loneliness, namely, harsh discipline, an externally
imposed order, the creation of restraints and ideals
in opposition to sexual activity, which in the collective
is particularly intense. Objections to education in a
collective usually stem from the fear that children
might become "bad," from a fear of their sexual
games, etc.

The impressions Soviet kindergartens made upon
me were quite contradictory. Old patriarchal forms
existed side by side with new, unfamiliar, promising
forms. Under the guidance of a teacher, the children
had to organize their own activities ("self-government"). The combining of manual work with intellectual learning no doubt effected not merely external but structural changes. The so-called work
schools in which, along with geography, mathematics,
and other subjects, the children also learned a trade,
are no doubt the basic forms of educational institutions
for the creation of collective structures. Until a few
years ago, there was a genuine camaraderie between
students and teachers. The "Diary of the Student
Kostya Ryabtsev" contains anecdotes about the everyday life of the children and their relationship
with their teacher, which reveal the liveliness of their
criticism and intelligence. The "flying kindergartens"
in the culture park in Moscow impressed me as a
model for creating life-positive structures. While in
the park, visitors could leave their children with
teachers and kindergarten workers who played with
them. In this way, the dull, dismal picture of the
child dragged along by his parents, bored and contrary,
disappeared. Children who were strangers learned
to know each other, formed quick friendships, and
separated just as easily and quickly. On occasion,
a friendship was continued. Children between the
ages of two and ten were brought together without

any particular order in a hall. Every child received some simple object—a key, a spoon, a plate, etc. A music teacher sat down at the piano, struck some chords, and created rhythms. Without being asked to, without exhortations or guidance, the children gradually fell into the rhythm, and in a few minutes the most wonderful orchestra had been created. It is not that the existence of a culture park is specifically revolutionary; there are culture parks even in the most reactionary countries. What is specifically life-positive is that children were brought together and entertained in such a marvelous way. The motor activity of the child was taken into account. And children who experience such joy from "unorganized" organized games will be structurally capable and ready themselves to develop work-democratic ideology instead of merely parroting it mechanically.

The question of handling the child's motor activity leads us to the focal point of pedagogic problems. In general it is a task of the revolutionary movement to free man's bound-up and repressed biological impulses and to satisfy them. This is the basic function of natural work democracy. Adequate and constantly increasing possibilities for the gratification of needs should enable man to develop his natural potentials. A child whose motility is free and uninhibited is scarcely, if at all, susceptible to reactionary ideology and ways of living. However, a shy child, inhibited in his motor activity, is capable of every ideological degeneracy. The efforts of the Soviet government during the first years of the revolution to give children complete freedom to criticize their parents also belong to the context of free motor activity. This measure was initially misunderstood and seemed shocking to Western Europeans; it was less so in the United States. Occasionally one heard that a child would call his parents by their first names, a fact that pointed toward free, unauthoritarian relationships. Thus both home and school began to adapt themselves to the self-regulation of children. This tendency, which we

could illuminate by many examples, was confronted
by a second one which unfortunately has prevailed.
It has recently triumphed to the extent that parents
have again been given the responsibility for raising
their children, indicating a retrogression to patriarchal
forms of child education. In the past few years, less
and less has been heard about the complicated problems of collective education. Family education has
again won the upper hand. It is hard to judge how
much of the original tendency has remained. But
the orientation toward patriarchal forms of education
has found unquestionably strong support in terms of
the children's political lessons at school. For example,
we read in pedagogic newsletters that schoolchildren
have to enter political contests. Questions like "What
was the nth thesis of the Sixth World Congress?"
show us that the external form of Communist ideological indoctrination has prevailed. Obviously a child
is not in the slightest way equipped to understand
the theses of a World Congress, let alone to judge
them. And even if he should win such contests by
memorizing and brilliantly reciting these theses, he
is by no means immune to Fascist influences. He
will just as easily swallow Fascistic formulas. In contrast, a child whose motor activity is completely free,
and whose natural sexuality has been liberated in
sexual play, will oppose strictly authoritarian, ascetic
influences. Political reaction can always compete with
revolutionary education in the authoritarian, superficial influencing of children. But it can never do
so in the realm of sexual education. No reactionary
ideology or political orientation can ever accomplish
for children what a social revolution can with respect
to their sexual life. In terms of processions, marches,
songs, banners, and uniforms, however, reaction undoubtedly has more to offer.

We thus see that the revolutionary structuring of
the child must involve the freeing of his biological
sexual motility. This is indisputable.

2. NON-AUTHORITARIAN STRUCTURING OF THE SMALL CHILD

The basic task required to create a non-authoritarian structure in man is the sex-affirmative upbringing of the child.

On August 19, 1921, the Moscow psychoanalyst Vera Schmidt founded a children's home in which she attempted to bring up small children correctly. Her experiences, which she published in 1924 in her booklet *Psychoanalytic Education in Soviet Russia,* confirm that what sex-economy teaches today about the child's development evolved spontaneously at that time as a result of a life-affirmative and pleasure-directed attitude. Vera Schmidt's work wholeheartedly affirmed infantile sexuality.

The basic features of the children's home were the following: The teachers were informed that the children would not be punished for anything. They were instructed not even to raise their voices when speaking to the children. Subjective judgments of the children on the part of the teachers were prohibited. Praise and blame were regarded as judgments that the child could not understand; they only served to satisfy the teacher's ambition and self-esteem. With these few basic rules, the authoritarian principle was eliminated from education. What replaced it?

What was judged was the objective result of a child's activities, but not the child himself. Therefore, one described a house built by a child as beautiful or not beautiful, without praising or blaming the child; during a fight the offender was not blamed, but the pain he had inflicted on the other was described to him. In the presence of the children, all teachers had to exercise the greatest reserve; they were not allowed to make any comments that might assess the peculiarities and conduct of the children. Likewise, they had to be very sparing with their affection and tenderness. The adults were strictly forbidden to indulge in emotional expressions of affection, such as warm kisses, tender embraces, etc. Vera Schmidt emphasized quite correctly that such expressions of affection served the gratification of the adults more than the needs of the children.

This broke with a second harmful principle of the moralistic-authoritarian rearing of children: anyone who feels justified in beating a child also feels justified in living out his ungratified sexuality with a child. Here the defenders of conventional family upbringing are usually the real culprits. If one does away with the stern treatment and moral judgment of children, it is no longer necessary to heal with kisses the injury caused by a beating. Toys and materials were selected in a way that took into account the child's urge to do something and stimulated his creative activity; if the children developed new needs, toys and work materials were changed accordingly.

The principle of adapting the material to the need, instead of the need to the material, was in accordance with the basic view of sex-economy, which can be applied beyond the kindergarten to all social existence (e.g., economic needs should not be adapted to economic institutions; rather the institutions should be adapted to the needs). In Vera Schmidt's kindergarten, this principle was applied as distinguished from the moral, authoritarian principle of the Montessori kindergartens, in which the children uniformly have to make do with prescribed material.

Vera Schmidt endorsed the following view: "If the child's adaptation to real external conditions is to develop without great difficulties, the surrounding world must not appear to him as a hostile force. We therefore try to make this reality as pleasant as possible for him and to replace every primitive desire which he has to forgo with reasonable, rational pleasures."

This means that the child must first learn to love the reality to which he will then voluntarily adapt himself. He has to identify joyously with the surrounding world: this is the principle of sex-economy. In contrast, there is the moral, authoritarian principle by which an attempt is made to adapt the child to a hostile world to which he is fundamentally opposed, not in loving identification with this world but under an obligation, if not with the help of moral pressure. For a mother or a teacher to conduct herself so that the child will spontaneously love her—that is sex-economic. For a social, religious, or legal command to say, "You must love your mother," even though she has not behaved lovably—that is moral, authoritarian regulation.

The necessity of adapting to the social community was facilitated for the children in various ways. Demands made on them arose out of everyday conditions and occurrences in the children's own lives and not from the arbitrariness of neurotic, sick, ambitious, or love-starved adults. What was expected from them and why was explained to the children in a reasonable way; they were not given commands. Instinctual gratifications which the child should correctly give up were replaced with other forms of gratification, such as love for adults or playmates. Self-awareness and feelings of independence were stimulated and supported because children with those qualities are most fitted to deal with the necessities of life. These policies would be completely incomprehensible to a drill-sergeant educator; yet they are self-evident. The sex-economic principle of voluntarily giving up instinctual gratification that is no longer socially acceptable was also applied to education in cleanliness. Prohibitions of any kind on the part of the teachers were strictly forbidden. The pupils of the children's home did not know that their sexual impulses could be judged differently from their other natural impulses. Therefore they gratified them quietly and without shyness before the eyes of the teachers; no different from hunger and thirst. This spared the children the need for secrecy, strengthened their trust in the teachers, furthered their adaptation to reality, and in this way created a favorable basis for their total development. Under these conditions, the teachers had every opportunity to follow the sexual development of the children step by step and to encourage the sublimation of individual drives.

We can be grateful to Vera Schmidt for pointing out that the educator has to work on himself. Restlessness and disorder among the children was regularly shown to be the result of neurotic unconscious behavior on the part of the teachers themselves. A sex-economic upbringing of the child is impossible so long as the educators are not free of irrational impulses or at least recognize and control them. This is evident immediately upon consideration of the specific content of this type of upbringing. For example, in so-called Western cultures mothers and educators cannot tolerate it if the child is not potty-trained before he is a year old. In Vera Schmidt's kindergarten it was not until the end of the second year that the children "at certain intervals" were put on the potty. But they were never forced to take care of their needs in precisely this manner; nor were they blamed when they wet themselves. This was passed over as something natural.

This central fact of infantile toilet training shows us what prerequisites must be fulfilled before one can even think of sex-economic structuring of the child. It is not practicable within the family; it can be accomplished only in a children's collective. Contrary to the harmful views and interference of ignorant physicians and pedagogues who believe that severe punishment should be meted out to the bed-wetting child (which only serves to fixate the problem), Vera Schmidt reports: A girl of about three reverted to bed wetting. No attention was paid to this relapse. It took three months before the girl spontaneously became continent again. This fact, too, will be totally incomprehensible to the authoritarian teacher. It is nevertheless self-evident.

"The attitude toward cleanliness is quiet and conscious; there is no noticeable resistance or moodiness. No feeling of shame or any idea of 'disgrace' is connected with these functions. Our method shows promise of protecting the children from serious traumatic experiences which so often result from an education which insists on controlling the excretory processes," Vera Schmidt writes. According to clinical experience, the most frequent source of severe disturbances of orgastic potency among adults is strict toilet training in early childhood. It causes a connecting of feelings of disgrace and shame with the genital function which, understandably, destroys the capacity of the organism to regulate its biological energy. Vera Schmidt acted correctly: small children who do not have any sense of shame or disgrace in connection with excretory functions also have no basis in later life on which to develop such genital disturbances.

The children in Schmidt's home were in no way impeded in gratifying their desire for movement; they fought, jumped, ran, and did as they pleased. This enabled them not only to live out their natural inclinations but also to utilize them culturally, which was in complete accord with the sex-economic view that the freedom of the infantile drive is *the* prerequisite for its sublimation, i.e., its cultural utilization, and that its inhibition through repression prevents its sublimation.

In our kindergartens, where children are made "capable of culture" and "adapted to reality" by inhibiting their motor activity, we notice, during the fourth, fifth, and sixth years, a disturbing transformation from natural, lively behavior to behavior that is quiet and subdued: the children have become cold. Anna Freud confirms this change in her book *Psychoanalysis for Teachers and Parents,* but she does not criticize it and accepts it as necessary, for she wants the child to be consciously educated to become a "respectable" citizen. This is based on the false assumption that the child's natural motility is antitheti-

cal to his capacity for culture. Exactly the opposite
is true.

Vera Schmidt's report on her pupils' masturbatory
practices is very important. The children masturbated
"relatively little." She correctly distinguishes between
masturbation conditioned by purely physical sensations in the genital organs and serving the gratification
of genital pleasure needs, and the other form of masturbation, which occurs "as a reaction to an offense,
disparagement, or limiting of freedom by the outside
world." The first form causes no difficulties for the
educator. The second is the consequence of an intensified vegetative excitability resulting from anxiety and
defiance which the child tries to relieve by means
of genital stimulation. Vera Schmidt understood this
better than did Anna Freud, who is of the opinion
that so-called excessive masturbation in children
results from "instinctual living out." We must remember that the masturbatory activity of children, under
conditions of instinct-affirmative education, took
place "without secrecy, under the eyes of the educators." In view of the masturbatory anxiety in educators, we must recognize that "the educator must first be
educated" before he can quietly observe the natural
instinctual behavior of the child.

The children also had complete freedom to satisfy
their sexual curiosity with each other. They were
allowed to examine each other; their statements about
the naked body, their own as well as their playmates',
"were quite sober and factual." "We noticed that
interest in the sexual organs did not show itself when
the children were naked but only when they were
dressed." The children's questions about sexual matters received clear and truthful answers. As Vera
Schmidt emphasizes, they did not know any parental
authority, any parental power, or the like. For them,
father and mother were beautiful, beloved, ideal
beings. "It is quite possible," writes Vera Schmidt,
"that these good relationships between parents and

children can only be effected when education takes place outside the parental home."

While in practice the children's home was administered according to the life-affirmative concepts of sex-economy, the theoretical concept was different. In establishing the guiding principles for the kindergarten, Vera Schmidt spoke of "overcoming the pleasure principle" and of the necessity "to replace it by the reality principle." She was caught up in the incorrect psychoanalytic concept of the mechanical, contradictory relationship between pleasure and accomplishment, instead of seeing in the realization of the natural pleasure principle the best foundation for sublimation and social adaptation. Her practical work contradicted her theoretical views.

In order to evaluate such attempts to structure the new generation differently, it is important to consider the ultimate fate of this children's home. Soon after it was founded, all kinds of rumors could be heard in the city. It was said that the most terrible things were being done in the institution; that the teachers stimulated the children sexually for purposes of observation, etc. The authorities who had approved the founding of the home started an investigation. Some educators and pediatricians spoke out in support of the home. The psychologists, of course, were opposed to it. The People's Commissar for Education declared through his representatives that the children's home could no longer be maintained; he claimed lack of funds as the reason for this decision. The real reason was different. In the Psycho-neurological Institute with which the children's home was affiliated there was a change in directorship. The new director, who had also been on the investigating commission, gave a devastating report. He even abused the administrator, the workers, and the children of the experimental home. Whereupon the Psycho-neurological Institute not only withdrew all support from the children's home but also hastened to detach itself from it ideologically.

On the very day the home was to be closed, a representative of the German and Russian mine workers' organizations appeared and offered to support the experimental home financially and ideologically. After April 1922 the children's home was given food by the German organization and coal by the Russian miners. The home changed its name to "The International Solidarity Children's Home Laboratory." But it lasted only a short time. Commissions, surveillance, and general withdrawal of all support put an end to it. Significantly, the dissolution of the children's home coincided roughly with the time when the general inhibition of the Soviet sexual revolution began to succeed.

We ought to mention that the International Psychoanalytic Association also opposed Vera Schmidt's experiments—sometimes with skepticism, sometimes with outright rejection. The later development of psychoanalysis into an *antisexual* doctrine was being expressed even then in this negative attitude. Yet Vera Schmidt's work was the first attempt in the history of education to give practical content to the theory of infantile sexuality. We may safely compare this attempt—even though of a different historical dimension—with the Paris Commune. Vera Schmidt was undoubtedly the first educator who, purely intuitively, had grasped, in a practical way, the necessity as well as the nature of the socialist restructuring of man. And as always happened throughout the Russian sexual revolution, authorities, "scholars," psychologists, and self-styled pedagogues helped the reactionary forces to win out, while the mine workers' unions proved that, even without theoretical knowledge, they fully understood the importance of the problem.

Now let us compare this correct attempt at structuring the small child with what an allegedly revolutionary pedagogue was allowed to do, undisturbed, at about the same time. It will teach us that, should another revolutionary opportunity arise, we must turn to the miners' unions and not to reactionary psychologists.

3. SHAM REVOLUTIONARY, RELIGIOUS EDUCATION

When the educator approaches the problems inherent in educating the growing child, no other area offers so many difficulties as that of sexual education. Although it cannot be separated from education in general, it confronts him with special difficulties. He himself has received a life-negating sexual education; he has been indoctrinated by parents, school, church, and the whole conservative environment with sex-negating views. These conflict with whatever life-affirmative conclusions he may have reached later in life. Therefore, if he wants to educate children in a life-positive way, he must detach himself from reactionary attitudes, form his own principles and apply them to the education of children. In doing so, he will borrow many essential elements from conservative pedagogy, reject much of it as antisexual, and modify other elements to suit his own purposes. This is a great and difficult task which has only just been started.

The parsons in the revolutionary camp presented the most serious problem. They were mostly sexually rigid intellectuals, neurotically motivated revolutionaries who only spread confusion instead of contributing knowledge. Among them was the Communist cleric Salkind, a member of the Communist Academy *and* the International Psychoanalytic Association. His views were strongly opposed by revolutionary youth in the Soviet Union, but they governed official ideology, even in Germany. His article "Einige Fragen der sexuellen Erziehung der Jungpioniere" [Some Questions of Sexual Education of Young Pioneers], published in *Das proletarische*

Kind (Vol. 12, No. 1/2, 1932), caused much trouble in the German Sexpol movement. We shall use this article to demonstrate the hopelessness of mixing revolutionary form and sex-inimical content.

Salkind begins with the correct statement that the Pioneer movement affects children "in their most important phase of development"; it has means at its disposal which family and school lack. But he proceeds from a concept of infantile sexuality which is equivalent to the Christian one. All other errors of Salkind and his followers derive from this attitude. He writes:

> Therefore [because the Pioneer movement has better educational capabilities than the family], it must be the principal antagonist of . . . *the parasitic shifting of growing children's energy to sexuality* [emphasis added].

Thus, Salkind assesses infantile sexuality as "parasitic." How did he reach this judgment? What does he really mean? What conclusions can be drawn from it for education? By "parasitic" he means something alien to the body. This sexual philosopher, whom the Soviet Union tolerates, seriously believes that the "shifting," of energy to the "parasitic," the "sexual," must be prevented.

> If the Pioneer leaders know how to offer children the material of Pioneer work in a form which corresponds to the needs of their age group, there will be no energy left for parasitic dominance.

Salkind believes that the sexual interests of children and adolescents can be entirely eliminated. He does not ask how the collective interests can be reconciled with the sexual ones, where they contradict each other and where they coincide.

What is the difference between Salkind and any Catholic priest or reactionary pedagogue who believes that sexual energy can be completely diverted? It is no longer possible to deny infantile and adolescent sexuality. Those convenient times are over. Today the talk is of complete diversion, which is merely the old element in a new form. It did not even occur to Salkind to ask why the Church does not allow infantile sexuality. He did not stop to think that, if he wants to provide rules for revolutionary education, he must first explain why his viewpoint is the same as that of the reactionary educator. He has some vague notion that his view of sexuality and collectivism as contradictory furnishes an explanation; he wants to eliminate sexuality in the interests of the collective.

> It is primarily the neglected, lonely children who fall victim to premature sexual drives, those children who have no active, lively contact with their contemporaries, who have been left to their own devices too often. . . . The more one becomes isolated from the collective and surrenders to loneliness, the closer one is to premature sexual parasitism.

These are ignorant slogans. What does "premature" mean? Is it premature for a four-year-old child to masturbate? Is it premature if a maturing adolescent of thirteen or fifteen gratifies himself? Is it premature if, sooner or later, he demands sexual intercourse? Salkind and his kind prove by their nebulous, sloganeering argumentaion that they have failed to descend from the upper regions of abstract ethics into the reailty of infantile and adolescent life. And those Pioneer leaders were absolutely right (and not, as Salkind thought, "absolutely wrong") when they turned their attention to sexual enlightenment as soon as they noticed manifestations of unhealthy sexuality in their groups. Every reasonable child and youth leader knows that it is not the "lack of collectivism" which causes so-called "sexual conditions," but, con-

versely, that it is the lack of clarity about childhood
sexuality, produced by such views as Salkind's, which
is the most important source of disturbed communal
life. No one will ever succeed in building collectivism
on the complete suppression of sexual life, except
by authoritarian measures. "The uninterrupted collective control of children's sexual and other behavior
should be the basis for a healthy sexual development,"
Salkind writes. When he says "healthy," he means
of course "without sexuality." Salkind seeks to accomplish this "Pioneer ethic" through "skilled organization of work." At this point we have had enough
of empty phrases, but let us visualize concretely what
has been suggested here. How long should adolescents
work? Uninterruptedly? Thus also at night when
they are in bed? So they will not touch their genitals?
And when children and adolescents play games,
should there be an "uninterrupted collective control"
so that the children will not fall in love, so that no
"amorous adventure" can develop? Salkind explicitly
speaks of "children" aged thirteen to sixteen years;
thus of sexually mature adolescents! Why should
these "children" not fall in love and have "amorous
adventures"? Because it disturbs collectivism? Or
because Salkind and his kind cannot bear to look
on? In Berlin, during public discussions, young Communists had established beyond any doubt that the
groups would disintegrate when there were not enough
girls; they kept together if boys and girls were represented in about equal numbers. Was this because
one might then exercise "uninterrupted collective control" without letting any "unnecessary amorous
thoughts" come to the surface? Or was it because
young people found congenial partners and love life
ceased to be a disturbing influence on the collective?
The Salkinds arrive at their absurdities because they
make no distinction between disturbed and undisturbed love life; because they do not investigate the
causes of "brutalized" love life; because they do not
see that since sexual drives can never be eliminated,

it is precisely the inhibition of love life which creates this degeneracy, which, in turn, makes a collective collaboration totally impossible. How arid, bureaucratic, and hostile to life is the following thesis:

> An active collectivism is the best means of indoctrinating the feeling of sexual equality; a co-worker does not evoke unnecessary thoughts of love because there is neither superfluous energy nor time for them.

What does "sexual equality" mean? We endorse the equality of the sexes; we fight political reaction with an ideology of sexual freedom. The Salkinds, however, endorse the "equality of the sexes" by not permitting them to have a love life. (This is precisely what the leaders of a Catholic youth organization would endorse, except that they do not oppose coeducation, not yet.[1]) But this is, precisely why they reach the point of absurdity. Specifically, what is to be done, according to Salkind's logic, if a boy and a girl have worked together and completed an important political or organizational project and, in spite of Salkind's Ten Commandments, fall in love? What should be done? Exercise collective control? "Smother" the love in further work? Or achieve sexual equality in abstinence? And this at an age which Salkind himself has described as "the most important phase of a child's development," "the stage of maturing sexual drives." What mendacity and hypocrisy are contained in the following sentences:

> Complete mutual confidence and mutual respect, complete mutual honesty—these are the main conditions without which a healthy educational system in the Pioneer units is impossible.

---

1 [1949] Several years ago, coeducation was discontinued in the Soviet Union. In the United States it is being encouraged.

How can the Pioneers have respect and confidence
in themselves and in the leader if one of their most
burning problems is not understood?

> The child of Pioneer age knows a good deal, if
> anything too much, about the sexual question, but
> he does not know where and how [such knowl-
> edge] would be needed. And the leader cannot ig-
> nore this aberration but must discuss it. But how
> to discuss it?

Well, how should the Pioneer leader talk about
it? We are eager to learn, and here it is:

> In any event, he should not give any lectures to
> the children on sexual questions. More than that, he
> should not talk at all with the children about any
> special sexual topics.

Does that mean he may discuss sexuality only in
connection with social and political questions? That
would be correct, but not so:

> By careful observation we can notice masturba-
> tion in individual children. [In "individual" chil-
> dren, only at the age of thirteen and sixteen, in
> the stage of ripening sexual drives.]

Only by "careful observation"! Furthermore:

> This requires the greatest caution on the part of
> the leader because the children are particularly
> sensitive [And rightly so WR] if one tries to
> fight such *damaging habits*. . . .

This is exactly how our German Father Hypocrite
spoke.

> In each case, entering the immediate sexual
> sphere of the child is permitted only to those

leaders who have been pedagogically schooled in this subject. [By whom? And for what? For stating that masturbation is a damaging habit?] A public discussion of such points of disagreement under the guidance of the leader of the group is absolutely inadmissible. The matter must be stifled in private. [What matter? The "scandal" that children masturbate?] In doing this, one should rely on the best activists whose conduct, sexually speaking, is irreproachable.

So this is what "complete mutual honesty" looks like! No wonder there was "sexual delinquency" in the Pioneer groups, i.e., split-up, confused, conflict-ridden sexual life!

The Salkinds have never understood what everyone, except the "sexually irreproachable" boy, knows intuitively from his own life: that sexual delinquency is never created by sexual activity in itself but only by inhibitions and educational methods à la Salkind, which contradict natural sexual needs. For instance:

Not . . . unless there is an emergency, not without previous alarm signals, can or should the leader touch upon the sexual question, among others.

How can any youth group leader find his way out of this mishmash of contradictory opinions!

Such pedagogues evade the enormous difficulties which immediately arise once the question of infantile and adolescent sexual life is thought through. We cannot enlighten children and adolescents and at the same time prohibit sexual games and masturbation. We cannot keep the truth about the function of sexual gratification a secret. We can only tell the truth and let life run its course completely free of interference. Sexual potency and physical vigor and beauty must become the permanent ideals of the revolutionary freedom movement. The revolution must reject the

pack ox and choose the bull; it should not choose
the capon but the cock. People have been beasts of
burden long enough. Castrates are not revolutionary
fighters.

4. THE NEW WAVE OF DELINQUENCY

Not only did the Russian revolution have to combat
the devastation left by Tsarism and the repercussions
of civil war and famine; it also did not have enough
trained educators, particularly those with correct
sexological training, to cope with the enormous
problem of juvenile delinquency. Moreover, the sexual castrates attached themselves to this problem
like milestones around the neck of a jumper. Finally,
in 1935, the lack of clarity about adolescent sexual
rebellion resulted in the intensification of the delinquency problem. It cannot be claimed that the new
wave of delinquency resulted from conditions during
the civil war years, because the delinquent children
of 1934–1935, were children of the new social system.
Thus, we should not be led astray by false history.
The Soviet Union had done everything imaginable
to solve the problem of delinquency. The film *The
Road to Life*, a documentary about revolutionary
educational work, depicted the first-rate pedagogic
accomplishments in the fields of work culture and
workers' education. But we must ask why the attempts
to solve the problem of delinquency failed. That they
did fail was proved by the June 1935 resolutions
of the Council of the People's Commissars of the
U.S.S.R. and the Central Committee of the Communist Party of the Soviet Union concerning the elimination of delinquency and the inadequate supervision
of children:

The Council of the People's Commissars of the U.S.S.R. and the Central Committee of the Communist Party of the Soviet Union have determined that the presence of delinquent children in our principal cities and other towns in the country—now that the economic and cultural situation of the working class has been substantially improved in town and country and the state has allocated enormous funds for maintaining institutions for children—must be explained primarily by the poor work of local Soviet organizations—Party, trade unions, and Komsomol—in liquidating and preventing juvenile delinquency. To this we must add the lack of organized participation of Soviet public opinion.

a) Most children's homes are not provided with sufficient funds and are educationally inadequate.

b) The organized fight against rowdyism in children and against criminal elements among children and adolescents is ineffectually directed and in some places does not exist at all.

c) Until now no measures have been taken to put children who are for some reason roaming the streets (who have lost their parents or left them, or fled from children's homes, etc.) immediately into institutions or to return them to their parents.

d) No countermeasures or punishments have been directed against parents and guardians who are indifferent to their children and let them run wild, indulging in rowdyism, theft, depraved morality, and vagabondage. The parents are not being held responsible.

It was not the "poor work" that was at fault! The state fell back on the responsibility of parents and measures which were no longer in accord with revolutionary principles. Had these educational principles themselves failed? No, they were merely incomplete; they did not include the principal problem and often consciously evaded it: the problem of children's sexual life. For *if collective social ideology and collective living of adults are maintained simultaneously with ascetic demands for children, sexual hypocrisy, and family education, they must of necessity lead to juvenile delinquency.*

It is quite inconceivable that, with a general liberating development, the sexual claims of children can be suppressed without damage to society and child. In 1935, the Soviet Union made a major effort to combat juvenile delinquency. In Ordinance No. 3, "On the Organization of the Fight Against Rowdyism of Children in the Streets," the leaders of the worker and peasant militia are ordered to step up this fight. The People's Commissariats for Education in the republics of the Soviet Union were obligated to accept the children in children's homes. The militia was authorized to punish parents for the vandalism and rowdyism of their children with fines of up to 200 rubles. Parents and guardians would be held financially responsible for any physical damage caused by their children. Parents who "did not properly supervise their children" would lose them and they would be placed in a children's home at the expense of the parents.

On June 16, 1935, the Norwegian newspaper *Arbeiderbladet* reported that the Soviet government had resorted to mass raids against delinquent children. In addition to describing acts of theft, burglary, and looting, *Arbeiderbladet* reported that these children were infected with venereal diseases: "Like a pestilential flood, these children carry the infection from one place to another." According to this report, public baths, children's homes, and hospitals could be used by the children free of charge, but they refused to use these facilities. Masses of children fled from children's homes. Almost daily reported *Arbeiderbladet,* there were announcements in *Izvestia* searching for runaway children. "Until recently, this kind of announcement had never appeared in the Russian press, but now it has become routine." The newspaper also emphasized the countermeasures taken by the Soviet government: hiring qualified teachers, providing tools and machines, educational films, and special instruction books. Beyond that, the government called for the mobilization of the whole population to master this problem.

In talking with the Soviet educators Vera Schmidt and Geschelina in 1929, I endeavored to point out the incompleteness and hopelessness of such attempts in themselves. It was obvious even then that the problem of delinquency in the Soviet Union had developed because of civil war conditions but was continually drawing nourishment from the confusion in sexual life. There was enough work in the Soviet Union. Unemployment had disappeared. Work therapy was highly developed. Children's homes and collectives were for the most part impeccably organized. And in spite of that, an increasing number of children were running away into the dangerous and destructive life of the street, preferring a form of unsociality to life in the children's homes. This tremendous problem can be solved neither with work therapy alone nor by blaming the romantic curiosity of the child's psyche. In Germany, we had numerous opportunities to study the true nature of delinquency and the preventive measures against it. When my efforts concerning the sexual health of youth became known, more and more runaway youth came to me because I understood their principal problem. They poured their hearts out, candidly and honestly, about their suffering and the true motivations of their antisocial behavior. I can affirm that there were fine young people among them, extremely intelligent and capable. Often I would think how much greater vitality these so-called delinquents had when compared to the "good" hypocrites in the schools; and this was true precisely because they rebelled against a social order which denied them their most primitive natural right. There were not too many variations on the theme. Time and again it was the same story: they had been unable to cope with their sexual fantasies and excitations. Parents had never understood them, let alone teachers and authorities. Therefore, they never managed to talk about their troubles to anyone. On the contrary, they had become reserved, suspicious, and vicious. They had kept their secrets to themselves and found understanding only among their contemporaries with similar structures and difficulties. Since they were not understood at school, they boycotted the school; since they were not understood by their parents, they cursed their parents. Since they were also deeply attached to their parents, unconsciously expecting help and salvation from them, they were torn by conflicting feelings of severe guilt and defiance. So they took to the streets. They were not happy there, but they felt free—until the police picked them up and put them in the custody of social workers, often only because girls of fifteen, sixteen, and seventeen had been caught with boys. I could establish that many of them were psychically healthy, with a sound critical capacity and justifiably rebellious, up to the moment when police and social workers got them in their clutches. From that moment on, they became psychopaths and were socially ostracized. The crimes that society commits against these children are endless. It was possible (and further proof for the correctness of my views) to gain the full confidence of such "delinquent" children and give them real guidance if one proved to them that they were understood.

Even in Germany the problem of children and adolescents was tremendously complicated. No wonder that the conflict in a country like the Soviet Union was aggravated, with its pressing demands of stormy sexuality and the deceit of society which proclaimed full freedom but left sexual suppression untouched. General collective life and the continuation of familial education necessarily led to social explosions. We also must not forget that Soviet mothers were included more and more in the production process; they felt reinvigorated as active members of society, and consequently produced a new contradiction in their relationship with their children. If mothers were in the production process, the children also wanted to participate in public life. The way into a life of work was open to them, but many of them did not want to go that way because the road to sexuality was closed to them. This, not the civil war situation, which by 1935 had become history, and certainly not the Soviet system itself, has always been the actual effective basis of delinquency in the Soviet Union. It may be said without reservation that juvenile delinquency is the visible expression of the subterranean sexual crisis in the lives of children and adolescents. And it may be predicted that no society will ever succeed in solving this problem, the problem of juvenile psychopathology, unless that society can muster the courage and acquire the knowledge to regulate the sexual life of its children and adolescents in a sex-affirmative manner.

Today we cannot predict what specific measures would have to be taken if we should be confronted with the task of solving this problem. We can only indicate general interconnections and necessities.

The solution of the problem of juvenile delinquency in particular, and the education of children in general, depends on whether and how children's incestuous and guilt-ridden ties of hatred to their parents, and those of parents to their children, are eliminated from the formation of psychic structure. It is logical that this cannot be accomplished if the children are not raised collectively *before* they form emotionally destructive ties to their parents, that is, *before* the fourth year. This does not mean destruction of natural love relationships between parents and children, but only of neurotic, pathological relationships. This task will certainly fail unless the contradiction between collective and family is resolved on a broad social scale. Parents should be able to love and enjoy their children, and children their parents, unimpeded by neurotic complications. Yet, paradoxical as it may sound, this presupposes the dissolution of the compulsory family and its educational forms. We will founder unless we can destroy the outlawing of childhood sexuality with its resultant feeling of being ostracized from society as a result of sexual desires and activities. We must do all we can to prevent the following kind of situation:

"Six-year-old Garik: 'For heaven's sake, what has happened?' Something absolutely unheard of! Eight-year-old Lyubka, who has scarcely learned to write, is in love and has smuggled to eight-year-old Pavlik the following note: 'My sweet darling, my bonbon, my golden bracelet . . .' 'To fall in love! What a petty bourgeois thing to do! After all, the times of Tsar Nicholas are over!' The matter is hotly debated, and Lyubka is punished by not being allowed to play for three days." In this way, Fanina Halle, in her standard work, *Die Frau in Sowjetrussland* (p. 235), seeks to prove the morality of the Soviet system and to rehabilitate Communism before the whole "moral" world.

Pedagogues and "socialist" sexologists who cannot bear the sight of two children fondling each other, who cannot understand the charm and natural matter-of-factness of their sexuality, are completely useless for the revolutionary education of a new generation, even if they have the best intentions. In the child's sexual impulse, in his sensual demonstration of love, there is infinitely more morality, truth, power, and vital will than in thousands of bone-dry analyses and theses. Here, in the liveliness of the child, lies the guarantee for creating a society of truly free human beings—here, and only here.

This much is established, but it would be harmful to think that the discovery of this simple fact has solved all problems. We must understand that the changing of human structure from the patriarchal, authoritarian to one that is capable of voluntary activity, joy, and delight in living will pose the most difficult tasks. Marx's dictum that "the educator himself has to be educated" is often quoted mechanically. It is time to understand it in concrete terms and effect it practically: the educators of a new generation— parents, teachers, leaders of the state, economists— must first be sexually healthy themselves before they will be able to countenance a correct sex-economic education for children and adolescents.

XIV

What Will Result from the Soviet Struggle for a "New Life"?

The functionary, the educator, the youth counselor, and all those who must master everyday problems will now insist on practical instructions for their work. This is understandable but can in no way be complied with. For the moment, it is possible only to learn from the failures and setbacks of revolutionary upheavals and to sketch the general outlines of the ways and means of revolutionary development which point in the right direction. We cannot know what the actual conditions will be in a new revolutionary upheaval in this or that country. What is always at issue is the application of general principles to specific conditions. Under no circumstances should utopian ideas be permitted; they merely block the road to reality at a given moment.

One of the many basic principles that emerge from investigating the inhibition of the Soviet sexual revolution is undoubtedly the explicit guarantee of all prerequisites and conditions for man's sexual happiness. Since Soviet sexual legislation from 1917 to 1921 tended in this direction, we would take over these laws with very minor changes. However, this would in no way suffice. Serious measures are needed to make these laws effective, i.e., for them to become part of human structure. Besides, the Soviet Union does not have many laws which would have channeled the spontaneous revolution in sexual life into orderly paths.

To safeguard revolutionary sexual legislation for all time, the sexual health of the population must be taken out of the hands of urologists and old-fashioned professors of hygiene. Every worker, housewife, peasant, and adolescent must understand that in conservative society there are no authorities in this field, that those who think of themselves as sexual hygienists and sexologists are permeated with asceticism and anxiety about "the moral conduct of man." On the basis of our work among youth and youth organizations, we may conclude that the average untrained but bright young worker has a better feeling for and capacity to judge questions of sexual life than have any of these "authorities." Therefore, the working people will surely be able to find in their own ranks the functionaries and organizations to resolve the problems of the sexual revolution.

The new ordering of sexual life must begin with a change in the education of the child. For this reason the educators must be retrained and the masses must learn to use their sound instinct in criticizing old pedagogues who have been improperly trained in sexology. It will probably be much easier to reeducate teachers than to upset the convictions of hygienists and demographers. In Western Europe and America, there are increasing signs that progressive educators are spontaneously looking for new ways of raising children and adolescents and in many cases have already developed sex-affirmative views.

This new ordering of sexual life will fail if the political leaders of the working-class movement do not pay proper attention to it. Political working-class leaders constitute a serious impediment if their sexual orientation is ascetic. We will have to convince those leaders who are untrained in sexology and frequently have sexual problems themselves that they must *learn* before they can lead.

Furthermore, it will be essential that spontaneous discussions about the "sexual question" are not shoved aside as a "diversion from the class struggle" but are integrated into the total work of building a free society. A victorious workers' movement must never again tolerate the authority of religious socialists, ethical intellectuals, pathological brooders, or sexually disturbed women in matters pertaining to a new organization of sexual life. It must be understood that it is these very people who, urged on by unconscious feelings, interfere in the debate precisely at that moment when utmost clarity is required. Thus the untrained worker is usually silenced because of his unjustified respect for the intellectual. Every mass organization will have to have functionaries who are well trained in sexology, for the exclusive purpose of observing the development of the organization in respect to sexual attitudes, functionaries who can learn from these observations and, in conjunction with a central sexological department, try to overcome the difficulties.

Along with positive legislation and measures for the protecion of sexuality, a number of other measures, derived from previous experience, are necessary.

For example, all literature which produces sexual anxiety should be prohibited. This includes pornographic books and crime stories as well as horror tales for children. These books will have to be replaced by a literature which, instead of arousing creepy chills, will describe and discuss genuine feelings for the unending manifold sources of the natural joy of living.

Experience clearly teaches us that every hindrance of infantile and adolescent sexuality by parents, teachers, or administrative authorities must be stopped. No one can say as yet just how this is to be, accomplished. But the necessity for legal protection of infantile and adolescent sexuality can no longer be doubted.

The best laws are worth no more than the paper on which they are written so long as there is no clarity about the difficulties that, given today's political conditions and human structure, will be encountered if the sexuality of children and adolescents is affirmed. If parents and teachers had not been badly raised themselves, if they were not sick themselves, and if the best educational conditions could be immediately guaranteed for children and adolescents, matters would be simple. Since this is not the case, two measures are needed simultaneously:

a) Model institutions for collective education would have to be established in various areas. Here, well-trained, realistic, and sexually healthy educators would observe closely the development of the growing generations and try to solve the practical problems that arise. These institutions will form the core from which the principles of the new order will spread out into society. It will be a long, arduous task but in the long run it offers the only possibility to get at the problem of submission in human structure. In addition to the model educational institutions, there would be research institutes, which would inquire into the physiology of sexuality, the prevention of emotional illness, and the prerequisites of sexual hygiene. They would not, as has been done previously, collect Indian phalluses and condoms of various kinds.

b) Outside of these centers, it will be necessary to prepare for the sex-economic, natural regulation of sexual life on a mass scale. The first principle to be recognized is that sexual life is *not* a private affair. This does not mean that any state functionary is entitled to pry into bedroom secrets; rather, that the concern for the sexual restructuring of man, for the establishment of the capacity for full sexual pleasure, cannot be left to individual initiative but is a cardinal problem of all social existence.

Depending on the existing economic possibilities, several measures could be carried out immediately in preparation for the new ordering of sexual life. (This presupposes, however, that the sexual life of the masses is no longer considered a matter of secondary or even of the least importance.) Good contraceptives should be produced with the same attention that is given to big machines. The contraceptives, under scientific guidance and free of profit-making motives, will be among the first measures if the sexual hygiene of the masses is the goal. The publicizing of contraception as a method of decreasing abortions should not remain merely a theoretical matter but must be accomplished practically.

A repetition of the Soviet sexual catastrophe cannot be avoided unless the problem of providing private rooms for adolescents and unmarried couples is tackled immediately after the takeover of power. From what I know of the young, they will gladly solve this problem in a practical manner without waiting for instructions from above.

The building of emergency homes for youth is necessary and it can be accomplished, provided that no powerful moralistic authority opposes it. Adolescents must be made to feel that they have every possibility of building their own lives. This will certainly not distract them from their general social work. On the contrary, if they can gradually solve the problem of private rooms themselves, they will accomplish their social tasks with enormously increased pleasure. The whole population must acquire the secure feeling that the revolutionary leadership is doing everything it can to guarantee sexual pleasure, without reservation, without any ifs and buts. The enlightenment of the masses on the harmfulness of abortion and the dangers of venereal disease will become less and less necessary as an understanding of the value of healthy, natural sexuality increases.

If the population feels that its sexual needs are immediately and practically understood it will also happily build machines, without coercion. A population that is capable of sexual happiness will offer the best guarantee for society's general security. It will rebuild its life in a spirit of joy and defend it against any reactionary threat.

If "sexual chaos" in the armed forces and the subsequent compulsion to resort to the law on homosexuality are to be avoided, it will be necessary to tackle beforehand one of the most difficult problems of social sex-economy: the inclusion of young women into Army and Navy life. This may sound inconceivable to military specialists today, but there is no other way to avoid the sexual degeneracy of serving in the Army. Clearly, this problem will not be easily solved, but in principle what has been said here is valid.

Theater, films, and literature will no longer be exclusively at the service of economic problems, as happened in the Soviet Union. The problems of love life which have absorbed 90 percent of literature since time began cannot be eliminated from this world; nor can they be replaced by the glorification of machines. The reactionary, patriarchal kind of love culture will be replaced by a life-affirmative one in literature, film, etc. This will spare us from regressing to philistine forms and to trashy sentimentality.

Work in the sexological field will not be left to the initiative or the confusion of untrained physicians or romantically disposed, ungratified women; it will be organized collectively and conducted unbureaucratically, like other forms of social life. It would be useless at this point to rack one's brain over the details of such an organization. The question of organization will resolve itself spontaneously if sexual life is placed in the forefront of social work.

Under no circumstances will the new order of sexual life be established by the decree of a central authority. A wide network of sex-political organizations will mediate between the life of the masses and the professional centers. Following the example of the German Sexpol, these organizations will hold discussions on the life problems of the masses and return to the masses with their solution. All responsible scientists and leading sexologists will be examined as to their sexual health and freedom from any kind of ascetic moralizing attitudes.

We will not fight religion but neither will we relinquish the right to secure the sexual happiness of the
masses and convey to them the insights of natural
science. Whether or not the Church is correct in its
assertion of the supernatural nature of religious feelings will then be seen. However, we do not conceal
the fact that we want to protect children and
adolescents from being inculcated with sexual anxiety
and guilt feelings.

In the process of the social revolution, the family
will disintegrate irrevocably; a return to the old family
order is impossible. Family feelings and ties must
be taken into account in that the problems arising
from them will be constantly discussed publicly and
overcome. Our position is the following:

The goal of sexual and cultural revolutionary work
crystallizes from the events at hand, without sophistry.

Man's vegetative function, which he shares with
all living nature, strives for development, activity,
and pleasure; it shuns unpleasure and is experienced
in the form of flowing, surging sensations. These sensations are the essential element of every progressive,
revolutionary world view. Even the so-called "religious experience" and the "oceanic feeling" are based
on vegetative phenomena. Recently, bioelectric processes in the tissues were detected in connection with
some of these vegetative excitations. This is understandable because man is a part of nature, and nature
functions bioelectrically.[1]

The religious feeling of oneness with the universe
therefore corresponds to a natural fact. But the
mystification of these physical sensations has blocked
and distorted them.

Basically, primitive Christianity was a communist
movement whose progressive, life-affirmative force
was turned into the opposite, into the ascetic and
supernatural, by its simultaneous sexual negation.
Having become an established church, international
Christianity, aspiring to the salvation of man, denied

---

1 [1949] The discovery of orgone energy has necessitated considerable
modification of this view. (Cr. *The Discovery of the Orgone,* Vol. I.)

its own origin. The Church owes its power to the vast, life-negating changes of human structure brought about by the metaphysical interpretation of life: it subsists on the life that it kills.

Marxist economic theory recognized the economic prerequisites of the progressive course of life. But its curtailment by coarse economistic and mechanical views caused a threatening change toward life negation, with all its well-known symptoms. In those years economism suffered and was exposed to violent political struggles because it condemned the growing knowledge of the spontaneous will of life as "psychology" and abandoned it to the mystics.

In the neo-paganism of German National Socialism, the vegetative forces of life again broke through. The vegetative sensations were better understood by Fascist ideology than by the Church and were brought back to earth. The National Socialist mystique of "surging of the blood" and "unity of blood and soil" amounted to progress as compared to the ancient Christian view of original sin; but it suffocated in new mystification and reactionary economic policies. Thus, affirmation of life was again twisted into negation of life in the form of asceticism, submissiveness, duty, and ethic isolation. Nevertheless, the doctrine of original sin cannot be defended against the mystique of surging blood; the "surging of the blood" must be propelled into a rational outlet.

Many misunderstandings arise from this relationship between ancient Christianity and neo-paganism. There are those who proclaim neo-paganism as *the* revolutionary religion; they feel its progressive tendency, but they fail to see its mystical perversion. Others want to protect the Church against Fascist ideology and think in so doing they are acting as revolutionaries. (Possibly this is politically expedient for the moment, but in the long run it leads to error. There are many socialists who do not want to dispense with "religious feelings"; they are right insofar as they mean vegetative sensations; they are

wrong insofar as they do not see the real distortion
and impeding of life. No one yet dares to touch the
sexual core of unfolding life. Everyone unconsciously
utilizes his own sexual anxiety to affirm life in the
form of religious or revolutionary experience while
in the next breath his sex-negative attitudes transform
this experience into a negation of life. Thus religious
Socialists and economistic Marxists complement one
another. The following diagram illustrates this development:

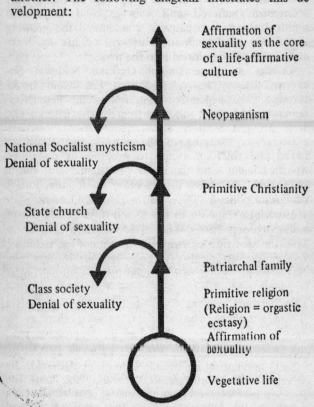

Affirmation of
sexuality as the core
of a life-affirmative
culture

Neopaganism

National Socialist mysticism
Denial of sexuality

Primitive Christianity

State church
Denial of sexuality

Patriarchal family

Class society
Denial of sexuality

Primitive religion
(Religion = orgastic
ecstasy)
Affirmation of
sexuality

Vegetative life

Diagram of cultural development

Proceeding from its basis in natural science and social processes, sex-economic research has drawn the correct conclusion: *the affirmation of life, in its subjective form as affirmation of sexual pleasure and in its objective social form as work democracy, has to be brought to subjective consciousness and objective development*. The struggle to achieve this must be organized. Its most powerful structural opponent is human pleasure anxiety.

Organic pleasure anxiety, caused by the social disturbance of the natural experience of pleasure, is at the heart of all the difficulties which mass-psychological and sexological practice encounter every day, in the form of modesty, morality, slavishness to the leader, etc. To be sure, impotence or the inability to make someone else's life happy is a source of shame, just as being a political reactionary is. Sexual potency has remained a high ideal, just as being a revolutionary has; every reactionary makes his appearance as a revolutionary. No one likes to hear that he has shattered his happiness, that a frittered-away future is already behind him. Therefore the aged always fight more fiercely against a concrete affirmation of life than do youth, and youth, as it grows older, becomes conservative. No one likes to admit that he might have arranged things better, that he now negates what once he affirmed, that to realize one's desires in life requires a transformation of the whole mode of living in the course of which many valued substitute gratifications and illusions are destroyed. One does not like to curse the executors of authoritarian state power and ascetic ideology when they are called "father" and "mother." One acquiesces, but one never resigns.

Still, the unfolding of life cannot be stopped. Its perversion in asceticism, authoritarianism, and life negation may succeed once more; but in the end man's natural forces will prevail in the unity of nature and culture. There is every indication that life is rebelling against the chains imposed on it. The struggle for a "new life" is only now beginning in earnest, at first in the form of severe economic and emotional disturbances of individual and social life. But whoever is capable of understanding life will not despair. He who is satisfied does not steal. He who is sexually happy does not need any "moral support" and his "religious experience" is true to nature. Life is as simple as this. It is complicated only by a human structure which is afraid of life.

About the Author

Wilhelm Reich was born in Austria on March 24, 1897, the son of a prosperous farmer. His early years were spent in a rural atmosphere close to animals and natural phenomena and this may well have determined his later interest in biology and natural science. After his service in the First World War, he entered the Medical School of the University of Vienna from which he was graduated in 1922. He met Freud in 1920 and soon became a prominent participant in the early psychoanalytic and mental-health movements. Freud's idea of a psychic energy, his libido theory, provided the stimulus for Reich's clinical and experimental studies in the exact nature of this energy, which was most vividly expressed in the orgasm function. These studies led eventually to the discovery of the life energy to which he gave the name *orgone*.

Forced to flee Nazi Germany in 1933, Reich pursued his work in Scandinavia until September, 1939, when he moved to the United States and established his laboratory in Forest Hills, New York. He later transferred it to Rangeley, Maine. In 1954, the Federal Food and Drug Administration filed a complaint for an injunction against him attacking specifically and clearly designed to discredit his discovery of orgone energy. He refused to be forced into court as a "defendant" in matters of basic natural research and a Decree of Injunction was issued *on default*. He was subsequently accused of criminal contempt in disobeying this injunction, and following a jury trial in May, 1956, in which his plea was "not guilty," he was sentenced to two years' imprisonment. He died on November 3, 1957, in the Federal Penitentiary at Lewisburg, Pennsylvania.

Index